I get by with a little help …

'We don't live alone.
We are members of one body.
We are responsible for each other.'
J.B. Priestley, An Inspector Calls, 1944

I get by with a little help …

Colleague support in schools

Bill Rogers

P·C·P

Paul Chapman
Publishing

© Bill Rogers 2006

First published in 2002 by Australian Council for Educational Research Ltd.
This edition published in 2006 by Paul Chapman Publishing

Paul Chapman Publishing
A SAGE Publications Company
1 Oliver's Yard
55 City Road
London EC1Y 1SP

SAGE Publications Inc
2455 Teller Road
Thousand Oaks, California 91320

SAGE Publications India Pvt Ltd
B-42, Panchsheel Enclave
Post Box 4109
New Delhi 110 017

Library of Congress Control Number: 2005938342

A catalogue record for this book is available from the British Library

ISBN-10 1-4129-2118–X   ISBN-13 978-1-4129-2118-3
ISBN-10 1-4129-2119–8   ISBN-13 978-1-4129-2119-0 (pbk)

Typeset by Dorwyn Ltd, Wells, Somerset
Printed in Great Britain by The Alden Press, Oxford
Printed on paper from sustainable resources

CONTENTS

SCOPE OF
THIS BOOK

CHAPTER 1 explores the immediate context of colleague support, particularly the current climate of change that is affecting schools. There are many factors that impinge upon, and affect, colleague support in a given school (for good or ill). These factors are introduced in this chapter and developed in subsequent chapters. The research methodology is briefly explained in terms of the teacher narratives that inform this book.

CHAPTER 2 examines the determinants of colleague support in schools. The potential in schools is for isolationist culture and practice to adversely affect colleague-coping and professionalism; the natural stress of teaching is explored through research on the positive (stress-buffering) benefits of colleague support, morale and supportive leadership and supportive teaming. Professional development is explored in supportive colleague cultures. The issue of personal and professional needs is also addressed in light of colleague support and how colleague support can enable change in school cultures.

This chapter is an exploration of the literature as it addresses the nature of social support and how such a concept is observed and expressed within colleague cultures in schools.

CHAPTER 3 develops a whole-school approach to colleague support through a proposed 'typology of colleague support'. This 'typology' is based on the degree, and level, of consciousness within a school culture as it seeks to meet the espoused needs of its teachers. The 'structures', 'forms', 'processes' and 'policies' that can enable colleague support are discussed as practical and professional ways of meeting such needs.

CHAPTER 4 looks at how teachers might understand colleague support in their school, based on direct – longitudinal – research from teachers in schools. This chapter discusses how colleague support can enable the meeting of needs from basic expressions such as 'creative whingeing', incidental sharing and humour, and purposeful teaming through to the *enabling protocols* of colleague support. These 'protocols' are the defining and enabling features of a supportive colleague culture. The 'protocols' illustrate how supportive colleagues manage coping, stress, failure, support and professional growth. Case examples from a variety of schools are utilised to illustrate the meanings and practices of colleague support.

CHAPTER 5 discusses how colleague support is 'built' in schools – how it is managed, affirmed and developed. Rather than merely leaving such support to chance, this chapter addresses how to constructively address support, particularly in areas such as behaviour management, discipline, challenging children and classes, 'struggling' teachers, and teachers who have to cover 'hard classes'. The issues of teams and teaming are addressed as significant features of supportive collegiality.

Professional development in terms of encouragement, professional feedback and elective mentoring (and coaching) is explored through case examples in supportive schools.

CHAPTER 6 addresses colleague support and the process of change: both natural, normative change and imposed external change. The typology of support in Chapter 3 is re-addressed in terms of the difference that conscious, collaborative, collegiality can make to change imperatives.

CHAPTER 7 explores and discusses the adaptive utility of the colleague support model and the typology and practices developed in chapters 3 to 6. A practical framework for needs-analysis and change is offered for school awareness-raising and needs-analysis.

CHAPTER 8 provides a brief summary of the key ideas in the book (sounds a bit like the teacher summary of a lesson!) and introduces two metaphors which (I hope) will emphasise the essential features of colleague support.

The APPENDICES offer needs-analysis options for addressing supportive change in the area of colleague support.

ACKNOWLEDGEMENTS

To my colleagues who are often the object and subject of ill-informed and wearing criticism, both in the media and wider society, yet who slog it out day after day in the classroom to bring some meaning, purpose and even some *joie de vivre* into the lives of children in their educational journey.

For their participation, goodwill, suggestions, ideas and understanding; this is their story and not just mine. To all my many colleagues who gave unstintingly of their time and themselves, this is their story; this book is a small return for so much given. My faith in the self-effacing aspects, and mutual regard, of my colleagues has been reaffirmed.

My thanks to Dr Neville Johnson for his ongoing support and encouragement; Felicia Schmidt for the patient typing of the handwritten drafts and redrafts; and to ACER Press for their support of this project from the start, particularly John King, Anne Peterson, Alex Watts and Siobhán Cantrill. My thanks to the team at Paul Chapman Publishing, London. To Marianne Lagrange and Jeanette Graham – many thanks for the enabling of this English edition.

To my wife, Lora, whose patience, understanding and support enabled me to realise why I even started this project in the first place: she too is a teacher. To Elizabeth, our daughter, also a teacher, who has given and often benefited from the kind of support written about here, and to our daughter Sarah, who has shared the kitchen table on many occasions with this book – a husband's and a father's thanks for your support.

William Arthur Rogers
December 2001
Revised UK edition, February 2006

INTRODUCTION

'What do we live for, if it is not to make life less difficult for each other.'

George Eliot (1819–1880)

'The thousand natural shocks that flesh is heir to.'

Shakespeare, *Hamlet* Act 3:1

'People must help one another; it is nature's law.'

Jean de la Fontaine (1621–1695)

It is 8:30 a.m., a busy secondary school staff room. The daily organiser is 'flat out' engaging a few last-minute changes with teachers. A few teachers are creatively, even purposefully, whingeing about 8D – the transitional whinge 'makes them feel a bit better', 'as if we're all in the same boat; a bit leaky, a bit rusty but roughly going in the same direction!' This is colleague support.

A colleague says to a harried-looking fellow science teacher, 'Look, I'll drop the photocopied sheets in your pigeon hole; we're covering the same unit of work.' The other colleague looks relieved as she runs off to her home group class (she was concerned about the last-minute rush to get 'that worksheet ready').

This, too, is colleague support; transitional, on-the-run, none the less valued for that.

Anne has a 'blazing migraine'. Janet notices this (it has happened before) and offers to take the class for Anne while she recuperates. On other occasions (not too many), Anne has asked for similar support – it has never been refused.

Fortunately, Anne is in a supportive, a collegially supportive school. In some schools, teachers will suffer physical and psychological pain; difficult classroom and playground management issues; uncertainties about teaching practice; rarely receive useful professional guidance and feedback; and not enjoy the opportunities for professional off-loading and problem-solving.

School cultures are significantly affected by their 'colleague culture' and how 'consciously' schools address the issue of colleague support.

'Gees Paul, you look sh__house!' Carl says with humour to a fellow teacher who does, indeed, look 'a little washed out' already at 8:40 a.m. 'Listen I'll grab you a coffee all right?'

'Thanks Carl ...'

A brief chat about 9C and the social studies class aided by a collegial cuppa gives Paul that 'coping edge'. It may not sound like much in the long haul, but this, too, is colleague support.

A colleague walks past a very rowdy class and looks through the glass that separates him from a very stressed looking colleague. After knocking on the door he asks politely if he can 'borrow one or two students, please?' His body language, and tone, indicate this is a 'collegial' expression of support (code for 'I'll take a few students – the most troublesome at present – and look after them till the bell goes'). His colleague is immediately thankful and supported by this courteous knock on the door, as distinct from a colleague 'barging in' and 'taking over'. Later that day the two colleagues sit and debrief and longer-term offers and options of support are explored.

Carmel taught a composite grade 5/6 class. Over several weeks (since the beginning of term 1) the class had become 'increasingly difficult to manage'. It was 'one thing after another': the general level of noise and rowdiness as students entered the classroom; the pushing, shoving and annoying comments; the inattentive behaviour during instructional time ('boys being silly', 'calling out, 'butting in'); general noise level during on-task learning time; and 'loss of active learning time'.

Carmel was new to the school and initially hesitant about asking for help; she was a little anxious, as an older teacher, that she not be seen as ineffective or, worse, incompetent.

The school is a very supportive school, however, and when a colleague noticed – one day after 3:30 p.m. – that Carmel looked more than 'a bit wrung out', it eventually 'all came out' and very quickly a 'support process' was offered that stopped the spiral of disillusionment and 'partial defeat'. It was an offer accepted, and an offer grounded in long-term support options. The support offered was genuine, caring and non-judgemental.

A 'fresh-start' program was initiated with the class that reviewed whole-class and individual behaviour concerns; *shared* rights, responsibilities and rules; core routines (such as seating plans, entering and *leaving* the classroom considerately, workable routines for class discussion and learning time); 'partner-voices' and co-operative talk during on-task learning time; and conferring routines for teacher assistance etc.

Classroom meetings initiated the 'fresh-start' process, and a colleague worked with Carmel to set up the initial meeting with the grade and to act as a supportive mentor to discuss, plan and review the process of change. A key feature of this long-term professional support was peer-coaching, a process that enabled Carmel to professionally reflect on and assess aspects of her teaching and behaviour management (see Chapter 5).

Carmel felt better, gained significant professional hope and coped more effectively with the class group. It took time, effort, goodwill – in effect, colleague support. It made a significant difference; I know, I was there.

All these examples from different schools embody typical features of colleague support: moral, 'structural' and professional support. All teachers recognise these expressions of support given by their colleagues, but colleague support is not limited by such expressions.

This book addresses the difference that colleague support can and does make to the individual teacher and to whole-school cultures. Colleague support can significantly affect stress and coping; the management of change (externally imposed and internally required); professional development (including professional feedback); the maintenance of effective discipline and classroom management and more.

This book came about as a result of an ongoing interest in how colleague support operates in schools and the difference it can make within a school. That 'interest' was further extended with a longitudinal research study (doctoral research) into colleague support that enabled me to more consciously address the effect of colleague support within and across schools. This research is discussed in Chapter 1 and referred to throughout the text as it is applied to aspects of individual and social coping, and the meeting of colleagues' needs within a school context.

A colleague

Colleague refers to a fellow person in one's professional life to whom one '... joins in alliance with, unites ... binds together [with] one who is associated with another in office or employment' (*Oxford Shorter Dictionary*, p. 619). It can also refer to one who '... is an ally – a confederate' (ibid). Colleague, in this sense, can have a meaning that carries degrees of affiliation and support association, through to 'ally', 'co-worker' and 'partner'. Indeed, much of the research on social support, as distinct from the terminology of *colleague* support, emphasises understandings such as 'alliance', 'aid' and 'emotional concern'. Indeed, the more common term used for support, in the literature, is 'social support' rather than 'colleague support'.

I have opted for the term 'colleague support' as it allies the understanding of the personal and relational more strongly than does 'social support'; though social support is a significant feature of colleague engagement in a social-professional setting like a school. It is within these accepted meanings that I have embraced this term. When using the term 'collegial', as an adjective, I mean it to carry the basic concepts of colleague support such as moral support, structural support and professional support – concepts developed fully in chapters 2 and 3. More importantly, in this text I have allowed my colleagues to define and shape their meanings of colleague support across the fundamental dimensions of support: moral, structural and professional. These dimensions are affected by several factors:

- the effect of stress and the reciprocal 'buffering' given by colleague support
- the coping mechanisms of individuals as they interact with their colleagues
- the negative effect of social and professional isolation
- how colleague support meets individual needs and interpersonal needs
- the nature of the school as an 'organisation' and a 'culture'
- how a school addresses and manages change
- the place of encouragement and professional feedback
- the role, and effect, of appraisal and mentoring in colleague support.

Figure A.1 (over page) represents the dynamic nature of the dimensions as they are affected by a school's organisation, structure and culture as it consciously seeks to address support.

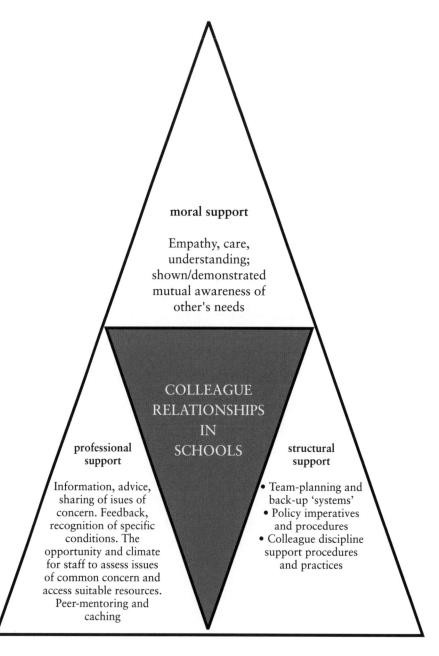

Figure A.1   *Dimensions of colleague support*

CHAPTER 1

THE IMMEDIATE CONTEXT OF COLLEAGUE SUPPORT

'I've been in some schools where there appears to be colleague support, at least on the surface – but it's more like a social club. People are not really working in teams or really supporting the kids. But there is colleague support and teaming here – and no cliques ...'

(Primary teacher, in Rogers, 1999)

'Even the basic moral support of "how's it going?" – they seem to know when you're run off your feet ... There are colleagues who, after school, I can informally bounce ideas off – even outside my faculty. I value their views, ideas, suggestions. I can compare this to schools where staff wouldn't even stay back after 3.30!'

(Secondary school teacher, in Rogers, 1999)

Teachers spend a third of their 'waking day' in schools, in an environment that is both demanding and stressful. They have a multi-task professional role where they have to juggle many demands – often simultaneously. The instruction-teaching role with over 25 students – in a small physical space – is combined with a challenging discipline and management role. They have to attempt to meet a range of learning needs and abilities and still cater for the preferred learning styles of their students. In any one lesson – especially in 'challenging' schools, where students may be 'reluctant learners' – there are a number of interruptions and diversions that distract and disturb overall teaching and learning: students who are late, homework not in, students without equipment, attentional and distracting behaviour, students in conflict with one another and their teachers, poor aesthetics ... All of this is *naturally* stressful as well as professionally challenging – why wouldn't it be? Beyond the classroom role there is the marking, lesson preparation and duty-of-care outside the classroom.[1]

Teaching, strangely, can be a lonely profession. Surrounded by other human beings (minors), teachers are often (effectively) cut off from their adult peers; peers who can offer so much in the way of moral and professional support.

When 'the bell' goes teachers are called off to playground duty, 'wet day' duty or bus duty, another class or another meeting. Even staff meetings, or team, or faculty, meetings do not always provide the opportunity to just talk through issues of common concern. Of course, teachers cover 'business' in such meetings, but we are often naturally tired from the day's teaching and follow-up that has to be done; this is coupled with the demands of time available to share those concerns. Now, ushered into yet another meeting it may not, in itself, offer the ongoing support we may need to realistically cope and manage in the teaching role.

Of course 'meetings' can be productive; they can – potentially – meet one's needs for emotional and psychological 'off-loading'. Meetings can even enable provision for support mechanisms to operate such as building in active problem-solving on issues of common concern over discipline, behaviour management, home-work, teaching and learning, and the management of 'crisis situations' in and out of class.

As a teacher, and a consultant, I have noticed that colleague support can significantly affect general well-being and professional esteem, as well as professional coping – it can significantly affect and enhance one's ongoing skills and abilities. How does it do that? What does a 'culture of support' look like within a school? What makes *colleague* support effective and why? Who initiates such support and how? How does such support affect personal coping and the ability to manage the day-to-day grind of teaching? How does colleague support affect longer-term issues such as professional feedback, appraisal of teaching, curriculum planning, lesson planning, as well as ongoing concerns such as classroom discipline and behaviour management generally? How does colleague support affect the impact and management of change?

As a consultant (Department of Education) in the mid-1980s (specialising in the area of behaviour management and school discipline), I was struck by the wide variance in how supportive schools were, both from the administration and senior staff levels to 'chalk-face' teaching staff.

Research basis

As a private consultant,[2] I have continued to observe the patterns and dynamics of colleague support in schools. I have spoken to many hundreds of teachers and principals about the issue of colleague support and the difference it can make. In 1994 I began a doctoral research study on colleague support in Australian schools. I was keen to see how teachers in schools perceived colleague support as operating in their school, what meanings it had for them and the difference such support made to their coping, their professional life and their sense of 'teaming'. I also researched how colleague support affected a school culture in its professional coping and in its management of change.

The principle research methodology used in this study was qualitative[3] and based in teacher narrative as developed in surveys, formal interviews and unstructured dialogue and long-term observation. Participant observation is an integral feature of this form of 'naturalistic inquiry', allowing continuing reflective observation on aspects and features of collegiality and colleague support that extended and illuminated the formal surveys and structured interviews that formed the core of this research. Colleagues often noted that they felt 'comfortable' and 'willing' to share both in the 'formal' setting of structured interviews and to discuss a range of issues relating to colleague support in the many unstructured dialogues. I believe this acceptance enhanced the depth, and range, of this research, as colleagues felt their 'voice' was heard and 'validated'. My role as researcher was to bring the research methodology to bear on that 'voice'; to hear and listen, to measure and compare and appropriately validate that 'voice' so that inherent and adaptive meanings were highlighted and theory-generation made possible.

Naturalistic inquiry and qualitative research seek to come to terms with difficult concepts like feelings, beliefs, attitudes and relationships by entering into the teacher's setting and 'world'. The emphasis on teacher narrative and partner-observation has given a longer-term view of colleague support in each of the schools I worked with and enabled a generative view of colleague support within school cultures and a sound basis for grounded theory.

Given the methodology used in this study, the relationship of researcher and 'researched' is important; as Eisner (1979) points out, one needs to be able to 'enter into the work'. Guba and Lincoln (1989) note that the qualitative researcher is 'situationally responsive' as a co-participant. Over several years with many, many, teachers I was able to not only survey and interview them as 'respondents', I often worked alongside them and observed (informally) how colleague support operated within a given school.

As Burns (1984, p. 238) points out, 'Qualitative methods such as participant observation and unstructured interviewing permit access to individual meaning in ongoing daily lives.' Hargreaves (1994, p. 54) further suggests that, 'Voices need not only to be heard, but also engaged, reconciled and argued with.' This I was able to do as colleagues supported my role as researcher *and* colleague. In this sense the research study and its outcomes are as much their story as it is mine.

The wider context affecting colleague support

In pursuing this study of colleague support I was also aware of natural and transitional demands made on the coping and support cultures in school.[4]

My colleagues frequently cited aspects such as:

- One's personal needs as they interface with one's professional role.
- The demands of one's individual role as a teacher.
- The daily demands of the local school setting – the *'realpolitik'* of the local, and daily, demands of teaching and managing in a given school culture.
- The transitional demands of society sometimes expressed in misinformed, and misleading, media reports.
- The demands of the Department of Education, particularly ongoing imposed and mandated change (see Figure 1.1).

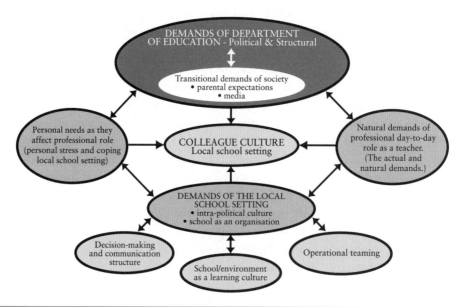

Figure 1.1   *Issues affecting colleague support*

Schools are also subject to frequent change; the impact and pace of change challenges a school's coping ability, affects teacher stress, and calls forth their accountability.[5] The pace and type of imposed changes on schools is often related to teacher accountability, but with increased accountability there is the potential for increased workplace stress. In many of the unstructured dialogues (as well as the interviews), in the schools surveyed for this study, staff recounted the recurrent anxiety brought on by performance demands that, in turn, affected whether they were to be seen by their peers as 'effective' teachers or (more disconcertingly) as 'teachers in excess'. In an ACTU survey of workplace stress (1977), job security was rated as a significant stressor directly linked to factors such as organisational change and restructuring, increased workload and lack of communication and consultation by management.[6]

In a survey addressing the status of teaching (Ashdown, 1997) conducted on teachers' perceptions about their careers, teachers largely spoke positively about their professional life (60 per cent) but were very concerned about perceived political interference, lack of community support and declining status – these were the most cited, and negative, aspects of their 'profession'.[7]

The survey went on to state:

> 'The dangers of devaluing education through "economic rationalism" was a common theme for teachers looking to the future. Similarly, some saw the need to protect the "ethos" of education against the "market economy".[8]

Schools normally value supporting children; whatever the outcome, whatever their background. Teachers do not always feel they, too, are valued by their Departments of Education for what they do. While this does not delimit accountability, the kind of accountability that is simplistically focused in 'accounting terms' will not deliver social and moral responsibility.[9] As one senior colleague noted (in an interview):

> 'We're told to implement departmental (Department of Education) policy – staff **are** aware of that, but on the one hand we're told to treat children as individuals yet we **must** do this or **that** aspect of the policy. There's a dichotomy there; asking schools to be self-managing and take on more and more responsibilities but this can be a pseudonym for more work!' (Colleague's emphasis)

Another interviewee notes:

> 'Today there's more emphasis on competition; the way schools are going teachers are even competing against each other … numbers, posting results, how early enrolment starts, *advertising* and *promoting* your school …!' (Colleague's emphasis)[10]

The media, too, impacts on teachers' sense of professionalism, self, role and even morale. In the interviews, and unstructured dialogue, teachers often commented on how media misinformation contributed to a perceived diminution of the professional status of teachers 'in the eyes of the public'. While the media informs, it sometimes feeds on misconception and misinformation, leading to misrepresentation. Whether it is the literacy debate, the 3Rs, civic education, social education – 'the schools do not do enough' or 'do not do it right' seems to be an easily targeted judgment on teachers.

Colleagues passed on to me many printed 'slurs' on their profession. A typical example, from a school notice board, of how the media bring unnecessary stressful demand into the public education sphere is:

'... They are experts at self-pity, self-justification and self-serving politics. They are also a tad more intelligent than most and a whole lot less adventurous. So they have taken safe jobs that pay about one-and-a-half times the average wage; jobs that force them to take boringly long holidays in which to brood over life's injustices. Nor, once they have been at it long enough, can they escape teaching because out in the real world employers know what blinkered lives they have led: school, training college, university, then back to school. Teachers, though, are superb at throwing up defensive earthworks and shouting at their critics ...' (*The New Zealand Herald*, 11 April 1997, p. 2).

I have read countless articles like this (more prevalent on the rare occasions when teachers go on strike). Another journalist, in a more sympathetic note, writes:

'A very bright girl with a TER of 96 mentioned she was going to be a teacher. My automatic response was, "But you can do better than that!" I'm ashamed of that response but it reflects what many people think – even though most of us aren't tactless enough to articulate it' (*The Herald Sun*, 1997, p. 8).[11]

I was encouraged by a recent 'public opinion survey' on education issues. Douglas (2001) indicates that:

' ... over 80 per cent of Victorians approved of the latest pay raise for school teachers and nearly 90 per cent thought teachers were doing a good job in difficult circumstances and that teachers are very professional in a very demanding and stressful occupation ... The results are very encouraging. [It] demonstrates that education has become an ever-increasing priority for the community, and any government that fails to keep faith with parents and school communities is likely to quickly lose public support.' (pp. 2–3).

The work of teachers and colleague support

The work of teachers is changing from both imposed change, from the Department of Education, and community expectations. Hargreaves (1997, p. 12) states:

'... we have probably never lived in an age where there has been a more systematic, unyielding and pervasive deprofessionalisation in the objective conditions of how teachers do their work.'

His theme was the raising of consciousness about the pace and impact of change and the way schools cope.[12] Regarding the pace of change and its mixed benefits, I am strangely encouraged by Tom Atlee's epigrammatic use of the ambiguity surrounding change and progress when he writes, 'Things are getting better and better and worse and worse, faster and faster.'[13]

The changes schools have had to face are certainly *perceived* as more taxing on an individual's, and a school's, ability to cope and manage. This sees:

- students staying at school longer;[14] what is offered in the years 11–12, the education of students post-16 years of age ... (and its heavy demands on the hours of processing, feedback and evaluation)
- the perceived demands from the Department of Education for teachers 'to do it better' (this often means longer time at school)
- the integration of technical and (formerly) 'academic' high schools into post-primary (unified) secondary schools. This factor was significant in the residual stress that some teachers felt about 'forced amalgamation' in the early to mid-1990s[15]
- uncertain employment futures in the information technology-driven future and the response schools have had to make to IT, making it a central feature of teaching and learning.

As I sat and talked through all these issues with teachers in their schools – within the context of colleague support – I noted the differences in school ethos and culture as different aspects and features of colleague support interfaced with these changes and demands.[16] Some schools felt somewhat 'under siege' from the perceived intensification of change, with teachers feeling they were 'fighting on too many fronts', with less time to induct and process the changes.

Teachers in such schools seem to operate virtually on their own; even autonomously. Staff room talk was negative and the staff showed a limited sense of control over what was happening to them – they seemed to evince the shared belief that the 'locus of control' regarding 'change', pupil management, curriculum implementation, was really 'outside' of them.[17]

Other schools acknowledged the same pressures but seemed to manage more effectively; they saw the 'locus of control' and management of change as manageable at the local school level. In this way, as individuals, they affirmed collaborative teaming and decision-making, and had developed a learning culture from within their shared colleague resources. Such collegial behaviour was clearly affecting their perception and level of stress, their coping ability and their professional empowerment in a positive way.[18]

Hargreaves (1993) suggests there may be a positive side 'to all this change' directed to schools when he notes:

'Externally imposed change is driving teachers to rely on colleagues and co-ordinate with them to an unusual extent' (p. 3). 'Imposed legislation can often indirectly and unintentionally, contribute to the empowerment of teachers through their reinterpretation of such innovations as appraisal and school-development planning, teamwork, and new approaches to management ...' (p. 12).

My research interest was to ask how such colleague teamwork, school-planning and management worked with imposed change. I was keen to address the 'consciousness' of colleague support as it addressed externally imposed change and expectations as well as normative change. How strong an advocacy was there in these schools for integrating colleague support when managing change?

Autobiographical context

During the years I was a teacher and later a consultant for the Department of Education (then the Ministry of Education), I had observed the sort of continuum of colleague support that schools seem to typify from broadly unsupportive to supportive (see Figure 1.2, p. 10). I also believed a school's 'colleague culture' could be expressed across a continuum of supportive colleague behaviour expressed in precept and practice. Such observations raised, for me, inevitable questions: Why was one school more supportive than another? In what way? And for what reasons? I had noted (How could one miss it!) the inevitable tension between external pressures on schools and their school-based responses to such pressures. What I began to realise, though, was that colleague support seemed to be a critical, integrating, factor, such that several schools with similar socioeconomic demographics exhibited differing characteristics regarding supportive behaviours in individuals and in groups of individuals.

Also in my work with schools I was keen to see if there were adaptive features, or principles, of colleague support that had wider utility beyond an individual school setting. If a school culture was more collegially supportive, along such a continuum, what adaptive features of their culture and practices could enable a 'less supportive' school to become a 'more supportive' school? I was also interested in what 'dimensions' of colleague support teachers identified as making a difference to their personal and professional coping.

The researcher's knowledge and interpretive focus

I have drawn widely on my own experience with countless schools, as well as the direct research focus of the schools researched in this study. This wider experience, coupled with the research focus, has given an 'integrating familiarity'; what Cooley (1964) called 'sympathetic introspection'.[19]

In naturalistic inquiry one is observing interactively, not passively or dispassionately. The reflection that has led to the 'grounded understanding' of colleague support in this study has come from what my colleagues themselves value and utilise regarding colleague support.[20] My role, as a researcher, and as a participant observer and writer, has been to bring a wider interpretive focus from my experience to theirs, as well as from their experience to mine and then to go on and share that experience with a wider colleague base.[21]

Listening to, acknowledging and affirming, the teacher voice – through teacher narrative – is not a naive acquiescence. As I interviewed colleague after colleague and discussed the issue of colleague support I was conscious of myself as researcher identifying any 'gaps', as it were, between the delineated 'voice' to me as researcher and the 'actual voice' that I observed and knew over time as a participant observer. It was the partner observation role that enabled some corroboration between 'outside' and 'inside' school cultures.[22]

There were many examples of frustration and concern in the accounts and stories my colleagues showed – this is natural; colleague support is not a neat, simple or easy concept. Those closest to us, by dint of professional role and location, can give, offer, refuse, invite or ignore colleague support. This study, in part, also gave voice to those frustrations, concerns and 'ambiguities'; most of all it has shown what teachers value and use within their understanding of colleague support they bring to their daily lives as teachers.[23] This study has served as a first-hand iterative journey.

I also saw first hand how colleague support can meet significant, as well as transitory, needs; how it can affirm social and professional identity; how it can soften and re-work the effects of imposed change and how it can enhance and strengthen professional practice. I also began to note those underlying features and practices that characterised supportive colleague cultures. These underlying assumptions and practices I have termed 'the protocols of colleague support'. It is these 'protocols' that I believe can give some adaptive facility to the findings developed out of this study. These 'protocols' are discussed at length in Chapter 4.

The research upon which this book is based has been a 'journey' as much as it has been an academic study. It has meant spending a lot of time directly, purposefully and incidentally, with many colleagues across many schools. I have been privy to, and party to, their experiences and 'their story'.

At all times I have been acutely sensitive to the ethical probity of research of this nature. I have been conscious not to include any references that might highlight any teacher or any school in this work. The direct quotes by teachers are all noted as colleague quotes and are taken directly from the research I conducted.[24] These quotes are used with colleagues' permission.

It's risky being a participant observer; neutrality is not always possible. One is subject to the internal dramas of a school when one is trusted as a confidante, but also as a colleague and friend. Each school has its range of personalities and its own cultural milieu; therein the risk. You hear lots of stories, names are mentioned, 'old wounds' not always healed resurface, and you are asked to be part of each colleague's struggle with their journey in their school.

Daniel Bar-on (in Josselson, 1996) affirms the responsibility of the researcher dealing with very sensitive and personal aspects of people's lives:

> '... we hold the meaning of people's lives in our hands. Our success will be gratifying, but our failures may be irreversible' (p. 20).

Josselson's work (1996) explores the dynamic nature of interpretation and authorship even when full permission is given. He exhorts that:

> '... there is no one "right" answer to the problem of speaking for others – we are left realising that writing, as an intentional act, is a moral responsibility ... as qualitative researchers we can more easily write as situated, positioned authors, giving up, if we choose, our authority over the people we study, but not the responsibility of authorship over our texts' (p. 28).

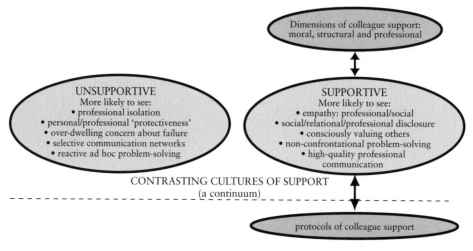

Figure 1.2   *Colleague cultures – contrast*

It was a privilege to share, for a while, my colleagues' world and – then – to write about it.

Experience is a great teacher but it is also a great resource. This study has been resourced directly from my colleagues' shared experience. These colleagues – teachers – are 'thrown together' in a particular school largely by chance. Their school-based professional community is not always planned; what is it they do, collegially, that makes a difference to the 'thousand natural shocks that flesh is heir to?' (*Hamlet*, Act 3:1). This study and this book is an answer to that question.

End notes

1 Even when one is 'technically' not 'on-duty' the need for conscious, school-wide, duty of care in out-of-class settings is important for all staff in a cohesive school management sense.

2 Working across Australia, New Zealand and the United Kingdom.

3 Blumer (1969), Bogdan and Taylor (1975), Braud and Anderson (1998), Burns (1975), Cambourne (1995), Curtis (1988), Ely and Anzul (1991), Glaser and Strauss (1967), Guba and Lincoln (1981) Hargreaves (1994), Howe (1996), Hughes (1980) and Peshkin (1993).

4 The interviews (and in many unstructured dialogues) alerted me to the impact on daily coping of the twin factors of an ageing teaching population and stress-related health issues. It was also clear that these factors can, in part, be ameliorated by the nature and quality of colleague support. In a radio interview the broadcaster Terry Lane referred to the 'longer hours' and 'expectations common in the workplace' labelling such as the 'overtime of self-preservation'. It is as if there is the unstated expectation that if you want to 'not only get ahead' but 'keep your job' you will need to 'work longer, harder, and more visibly'. (ABC 3LO, 2 January 1999). This could easily be a description of many of my teaching colleagues!

5 O'Brien (1998, p. 109), writing from a British perspective, notes:

'The stream of Government initiatives arriving in schools over the past decade has placed immense pressure on schools to change. Teachers have been bombarded [sic] by linear concepts of progress, attainment defined within the parameters of "normal" cognitive development and an overloaded curriculum. Externally enforced change, particularly when it seems to ceaselessly cascade down from a non-consultative hierarchical structure will demoralise those who are expected to implement the change.'

6 As Hannan (1997) notes:

'Workplace pressure has forced one in four Australian employees to take time off to recover' (Australian Council for Trade Unions Survey October, 1997; *The Age* Employment section 18 October 1997, Stressing the Obvious (p. 2)).

7 *The Education Review*, 'The Status of Teaching', March 1997 (p. 2).

8 *The Education Review*, October (1997) Ibid.

9 It is not uncommon to hear Australia spoken of (in the political arena) as 'an economy'. This easy slippage into the associative 'verb to be' is disconcerting when the purpose of education is at odds with values so easily tied to corporatist language and rationale. We 'have' an economy; we are not 'one'. We are 'a society'. Where economic growth is the overriding *leitmotif*, and where government is primarily concerned about economic management, it communicates a disturbing 'social' message. As Theobold (1997) notes:

'The reduced services which seem separate, in accounting terms, actually affect individuals, families and whole communities in ways which compound exponentially. Our relationship (as citizens) is not tied to purchase or value for money, but to responsibility.' (taped lecture)

10 The interviewee, here, was referring primarily to the Professional Recognition Program – an accountability/review process mandated by the Victorian Department of Education.

11 In one of the interviews a colleague noted: 'When I'm out I try not to admit to being a teacher.' I found this disconcerting but understood what he meant. I believe this to be due perhaps to the particular colleague ethos in such schools.

12 Commenting on the report 'Skilling the Australian community', Noble and Watkins (1988) noted, 'the morale of educators in general is sagging as they face almost impossible demands and uninformed criticism from the public' (p. 12). This is a little overstated but the meaning is clear.

   A frequent sub-theme in the interviews, as well as the surveys, were the expressions of frustration, a sense of powerlessness at times, and even anger about the stresses perceived as 'created by the Department of Education' cutbacks to educational funding and impositional change.

13 In Theobold (1997) *The Future of Work*, ABC audio tapes.

14 As the report *Teacher Stress in Victoria* (1989) notes, 'Schools have become the sharp end of a government policy which has been formulated on the assumption that it is a good thing to stay in school after the age of 16. This change in social demands and practices has changed the expectations which society places on schools, and therefore on its teachers' (p. 43).

15 In some of the high schools I surveyed for this study, this forced amalgamation still saw colleagues experiencing residual frustration over loss of control in their teaching several years afterwards, as formerly 'Trade' teachers ('Tradies') now mixed, and sought to work, with the 'Academic' teachers in the changed school organisation.

16 Colleague support expressed in common aims, practices and shared understandings is crucial to how cohesive a collegial culture is (see Chapter 6 and Appendix 2).

17 See, again, Figure 1.1. One of the more disconcerting comments made by the Government recently has been that of publicly highlighting failing schools. Such labelling is hardly going to engender any confidence in such a school's ability to take on any external support or utilise whatever internal support it believes it has.

18 This is more than a 'degrading survivalism', it is a conscious effort, within a school culture, to take charge of what is happening to them (see Rogers, 1992, 1995). In one of the schools I researched, a colleague rose above 'survivalism' when he noted (with a wry grin and Pythonesque humour) 'We're all in the same boat here ... a rocking, leaking, boat ... by talking things through it makes you feel (at least) part of a team; a broken, beaten team [sic] ... **but still a team**'.

19 'Insight and intuition can also provide reliable knowledge about reality and taken with other "forms" of knowledge support validity and ascribed meaning' (Peterson, 1989, p. 19). As Winter (1989) observes:

   '... in social science(s) the person being observed is interpreting the investigator, the events of a social investigation are always an *interaction* whose effects are thus never entirely within the control or awareness of the observer', in Carr (1989, p. 191). See also Loughran (1996).

20 Within this research frame 'grounded theory [is] the building up of an explanatory

framework through conceptualisation of the data' (Symon and Cassell, 1998, p. 60). Theory 'verification', as such, was not my aim. I wanted to develop grounded theory based on a grounded understanding, revealing dimensions about colleague support that are likely to have a greater 'explanatory power than could be revealed by a large-scale survey though of course the latter may be useful for some purposes' (Chell, 1998) in Symon and Cassell, p. 69). See also Glaser and Strauss (1967).

21 See Appendix 1.

22 What Shratz (1993, p. 3) calls, 'Listening to the silent voice behind the talk.'

23 Hargreaves (1993) notes:

'...the teacher's voice, says Goodson (1991), articulates the teacher's life and its purposes. To understand teaching, therefore, either as a researcher, an administrator or a colleague, it is not enough merely to witness the behaviour, skills and actions of teaching. One must also listen to the voice of the teacher, to the person it expresses and to the purpose it articulates. Failure to understand the teacher's voice is failure to understand the teacher's teaching. For this reason, our priority should be not merely to listen to the teacher's voice, but also to sponsor it as a priority within our teacher development work' (p. 53).

24 Unpublished Doctoral dissertation (1999)

CHAPTER 2

DETERMINANTS AFFECTING COLLEAGUE SUPPORT IN SCHOOLS

' ... the private sphere, the sphere of individual actions and feelings, is everywhere com-mingled with the "public" sphere, with the human and non-human environment. We cannot really separate individual endeavours from social endeavours ...'

Oliver Sacks (1990, p. 268)

*'I worked in a school where I dreaded walking in the gate because of the lack of collegial support – and I worked in others schools where I enjoyed spending the day there **because** of the staff ...'*

Secondary teacher (cited in Rogers, 1999)

An isolationist culture by history?

When I first went into teaching, colleague support was incidental; dependent on which mix of personalities were thrown together – often by chance – in a given school. Sometimes one would 'score' a supportive principal, sometimes not. The pre-vailing culture in teaching was that one did *one's own* work in *one's own* classroom; the concept of shared planning in teams was not typical practice or seen as valued colle-gial activity. Schools, then, were often quite hierarchical in terms of leadership decision-making and communication. 'Cells and bells' was a common, at times cyn-ical, description of how one often taught in one's own domain, not sharing one's concerns *too* widely. When the 'bell' went one raced off to duty or staff room.

There was, in those days, the sense that if one wanted to be seen to be 'a good teacher' it was not prudent to talk about 'struggle', 'concerns' or 'problems' – par-ticularly discipline problems; this might suggest one could not cope or was not a 'good' or 'effective' teacher.

Once inside one's classroom a teacher could be struggling, dispirited, mis-cueing and no one would really know. I saw too many colleagues only get recognition of their struggle with their challenging students (with emotional and behavioural concerns) when they finally 'broke down' in the classroom or the office. Teachers did not want 'censure' or 'blame', so they did not easily present their needs, anxious not to be seen as a 'problem teacher' or a 'non-coping' teacher. Fortunately, school cultures have changed in regard to these uncaring perceptions of self-protectiveness ('people must not see me struggling, I must be able to get it right ...').

The literature on colleague cultures often refers to the issue of isolation or isolationism in the teaching professional.

Fullan and Hargreaves (1991) call teaching 'the lonely profession'[1] – though it might be more accurate to describe it as a professional role where one often works 'alone' as an adult. Rudduck (1991, p. 31) has graphically described '... education (as) among the last vocations where it is still legitimate to work by yourself in a space that is secure against invaders.' This point is echoed by Leiberman and Miller (1990) when they say that:

'... loneliness [sic] and isolation are high prices to pay but teachers willingly[2] pay them when the alternatives are seen as exposure and censure. By following the privacy rule [sic] teachers forfeit the opportunity to display their successes, but they also gain the security of not having to face their failures publicly and losing face' (in Miller, 1996, p. 94).

The Elton Report (1989) commented on this reluctance by teachers to disclose concerns (notably in discipline and teaching practice) and seek colleague support. Elton (1989) speaks of a 'tradition of classroom isolation that contributes to teacher reluctance to share concerns about teacher-management and discipline', and suggests such 'reluctance' affects teachers in two fundamental ways:

'Good teachers may get little or no recognition from senior staff for their achievements; this is demotivating. Professional etiquette may also leave teachers who are having difficulty to suffer regular humiliation in the classroom' (pp. 76,78).

As one colleague said to me recently:

'There's this ludicrous idea that when someone is really struggling we have this "hands-off mentality" – just in case we do, or say, the wrong things. It's stupid especially when we **know** they need help' (senior secondary teacher, colleague's emphasis).

Fullan and Hargreaves (1991) suggest that a root cause of such 'individualism' has to do with the 'impossibly high expectations' many teachers set for themselves in a job with 'poorly defined limits'. The typical thought I have heard from some teachers in more relaxed moments is, 'If I'm not able to meet my (or society's, or the Principal's, or the media's) expectations why not work in an isolated way – at least my failures are private.' This sort of ambivalent uncertainty, experienced alone, is unhealthy and can lead to a stressful 'survivalism' in one's teaching practice.

As Hargreaves (1993) argues:

> 'The culture of individualism means that most teachers are content to do their main work, classroom teaching, on their own. Sometimes this leads to isolation, loneliness, and lack of practical and moral support; but it also means being able to have one's own way without interference or hindrance from a co-professional. Not surprisingly, many teachers feel ambivalent about this professional autonomy, but will not readily choose to work with another teacher in the classroom because of its high risk of tension, disagreement or conflict' (p. 4).

It depends, of course, on what is meant by 'enforced isolation'. It further depends on what the school encourages (or not) as colleague support, collaborative practice and professional development.

Little (1985) notes that there is often an etiquette, in teaching, about not giving advice about professional practice:

> '... in their reticence to give advice, advisors were responding to the prevailing professional etiquette among teachers: advice is not highly prized. Offering advice, especially unsolicited advice' (p. 35).[3]

This, naturally, has implications for how colleagues can more effectively give support through professional feedback (or even appraisal) in a way that does not unnecessarily, adversely, affect a colleague's self-esteem. As one school principal noted:

> 'I don't think they start out (at least as far as professional school teachers are concerned) being isolated; it comes more over time, when the pressure is on, when the changes of classes occur that are the really hard classes ...'

While 'isolation' (or more correctly the attitude, or culture, of isolation*ism*) may be a feature of teaching practice, it may also be a *habit* in some teachers and schools; what might be termed professional 'privatism'. Such 'privatism' may be ingrained in our working routines: preparation time, planning time and in our management time.

While physical isolation may be architecturally unavoidable at times, professional isolation is clearly avoidable. Worse, such professional isolation may contribute to the stress of wanting to share with colleagues but being reluctant to do so because of possible censure; this can also affect one's coping ability and psychological well-being, as Morgan (1991) notes:

> 'Each one of us working within these stressful situations (in difficult, challenging schools) needs a "mentor", someone we can turn to and trust to provide help and wise advice when needed' (p. 221).[4]

While many educational writers extol the virtues of professional collaboration, my concern is also with psychological coping arising from isolation and isolationism. Seligman (1991), in his psychological studies on both 'learned helplessness' and 'learned optimism', has noted that a society that 'extols the individual' and individualism sees 'an increase in depression'. He further links this to the factor of meaning:

'One necessary condition for meaning is the attachment to something larger than you are' (p. 287).

'Concepts like "meaning", "hope", "identity" and coping ability in failure and struggle actually need the longer term setting, the commons [sic]' (p. 285).[5]

The anomaly is that the very people who can assist (us) in so many ways are, in some schools, not offering to give assistance and support. Our colleagues, after all, are alongside us – daily. They know the daily irritations, demands and problems. They share the same 'knowing'. As noted, later, the lack of dependable and trusted support in a school owes much to how consciously a school values and endorses practical expressions of support in its ethos and culture (see Chapters 5 and 6).

According to a study by Miller (1996) there is (in a teacher's daily role) some 'ambivalence' between the wish for 'boundedness' and the 'search for assistance'. This ambivalence can mean that while teachers see their colleagues as a powerful source of ideas, they also see them as 'mirrors' in which they may 'assess their own performance' (pp. 95–8).[6] The concept of 'mirror' intrigues me, especially when I see (and hear) teachers using another teacher's professional behaviour, and knowledge, in terms of a negative comparative perception. While 'comparing' with a colleague can be positive, it can be used as a self-denigrating feature of professional life compounded by physical (and professional) isolation.[7] Colleagues I discussed this with said that they had experienced *both* the positive and negative aspects of such comparisons. (Rogers, 1999). As one colleague notes:

'What does the Principal think of me when he walks past my really noisy year 8? It's taking me a while to get through to this class ... I wish I had known a few of these techniques (on classroom discipline and management) a few years ago when I very nearly joined the stress statistics, due to trying to handle a very tough class using the "power-struggle" approach. I was also too proud and too naive to discuss my problems with any of my colleagues, **who seem to be handling things so well**'[8] (in Rogers, 1999, colleague's emphasis).

This is typically the sort of 'conversation' I have had countless times related to the issue of 'isolation' in the teaching profession. When one 'mirrors', in isolation from others, 'the mirror' may well easily 'distort' what the principal, or other colleagues see, and – conversely – what my colleague thinks about what he sees may well be distortion in 'the mirror'. Comparisons are not, of a necessity, bad; our colleagues can serve as 'positive', as well as 'negative' role models. A more crucial point, to my mind, is how can 'the collegial mirror'[9] be more authentically face-to-face, whether it is an airing of ideas, 'invited' advice, or even plain 'whingeing'? The degree of 'risk' and 'trust' here will depend on how collegially supportive the other colleague perceives his or her peers to be. It is risky exposing one's failure, fallibility, and uncertainties.[10]

From my experience these colleague concerns illustrate, in part, the natural by-product of a one-to-twenty (plus) ratio of children to adults, where a teacher (especially at primary level) becomes what we might term 'naturally protective' against others who might not 'really understand' 'what goes on here'; 'in 'my place' (even when those 'others' are collegial peers).[11]

Stress in teaching and colleague (social) support

Russell et al. (1987) in their major study of job-related stress, social-support and burnout among classroom teachers have indicated that different aspects, and facets, of social support can affect stress and burnout in positive (buffering) ways:

- Job-related stress, and feelings of stress and demoralisation 'decreased as the level of supervision support increased (p. 271).[12] According to 'the moderating hypothesis', individuals who have supportive social relationships are able to rely on others to aid them in dealing with stressful situations (p. 269). This is an important finding as it relates to the crises-management strategies used particularly in schools for students with emotional and behavioural disorders.
- Quoting a study by House (1981) they conclude that thoughtful, positive support from supervisors was 'consistently predictive [sic] of measures of physical and mental health' (Ibid).
- Teachers who indicated that when others (in their school) 'respected their skills and abilities' they reported 'less emotional exhaustion', had a 'sense of greater personal accomplishment' and their 'feelings of depersonalisation' were lessened.

This is related to what Russell et al. (1987, p. 272) term 'reliable alliances' [sic] where colleagues are available to give feedback, advice, encouragement and direct support. Iscoe (1974) refers to this aspect of support as describing 'the competent community' – the kind of community that fosters 'healthy connections among people' and 'catalyses and nurtures their linkages ...' (in Hobfall, 1998, p. 203).

Of course, this kind of research does not simply conclude that benefits to stress reduction are directly, causally, related to colleague support. It can be inferred, however, that there is a relationship – a positive relationship – between 'stress buffering', 'stress reduction', 'increased coping ability' and 'social support'[13] (from one's colleagues).

'Burnout'

'Burnout' says Morrow (1981) is the perfect disorder for an age that lives to some extent in the 'Doctrine of Discontinuous Selves'. He adds, sardonically (even cynically), 'Burnout runs through the teaching profession like Asian Flu – possibly because it depresses people to be physically assaulted by those they are trying to civilise' [sic] (p. 90).[14]

Many of the *symptoms* of burnout, as noted in the literature, can be managed, perhaps even ameliorated, by social support. In a large high school, for example, the complex nature of tasks – balancing time demands and organisational structure – can negatively affect collegiality, which is why a 'sense of solidarity, teamwork and mutuality of purpose is essential to the effectiveness of the individual worker' (Green, 1983). Green argues that burnout has a relational, social causation, as well as psychological causation, where, for example, individuals have cynical or negative feelings about those they work with. I have postulated that a school where there is a less *conscious* awareness of, and commitment to, colleague support these negative expressions of relational colleague behaviour are more common (p. 64f).

Kahn and Katz (in Rutter et al., 1979) have noted that supervisors in highly productive working groups were generally felt by employees to be supportive, understanding of difficulties and, most importantly, interested in them as individuals. Matathia and Salzman in Macken (1998) note that in an increasingly 'stressed' and 'information overloaded' society, the 'search for community has emerged as a dominant theme for the 1990s. In a 'workplace society' where basic needs still have to be met (whatever the managerial organisation or workplace structure) it is the 'sense of common community' that can serve as an 'antidote' to social and workplace 'isolation' (pp. 15–21).

Morale and supportive leadership

Hart, in his studies on stress, distress and school morale (1994, 1995) notes that if a school has poor management practices this will be reflected in both the levels of distress and overall staff morale. Supportive leadership provides the structures that underpin all other areas of staff management and can be seen as 'the anchor variable that can increase or decrease general staff morale'[15] (Hart et al., 1995, p. 31). One of the aspects of such leadership, relative to morale, is that it is necessary for school leaders:

> '… to develop a professional work environment that enables teachers to participate in the important decisions of the school, and develop professionally by working together and receiving feedback on how they are performing their role' (Hart et al., ibid.).

Studies by Hart et al. (1996) further indicate that while the effort to reduce teacher stress by changing student misbehaviour is laudable, the more appropriate focus should be on the development of a supportive organisational climate that enables teachers to cope with the student misbehaviour confronting them.[16] This is similar to a theme redolent in those schools I have noted as being 'characteristically supportive'. Fundamentally it is observed in how the commitment to the individual is practically evidenced, and how value is communicated in the day-to-day practice of a teacher's role by their senior colleagues (see Chapters 4 and 5).

Interpersonal control and stress

The degree to which the group, as well as the individual, believes it has relative control over the stressors in the workplace can also affect individuals and their social coping with stress. This is particularly relevant when a characteristic of the school culture is its ability to cope with external and mandated changes within the school setting, bringing its own, school-wide belief in colleague control to the mandated change and the management of those change requirements.

Social support is a key feature in an intra-personal sense of 'control' (Paulhus and Christie, 1981 in Parkes, 1988). Antonovosky (1979) suggests that this 'sense of control' is linked to 'a personal (and social) sense of coherence and global orientation' ... where 'feelings of confidence that one's internal and external environments are (relatively) predictable that things will work out as well as can be reasonable expected' (p. 12). Again, *relative* predictability is further related to the trust the individuals can reliably invest in both their colleagues as individuals and school-based 'systems' of support that can meet moral and professional needs (Rogers, 1995).

Some school groups meet imposed change in 'self-defeating' ways, as if they, as individuals and a school, had no 'real control' of events. It is the perceptual difference between being 'at cause' and 'at effect' that affects control of stress and coping (Greiger, 1980 in Bernard, 1990). Kyriacou (1986) notes this concept of 'control' as operating on a continuum ranging from those who believe that things are largely within one's control and those who believe that they are generally outside of one's control and 'primarily influenced by luck, fate, or powerful others [sic] a belief in external control.' Kyriacou further suggests that increasing recognition has been paid (in research) to the importance of social support within the school (from colleagues ...) as affecting a sense of positive control over stressful events and circumstances (p. 149).[17]

How much do staff perceive and believe they can manage the change within their setting by the way they perceive what 'their relative control' involves, individually and collectively? Even if they cannot directly control the fact that external change has been imposed (say by the Department of Education), they can at least control and affect how they 'work the change' at their local level (as one principal nicely put it).

The importance of 'the incidental' in colleague coping

Lazarus (1981), researching the effects of stress, noted that in contrast to the big stressors of life (marriage, divorce, losing one's job, death of a close friend) it is often the 'daily hassles' 'that are more closely linked to normative stress and may have a greater effect on our moods and our health than the major misfortunes of life' (p. 58).

Certainly, in teaching, it is the *frequency* and sometimes the intensity, of 'daily hassles' that teachers find most stressful: student behaviour such as lateness; homework not completed; students without equipment; behaviours such as talking while the teacher is talking; calling out; general noise levels; following up of classroom and playground discipline incidents; photocopiers breaking down; even toilets that are both inadequate (and placed too near the easy hearing of others); the frequent meetings and marking of student work ... The list could go on: small issues in themselves, but when they occur frequently they increase normative stress.

Lazarus points out that 'daily uplifts' can counter the negative effect of 'daily hassles' (1981, p. 58). It is here that much of the 'incidental colleague support' can, at least temporarily, buoy up the spirit and re-engage daily motivation.[18] The typical 'uplifts' can even 'sustain or restore when psychological resources have been run down during stressful periods ... (and) may act as psychological protection' (1981, p. 58). Those that are workplace-focused, he notes, are as 'basic' as:

- relating well to others on a daily, transitional, basis
- 'small' acts of support. I have noted countless times that colleagues value highly a fellow colleague's photocopying of 'those worksheets that one didn't get time to do(!)', the 'covering of class' when one is running late, the note or phone call of encouragement or going out of one's way in a 'free period' to visit a colleague to encourage or just chat about an issue of common concern
- visiting, writing or phoning someone (colleagues often appreciated a small thank-you note or token of appreciation)
- completing a basic task (that sense of 'completion of')
- meeting basic professional responsibilities
- a pleasing workplace (school), environment. (Even decent tea/coffee-making facilities and staff room furniture ...).

Social support as colleague support

Fundamentally, social support refers to the availability of people (both inside and outside of a social setting) to give support in the sense that such support is both helpful and can be relied upon. That support can vary from ideas and information shared, recognition and feedback through to advice, emotional support and direct support assistance. In short, Maslach (1982) says, 'People can provide many things you cannot (always) provide for yourself' (in Bernard, 1990, p. 287). A 'social support system' in a school environment addresses emotional and empathetic aspects of sharing (and problem analysis support), and instrumental support where someone can (and will) take some form of direct action on your behalf (O'Brien, 1998, Rogers, 2000).

Sarros (1989, in Bernard, 1990) has linked sources of stress in schools (including burnout) to how social support buffers stress, and has noted particularly that emotional support, listening, sharing-in-trust and demonstrations of concern helped teachers feel they were not alone in both having concerns and problems, but also in being able to work through these problems. This is consistent with studies noted in Elton (1989), Russell et al. (1987), Weiss (1974) and Rogers (1999). Bernard (1990) also notes:

- In terms of the frequency of support from different people, peer group colleagues provided the most support followed by family and friends inside and outside of school. Principals (in general) provided the least amount of support followed by the vice-principal, faculty head and year level co-ordinator.
- In order of importance, the types of support received by teachers were listening (emotional), time, feedback, advice and information (instrumental).
- Female teachers generally tend to give and receive more support than male teachers.
- The more support provided by principals, the lower the levels of teacher burnout.
- Peer group support was related to lower levels of personal accomplishment burnout.
- The more time teachers spent providing emotional support to others the greater their emotional exhaustion (pp. 291–5).

Johnson (1972) summarises the positive aspects of 'social support' and links it to the psychological and social-relational benefits:

> 'Positive and supportive relationships provide the caring, information, resources and feedback you need to cope with stress and flourish physically and psychologically. They decrease the number and severity of stressful events in your life. They reduce your anxiety and help you appraise the nature of the stress and your ability to deal with it constructively. Discussions with supportive peers help you perceive the meaning of the stressful event, regain mastery over your life, and enhance your self-esteem' (p. 11).

O'Brien (1998) makes a strong plea for 'institutionalising systems of collegial support', not by mandate, but by a conscious need for (such) support that:

'Can operate on grounds of professional responsibility as well as goodwill. Teachers should seek **and** expect support during difficult times; it should not be seen as something that is unusual or an imposition of the time of colleagues, especially those in a management position' (author's emphasis), (p. 97).

Dunham (1987) indicates that a mark of a 'healthy school' is 'pastoral care'[19] for teachers as well as pupils' (p. 15). In seeking to develop such a culture, Dunham emphasises that pastoral care support needs to be multi-dimensional rather than hierarchical if it is to enable colleague coping (p. 21). This multi-dimensional aspect is noted later, in Chapters 4–6.

To adapt a metaphor used by Stephen Glenn (1987), social support can provide a 'network of fellow travellers'[20] that assists in:

- lessening the feelings of isolation
- providing moral and professional support
- providing a forum for problem-sharing, problem analysis and problem-solving
- giving that essential stress-relieving support in the management of particularly difficult and disruptive students such as 'time-out' procedures (for staff and students) (Rogers, 1999).[21]

In a study on 'the moderating effects of social support on stress', Etzion (1984) notes that a number of features are identified in social transactions of support: 'emotional concern', 'instrumental aid', 'information and appraisal' (pp. 616–20). Kyriacou (1981) has also noted that the degree of social support available in a school is a crucial factor in 'mitigating stress' in both a 'palliative and direct-action way' by:

- allowing individuals the opportunity to receive advice about direct-action approaches to their stress-related issues
- addressing the issue of perspective on problems and conflicts
- social interaction as a provision and an outlet for tension relief (p. 197).

When linked with emotional coping and reduction of stress in the workplace, Maslach (1976) has found that:

> '… burnout rates are lower for those professionals who actively express, analyse and share their personal feelings with their colleagues. Not only do they consciously get things off their chest, but they have an opportunity to receive constructive feedback from other people and to develop new perspectives and understanding of their relationship with their clients' (p. 10).

Etzion (1984) adds that the effect of social support in 'moderating stress' and reducing burnout is due to 'adding positive need-fulfilling elements into one's life' (p. 620).[22] As explored later, to enable colleague support to be more than incidental or fortuitously dependent on a given individual (or individuals) being present, a school can enhance colleague support through whole-school initiatives.

Weiss (1974) in his major study on 'social provisions' outlines six relational aspects relevant to social support provision:

- attachment: a relationship factor in which the person receives a sense of security and safety
- social integration: provided by a network of social relationships in which individuals share interests and concerns
- reassurance of worth: provided by relationships in which the person's skills and abilities are acknowledged
- guidance: provided by relationships with trustworthy and authoritative individuals who can provide advice (both inside and outside the school setting)
- reliable alliance: derived from relationships (in which trust and rapport operate) the person can count on for assistance under any circumstance. This issue, for me, was fundamental in considering aspects of 'crisis-coping' and colleague support in 'behaviourally challenging schools'[23]
- opportunity for nurturance derived from relationships in which the person is responsible for the nurturance (and well-being of) another.

These 'provisions' (as Weiss terms them) describe a culture, or ethos, of support; they are the enabling provisions. In Chapters 4 and 5 these 'enabling provisions' are discussed in some detail.

Affiliation and social support

Studies in affiliation (from the late 1950s) have focused on several key ways in which affiliative motive and supportive behaviour operate.[24]

- The reciprocal nature of affiliation and the 'need to belong'.
- The increase in affiliation in times of stress and the enablement to cope gives shared assurance, reduction of anxiety and an increase in 'relative certainty' as people share common needs, experiences and solutions (Middlebrook, 1974).
- The need for assurance in needs-coping and professional coping. One of the consistently valued aspects of colleague support noted by participants in my research study was that of 'sharing of experiences and concerns in the teaching journey 'without censure or blame'.
- Consistent with studies noted earlier, positive, social-professional affiliation can have a 'buffering' affect on stress.[25]

The correlate here is that when people decide to affiliate there is an increase in psychological assurance and (one could postulate) professional assurance and a reduction in anxiety; in both psychological and role anxiety.

There also seems to be a strong association between the basic needs of 'belonging' (Dreikurs, 1968, 1982; Glasser, 1992; O'Brien, 1998) and 'social identity' through affiliative function. This raised for me the question, 'What sorts of affiliative function are noted and valued in colleague support teams in schools?' At its most fundamental level 'the affiliation need' expresses the need to be a social being. This 'need' is held in natural tension with the need (at times) to have professional autonomy. Some colleagues shared that sometimes they had the need to withdraw from the 'interpersonal frictions', the 'occasional boredoms' and 'psychological incompatibility' (as when meetings with others is a mere 'formal necessity'). Affiliative needs probably lie on a continuum from a 'high' to 'low' need to affiliate, since such needs relate to personality and temperament and how reciprocal trust operates between persons in a given school setting.

In a study on affiliation, Sermat et al. (1970) note that those (in their 'social' groupings) who were characteristically dogmatic, manipulative or judgmental towards others and who attributed responsibility for their problems to others were not liked as well as 'participants' who scored higher on *social skill* tests (Sermat, Cohen and Pollack, 1970, in Middlebrook, 1974, pp. 252–3). In this sense *de*-affiliation (by others) and *unsupportive behaviour(s)* act on each other reciprocally, and self-defeatingly, and are often an indicator of an unsupportive workplace.

For example, when a school culture addresses factors such as teaming, collaboration and shared decision-making, 'de-affiliative' behaviours can have a significant effect on the sense of common good and mutual regard for all (including the students). Without some shared sense of what Johnson (1972) terms 'consensual validation', the events, and even people's behaviour (around us), are often ambiguous and open to a variety of interpretations. Johnson suggests we need 'some affiliation' to affirm 'common goals, interests, activities and values and practices, to both compare with self and validate self' (p. 33).[26] It may well be this aspect of affiliation that is a feature of a more 'consciously supportive' school culture. (Rogers, 1999 and p. 64f).

Coping and support

Coping, at its best, is more than 'mere' coping or, as Freeman (1987) argues, 'defensive behaviour such as distortion of reality' (p. 37). 'Coping' includes 'adaptation' and 'mastery' as well as 'survival'. It includes the immediate and longer-term aspects of coping; immediate coping often includes crisis-coping, whereas long-term coping is significantly affected by the dependability of structures, policy and procedures one can depend upon to give adequate and necessary support.

Antonovsky (1979), Freeman (1987), Rutter (1981) and Kyriacou (1980, 1981) all link 'coping effectively', and the 'range of coping', to the amount and degree of social support available. Freeman (1987) suggests that one needs to examine coping from the perspective of 'personal appraisal', 'coping resources' and 'coping context' (pp. 38–9). This has implications for appraising how collegial culture addresses coping as a feature of colleague support. As a correspondent wrote (to me), 'Peer support has really helped, I have listened to my peers, their ideas and advice. They've especially helped me when I've had to use some time-out procedures with challenging students. In summary, my stress level is more under control'.

Freeman (1987) also cites three major stressors in the teaching profession that affect coping: 'isolation in the classroom', 'job satisfaction' (this also relates to the kind of feedback a teacher receives from pupils) and 'perceived incompetence'.[27] This last factor often relates to perceptions about perceived ability to manage, even control, a class. Freeman suggests that social support, 'would seem to be of great importance in the (self-) appraisal process. Appraisal of a stressful situation takes into account expectations that others have the resources available to the individual' (ibid.).

Little (1990) – in Miller (1996) – suggests that although teachers may provide a 'range of affiliative functions they do not (always) serve stimuli and agents for each other's professional development' (p. 199). While this may be true, what Little (1990) may not countenance is the very high value teachers place (in colleague support terms) on 'affiliative function' [sic] *in itself* as a feature of coping support. The issue of professional feedback is discussed in Chapter 5.

Interpersonal needs and colleague support

Maslow (1968, 1985), in his hierarchy of needs, describes the 'lower' level needs as 'pre-potent': the needs for food, shelter and then the needs for safety and security. He further describes the social–relational needs as 'higher-order': belongingness, affirmation and love. What is interesting, in terms of daily interaction in the teaching workplace, is that it is important to seek to meet and satisfy the lower needs in order for the 'higher' needs to be adequately met as well: cognitive curiosity, understanding and challenge; and the need for achievement, competence and mastery and the move towards self-actualisation.[28] In some of the schools I have worked, it seems that even the basic needs such as decent classroom furniture, materials and resources, assurances that 'one is on the right track', a fair timetable and back-up resources are real expressions of 'need' that affect daily coping. They are also indications of how supportive the administration is to their teaching colleagues.

Erikson (1968) has noted that one's *self*-esteem is significantly related to the 'reflected appraisals' of others. These reflected appraisals can also affect one's sense of acceptance and belonging; after all, we spend (as teachers) a significant part of our working day with our professional colleagues. Even if an individual does not naturally 'feel' a significant sense of social belonging with his peers at school, the fact that a school is an educational *community* requires some sense of requisite, professional, collegiality in order to engage its mission.

This operational feature of needs (even the so-called 'lower' needs) is an important feature in collegial life in a school – it can easily be taken for granted. In one school I worked (a few years ago) I asked a colleague what cup (etc.) I should use and he asked if I'd 'brought my own milk'. I thought, at first, he was 'winding me up', but no, in this school this protective individual ownership of milk (a number of different labelled containers in the fridge!) was, to me, symptomatic of a deeper feature of their collegial life. I have spoken to countless supply teachers (relief teachers) who have said that the degree to which they felt they belonged in a 'new' school environment was often affected by the 'small things' like being hassled because you took the wrong cup(!) in the staff room, or sat at the 'wrong' table, whether you were welcomed in the staff room, and whether you had a 'pigeon hole' and a photocopy number.

Glasser (1992) has indicated that one's physical and psychological needs are interrelated, such as security and comfort as they relate to belonging(ness) expressed in social and group membership. Dreikurs (1968), like Erikson (1963, 1968) and Maslow (1985), affirms the importance of the 'need to belong' as a central (if not the central) social need. This need, within a social network like a school community, is affected – even met – by how supported one feels relative to that sense of personal and professional belonging.

O'Brien (1998) contrasts this kind of individual need 'to belong' with 'common' and more distinct needs such as those relating to particular contexts such as a school setting and roles. O'Brien outlines 'needs' in three ways as they relate to the provision, or 'service', of needs in the school setting.

Table 2.1 *Needs and provisions*

Common needs	Those needs relating to self and self in relation to others; for example, self-determination, belonging, social interaction, safety, security, freedom ...
Distinct needs associated with being a member of a group or community	Needs as they relate to one's role in a particular school setting.
Individual needs that relate to a particular person at a particular time.	*This* teacher in *this* place at *this* time.

Adapted from O'Brien (1998) pp. 14–16.

Johnson (1972) sees these kind of needs operating, fulfilled and met, in the *'humanising'* of relationships:

> 'In humanising relationships, individuals are sympathetic and responsive to human needs. They invest each other with the character of humanity, and they treat and regard each other as human. It is the positive involvement with other people that we label as humane. In a dehumanising relationship, people are divested of those qualities that are uniquely human and are turned into machines and objects. In the sense that they are treated in impersonal ways that reflect unconcern with human values' (p. 12).

Scott-Peck (1997) notes that the concept of 'personal value' is also related to 'social engagement'; a 'feature of belonging essential to mental health' (p. 23).[29] This 'social-engagement is affected, further, by the historical aspect of classroom teaching as an isolated role experience; isolated from adult peers but ensconced with minors in classrooms.

Dreikurs (1992) also, intriguingly asserts that 'fun' is an important 'need'. I have noticed, countless times, how in schools where a healthy sense of 'fun', humour and laughter is present a positive camaraderie and morale are a characteristic feature of the school culture. Burford (1996) speaks of 'humour' and 'laughter' as playing a major role in the coping strategies of teachers and students alike (p. 29).[30]

Power, too, is acknowledged as an important need in the sense of both personal power (as an individual's ability to influence and effect events and to be accomplished and recognised for one's abilities) and relational power; the power to interact positively and supportively influence others. This need also relates to a sense of personal and social values relative to that influence (Bradshaw, 1981; Dreikurs, 1968, 1982; Glasser, 1992). The degree to which this need (as any need) can be both manipulated and abused is obvious. For some, 'power' (as a need) means the exercise of power *over* others, rather than using one's relational, and psychological power *for* and *with* others; this social dimension of power is a significant determinant in a supportive colleague culture.[31] This need for 'power' is also related to freedom; the need to be free to make choices in our personal and professional lives. For some, this need is higher, say in the need for some professional autonomy (and expression of professional freedom and 'power') than in others who prefer a more directed professional life.

It might well be hypothesised, then, that colleague support can affect, and assist, in the meeting of both common (or fundamental) needs, as well as more distinct and individual or specific needs relating to time, place and context (see Weiss, 1974).

I have proposed a model that illustrates this probable interaction in Figure 2.1.

Self-esteem and 'belonging'

Stanley Coopersmith (1967), in his seminal work on self-esteem, relates one's self-worth, self-respect, confidence, identity and purpose (as an individual) with a fundamental sense of (and need for) security in one's environmental and social relationships. He further highlights the importance of self-esteem as relating to approval by people who are important to oneself. Like Glasser (1992) he also relates self-esteem to 'power' in terms of the extent to which one can influence one's own and other's lives in a positive way.

Figure 2.1 *Colleague support as an expression of needs-fulfilling/needs-supporting*

This, it seems to me, has implications for the kind of colleague culture we seek to develop and encourage in our schools. Because self-esteem is related to 'other-esteem', a collegially supportive environment ought to be able to affect a personal sense of value (both as a person and a professional). This, one could speculate, would affect one's coping behaviour in a positive way, as well as supporting one's professional role (Russell, et al. 1987; Weiss 1974).

It has been my experience that where teachers seem to feel reasonably confident in their personal and social identity (as a 'self-in-relationship-to-others') that, in turn, has a positive effect on others; there is a reciprocal effect of esteem to esteem, self-to-other self, as it were. It has also been my experience that low self-esteem among teachers can also be affected negatively by the kinds of colleague support available in a school. As one correspondent (writing to me personally) notes:

> '… of the last thirteen years of my teaching, I look back to the first eight with satisfaction, the last five with sadness. The difference between two periods doesn't really relate to major differences in the type of kids … I have always worked in the "rougher" areas of Melbourne. What was different was the atmosphere of the school – in particular, the support and camaraderie of the staff and the genuine concern of the principal for the staff (compared with my most recent school). It strikes me as comic, on reflection, how may times I have sat on committees and written up lovely ideals about pupil self-esteem, encouragement of pupils and effective conflict resolutions – often this was done in the staff room where people were divided by fear or resignation. We were meant to develop these positive aims for students in an atmosphere of destructive staff morale' (used with permission).

Self-esteem is often linked with the need for 'affiliation' and 'belonging' – Dreikurs (1968); Erikson (1963, 1968); Maslow (1985); Middlebrook (1974). It seems to be affected for positive good, or not, by a number of factors relevant to the kind of support both available, encouraged and maintained within a school context:

- Opportunities (both formal and informal) to collaborate on issues of common concern, as well as those issues directly related to curriculum and lesson planning, in a climate of non-judgmental sharing.
- Common aims, objectives, policies and action planning (Breheney et al. (1996); Hart (1994); Hart et al. (1993), Axworthy et al. (1989) and Rogers (1995)
- Positive encouragement and descriptive – non-judgmental – feedback.

The general cultural 'norms' (stated and/or unstated) can be observed in teacher behaviour that sees teachers 'looking out' for one another, demonstrating acts of caring (even 'small' acts of caring), and reciprocal collegial trust (Johnson, 1972). Self-esteem is clearly affected by *other-esteem* – how others in the school value you; this sense of 'reciprocal value' of an individual is seen as a key factor in staff morale. These factors also affect what might be termed school-wide 'colleague esteem'; affecting (and being affected by) the consciousness of colleague support embedded in the school culture (Elton (1989) and Rogers (1992, 2000)).

Whingeing – 'off-loading'

Whingeing can be a positive and constructive feature of collegial coping; it can also be 'self-sabotaging' or 'other-sabotaging' (Bramson, 1981, p. 56). Myss (1988) suggests there are some good reasons the sharing of gripes, moans and personal struggles can be rewarding and supportive. She suggests that 'gripe-sharing' between colleagues is a form of social-intimacy; a way of 'developing' or 'affirming' trust (p. 14). This is often expressed, in typical dyadic forms, in schools, as teachers validate common feelings of frustration (difficult students, timetables, another meeting, a difficult parent etc.) – a shared frustration that can 'bond' – as the temporary relief validates 'one's common lot'.

There is a kind of moaning that can 'bond', validate one's feelings, enable coping and relieve stress, as well as act as a 'clearing house' for problem analysis and resolution. As one colleague noted in an interview:

> '… the grizzling and the whingeing release the emotion, the frustration that builds up about the unknown, especially with all the changes we have to cope with (!); and because something new is thrown at you [sic] you have a bit of a grizzle, you let off steam, and you feel better about it. We all do our grizzling and we all share our thoughts and pool [sic] our resources and with that I think we can cope because we share the **same sorts of feelings** and we can cope better …' (in Rogers, 1999, colleague's emphasis).

Negative whingeing[32]

Negative whingeing – a combination of whingeing, complaining and moaning – can become very draining on other colleagues' goodwill and patience. Frequent and pervasive moaning can be both a symptomatic, and a characteristic, feature of an unsupportive school ethos. Almost all respondents (Rogers, 1999) mentioned this feature of school culture and related it to incompetence, laziness, abuse of the system and lack of peer (colleague) support.[33] Bramson (1981) describes those who exhibit this negative whingeing as 'the complete complainer' and makes the point that (such):

> 'Complainers do not feel they are whining. Their complaining is a doomed effort to warn about anything gone wrong that someone else must fix. Complainers persist in their complaining in order to validate their feelings that they themselves are not responsible. They are not responsible for doing anything differently or seeing things in a different way' (p. 43).

The moaning of some in the workplace may be an expressed need to validate feelings of withdrawal or of avoiding responsibility. Markham (1993) describes this kind of moaning and complaining not merely as draining (on others in the workplace) but that when the complainer is typically complaining it may be an expression of a 'strong need' to be negative, 'in advance', to protect themselves from future disappointment.

It is, essentially, the difference between the sort of 'whingeing', or complaining, that adds to individual (and social) stress and the sort of whingeing that helps relieve stress and enhance coping.

The tension of 'individualism', 'collectivism' and collegiality

There is a creative tension regarding collegiality and collaboration, when it addresses isolation as if it is a 'one-side solution' and 'collegiality as automatically good' (Fullan, 1993). 'Pushed to extremes becomes "group think, uncritical conformity to the group, unthinking accepting of the latest solution, suppression of individual dissent"' (p. 34).

Fullan and Hargreaves (1991) note that in response to the problem of isolation 'greater collegiality is becoming one of the premier improvement strategies of the 1990s' (p. 43). They go on to note that in seeking to eliminate 'individualism' (habitual patterns of working alone), we should not eradicate 'individuality' (voicing of disagreement, opportunity for solitude). Individuality (not mere autonomy) can generate 'creative disagreement and risk' that can 'be a source of dynamic group learning'. Hargreaves (1994) asserts that:

> 'Singular models of mandated and specific kinds of collaboration is not empowering but disempowering. Contrived collegiality (is) a form of collaboration which is forced rather than facilitated, which meets the implementation needs of bureaucratic systems rather than the development needs of teachers and schools, which is designed to be administratively predictable in its outcomes' (p. 57).

This sort of collaborative teacher 'culture' includes 'high discretion' over the kinds of collaborative work pursued; 'trust and patience' are key attitudinal factors in 'building supportive relationships' which can (and will) have both 'formal' and 'informal' features in supportive structures.

Collaborative cultures

In a collaborative culture there are common features about collegiality and support that are present:

- Communication is characteristically supportive whether at the level of staff room 'chatting' or as a means of expressing shared coping and understanding. Communication that addresses professional issues, needs and concerns is 'open' and tolerant of differences among staff (Rogers, 1995, 1999).[34] Nias et al. (1989) note that whether transitional, incidental or more extended in form, collaborative communication facilitates 'the development of trust' that leads to 'mutual openness' and can enable 'shared meanings' across both 'mundane' and 'complex ideas' (pp. 79–80).
- Collaboration also relies on professional trust. Nias et al. (1989) suggest that

trust has two dimensions: 'predictability' (of other's personal behaviour and work-related behaviour) and 'common goals' (p. 130). Such trust is able to positively affect the resilience of the culture in coping with normative stress and change.

> 'Shared understandings and agreed behaviours enable staff in schools where this culture is dominant to trust and learn from one another. The relationships which they create in the process are tough and flexible enough to withstand shocks and uncertainties from within and without' (1989. p. 74).

- These 'shared understandings' are noticeably present in the management of conflict and change where staff do not allow natural 'differences' – even 'disputes' and 'dissention' to disrupt ongoing colleague relationships. *Collaborative conflict management* acknowledges and accepts differences of opinion, ideas, even teaching practice within shared norms.

- When coping with and managing change in a school, it is collegial interdependency within common goals and shared beliefs that is the overriding, enabling factor in managing difference and disagreement (Rogers, 1995).[35]

- The relationship between the individual and interdependence is demonstrated in how individuals are valued 'as people'. 'Individuals should be accepted and valued ... So too should interdependence because individuals exist only in a social context' (Nias, 1989, p. 72).[36] 'Valuing individuals' is demonstrated in the nature and kinds of communication operating in the school, the nature of 'trust' and 'openness', minimising unnecessary 'status divisions' and acknowledging the 'contribution of others' (ibid.).

- Valuing interdependence and working as a team is a central, even defining, feature of collaborative cultures. This involves both a recognition of the importance of others' contributions, as well as the concept of collective responsibility within the school's aims and purposes. In one of the more 'consciously supportive' schools I researched, a respondent notes, 'In our school we are purpose-driven not merely task-driven' (Rogers, 1999).

- Interdependence also involves collaboration and shared learning. Nias et al. (op cit.) (1992) in their work on whole-school curriculum development outline the importance of 'teachers as learners' in relation to their colleagues. This aspect of collegial learning and continual professional development within a school culture has important implications in areas such as professional sharing and feedback, needs-analysis in areas such as curriculum and lesson planning, and evaluation and appraisal.

Teachers need to feel that they can engage in professional discussions both informally and more formally with high trust. In this way their ongoing learning is occasioned from supportive feedback and sharing through to supportive appraisal. In such 'consciously supportive schools (Rogers, 1999) there is a shared belief that teaching and management practice can always be improved by shared professional reflection; in this sense (like our students) we are life-long learners.[37]

Autonomy, freedom and trust

> Sally is a senior teacher, recently appointed to the position of curriculum director of a large high school. In a discussion on colleague support she made an important distinction between autonomy and support:
>
> > 'I value being given autonomy to develop this role; it demonstrates the trust I've been given within my skills and abilities. This doesn't mean I am autonomous but it does give me autonomy – the freedom to develop "my" ideas about curriculum, as well as work with my colleagues. This professional freedom is important to me – not having to constantly check with senior staff about whether I'm doing the right thing or not – it's about professional trust.'

Some teachers appreciate the assurance that can come from such autonomy, others appreciate direction and structure – and there needs to be both in a school. Within structure and guidelines, though, teachers also value the opportunity to have professional autonomy (with its natural 'risks') to 'get on with their job'; this is quite different from being autonomous.[38] As one primary colleague notes:

> '... being able to say "I don't want to ..." and it's okay to say "no". Your individuality is respected. I've been in schools where it is the opposite. Here I can say what I like (if you know what I mean).' (in Rogers, 1999)

Teachers, in this study, noted these differences, acknowledged them as normative but drew a distinction between 'autonomy' and 'privacy' – privacy was valued by many, as the 'small personal moments' alongside the need to affiliate, to find support in the social and professional domain.[39]

It is as important to respect privacy and appropriate professional autonomy, as it is to endorse, encourage, invite and even 'structure' colleague support – without imposing it.

Nias et al. (1989), suggest that collaboration is characterised more by pervasive qualities and attitudes than formal meetings or its bureaucratic shape; it is demonstrated in how colleagues give help, convey support, communicate and engage trust and openness (pp. 98–9).

Teams and groups and teaming as colleague support

Little (1990) in Fullan and Hargreaves (1991, p. 47) identifies typical collegial relations as 'scanning and storytelling', 'help and assistance', 'advice and reassurance ...'. While these are helpful, she suggests that another kind – joint work – is perhaps the strongest 'type' or 'form' of collegial collaboration. '... joint work implies and creates stronger interdependence, shared responsibility, collective commitment and improvement, and greater readiness to participate in the difficult business of review and critique.' This, says Little, 'is the kind of collaborative work and culture most likely to lead to significant improvement. In the quest for improvement, other kinds of collaboration may support this basic thrust, but by themselves are likely to be poor substitutes for it' (ibid.).

Teaming, in the sense of a group operating and working for a shared purpose, has become a more common feature of Australian schools in the past 10 to 15 years – particularly at the primary school level where the shift from individual planning to team planning is more frequently the norm. Such teams are based generally in year-level or multi-age level teams, (at primary level).

Johnson and Johnson (1989); Bernard (1990); Fullan and Hargreaves (1991) and Rogers (1996) note that collegial teams can:

- enable individual, professional, empowerment (not available in prior individualistic contexts)
- enable communication that (can) support real problem-solving and initiatives by developing shared goals and approaches
- enable and develop the individual's ideas and skills in an interdependent way (that values individuality and group aspects of professional contribution)
- provide a social, not merely a talk-focused, dimension to work
- potentially reduce unnecessary stress, conflict and competitive behaviour.

Such teaming is based on a basic premise that most individuals want to make meaningful contributions to the effectiveness of their school. As Heller (1976) suggests:

> 'There is special virtue in group association which they cannot extend to a relatively solitary activity. [This] concept of participation finds its theoretical roots in [the] human relations approach to management that emphasises power equalisation and social interaction' (in Leana, 1987, p. 228).

Within these parameters and descriptors a team (not merely group) can support professional collegiality. It is important to note, though, that in developing, building and sustaining team*work* the process of shared communication and decision-making allows differences of opinion and position to be aired, even explored, as colleagues participate in group discussion, consultation, review and decision-making. It is the differences of opinion, approach(es) and even perspective that can actually enhance both the decisions reached and the value (itself) that endorses individual difference in a shared enterprise. This can often allow for a more creative decision overall.

Without this value position, group participants can end up merely arguing for their 'own' positions, not engaging in perspective-taking of another's position, and balancing their own views and perspectives within *shared* aims, objectives and common needs. This point is taken up by, Stacey (1992):

> 'People do not provoke new insights when their discussions are characterised by orderly equilibrium, conformity and dependence. Neither do they do so when their discussions enter the explosively unstable equilibrium of all-out conflict or complete avoidance of issues ... People spark new ideas off each other when they argue and disagree – when they are conflicting, confused and searching for new meaning – yet remain willing to discuss and listen to each other' (in Fullan, 1993, p. 27).

Scott (1992) notes that 'over concern' about 'spoiling the atmosphere', by not letting team members have 'differences of opinion' is one of the ways effective teamwork can be ruined.

The key aspects of team-building revolve around aspects of colleague support such as shared aims and targets; quality professional relationships (especially the feature of being able to disagree without resentment, and expressing feelings with professional tact); 'pulling together' when engaging in tasks that are 'more than the individual can manage'; 'balanced leadership' that includes 'sensitivity to individual differences'; the ability to 'balance demands of a task, building workable team cohesion and meeting individual needs' (Finger, 1993 and Johnson and Johnson, 1989).[40]

This places some demand on team leaders for key skills in information-gathering in groups, facilitating natural tensions and pressures in group dynamics; managing natural conflict; giving feedback and testing assumptions (without unnecessary critical judgment); and drawing a group together with their common ideas, concepts and positions within common values.

Not all groups, even working groups, are necessarily *teams*. In a team there is a physical group based in meeting (regularly) for a shared and common purpose, with common aims and complementary and interdependent skills. They also see that their individual accountability is balanced with collective responsibility and interdependency. The concept of 'teaming', as distinct from 'being a team', can occur at both a dyadic level as well as within a 'formal' team. This 'form' of loose-teaming is prevalent in many schools, it has a loose-coupling 'form' and tends to occur 'transitionally' as needs arise.

Peer support groups: teaming for direct colleague support

Peer support groups have been noted in the literature as a forum for 'reducing iso-lation', enabling professional 'sharing and support', 'improving self- (and group) esteem', 'reducing unnecessary competition', providing a forum for 'analysis and solution of problems', improving teamwork, as well as directly improving skills in areas such as curriculum planning, teaching practice and behaviour management (Rogers, 1996, 1999, 2000 and O'Brien, 1998).

Such groups can also provide a 'structure', a 'forum', (as distinct from a 'team'), that gives an opportunity for direct problem-solving and solutions matched to individual needs, as well as a forum for ongoing professional development. This is consistent with research conducted by Bernard (1990), Johnson and Johnson (1989), O'Brien (1998), Rogers (1996) and Parkes and Rogers (1987). Peer sup-port groups are a form of 'incidental teaming' that can cross faculty and grade boundaries, can exist 'ad-hoc' or on a long-term basis.

Johnson and Johnson (1989) see these 'semi-formal' groupings as direct partici-pation in collegial support aimed at engaging staff in a joint venture that increases their beliefs about the positive assistance arising from collaborative (peer) sharing, encounter and practice:

> 'Increasing teachers' belief that they are engaged in a joint venture ("We are doing it"). A public commitment to and by peers to increase their instructional and managerial expertise ("I will try it"), peer accountability ("They are counting on me"), a sense of safety ("The risk is challenging, but not excessive") and self-efficacy ("If I make the effort, I will be successful"). It is this balance of personal commitment and support (not authority) that energises change efforts by teachers' (p. 17).

This kind of 'grouping' can meet both distinct needs (the more professional needs), as well as the more fundamental needs such as 'esteem' and 'belonging'. O'Brien (1989) notes:

> 'It was important that the meetings were not an organisational structure for group coun-seling and psychotherapy and most importantly it was not, and never should be, a "moaning monster"' (p. 116).

> 'In such groups there was not always an "agenda" but there was a "provision", an emphasis, on "gentle direction" [sic], especially in the management of "fair share of time", and "managing tension"' (p. 117).

The most common experience generated by such groups was that its members found the peer-support group enabled both the sharing of 'new strategies and ideas' and the sense of 'having been listened to, and heard' (Rogers, 1997). This meeting of needs, therefore, enabled both the reduction and management of stress and professional sharing and the re-directing of problems to purposeful solutions. Sometimes the meetings focused on the recognition of positive achievements; this 'boosted morale' in a natural rather than artificially contained way. O'Brien (1989) adds that, we do not spend 'enough time' (as a profession) 'praising or complimenting each other on our practice' (p. 119).

In one school-based study on peer support groups (Parkes and Rogers, 1987) participants noted these benefits:

- confidence, enjoyment and pride in one's profession; that is, *being a teacher*
- the development of the qualities of enthusiasm, optimism and persistence, with a range of staff preparing to take the leadership roles (in a climate of trust)
- the emergence of a 'strong group of teachers who are now interested in both the classroom and the running of the school' [sic]
- security: (the) feeling of not being isolated but of (the) group sharing (and) being able to discuss real discipline problems without fear of criticism, and finding workable solutions (pp. 7–8).[41] Of course, any such trust is built over time, modelled, and occurs between persons in the system; *not simply because of the system.* Also such groups (unlike, say, formal faculty teams) occur from elective engagement
- learning how to respond to difficulties by sharing what has happened in one's professional life; 'You get a voice and you are actually taken seriously' (ibid.)
- reducing stress levels, and increased confidence in one's abilities through the sharing of common concerns and suggested responses. This finding is confirmed in the work of Sarros, 1989 (in Bernard (1990) and Rogers (1996, 1999))
- 'There is a secure base from which to build relationships with colleagues whom you hardly see in the busy atmosphere of a (special) school' (O'Brien, 1998, p. 120).

Johnson and Johnson (1989) note that such peer groupings can increase teachers' sense of moral and professional support; and promote committed and caring relationships among staff.[42] These 'forms' of peer-support groups can also empower staff through teamwork; being part of a 'team' can 'increase confidence', 'self-esteem', 'risk-taking' and experimentation.[43] From this, one has a collegial 'base' (not the only one) for 'professional development and growth'.

One of the aims of peer-support groups is to further extend professional development from group-sharing, to peer observation, mentoring and peer-coaching. Members of a peer-support group may elect to mutually observe one another's classes. Through agreed agenda and focus, they give thoughtful, descriptive feedback on 'what they heard, what they saw and how they felt in the colleague's class'. This feedback is valuable data for increasing professional awareness and generating change. Peer-members may also elect to rehearse skills prior to classes and ask the 'peer-observer' to give feedback. This 'observation phase' forms an invaluable link between workshop discussion (in the groups) and modelling and the application of knowledge within one's classroom setting. Many members, after several peer-group meetings, feel comfortable enough to share their experiences (often with quite judicious humour!) with the whole group – again, this is invitational (Parkes and Rogers, 1987, pp. 7–8).

Participants recorded (in their ongoing journal) some of their self-talk in relationships to their peer-support group experiences:

> 'Oh God … These kids are horrible, these kids aren't normal! No one could control these kids. Other teachers don't feel like this. They cope … they are just fine … they are even laughing in the staff room … It must be me … I'm no good at this … Oh God.'

> 'Oh God … Now they're going to tell me (at this meeting) what I should be doing if I was any good … Give me a magic formula …HMPH! It won't work for me, I bet!! **Well how about that, they feel the same way as me!** I'm not hopeless after all. That was a good idea what he said … I might try that …. Teaching isn't that bad after all' (colleague's emphasis).

> 'Peer group support, although initially yet another onslaught to the battered ego, has proven very useful. I found it de-mystified the 'successful' teacher, offering objective advice, techniques and skills. Despite my initial hesitation there was never any pressure to attend or to practise what was discussed, which gave a friendly informal feel to the group. Extremely valuable' (Parkes and Rogers, 1987, p. 8).

Beginning teachers – colleague support

Beginning teachers, particularly, find their first year of teaching difficult (especially in hard-to-manage classrooms). In a study by Watson et al. (1991) those teachers who received ongoing colleague support from fellow teachers through 'formal' induction rated such support as a *crucial* factor in first-year teacher adjustment. Those who had been helped by staff at their school of first appointment were more than likely to be more 'well adjusted' than teachers who had not received such support.

I have heard many sad accounts (too many) of first-year teachers having to engage the twin cultures of 'teaching as a profession' and their first 'particular school' in an unsupported fashion; some are even 'thrown to the wolves'. It seems that in those more 'collegially unsupportive schools', colleague support for first-year, new, teachers is not taken seriously. The groups I have been involved in have summarised some key aspects of first-year colleague support (in Forristal and Rogers (1988) and Rogers (1998)):

- opportunity and time through structured meetings to share typical 'early' concerns and common issues facing first-year teachers
- a *planned* and *ongoing* forum that acts as an 'emotional clearing house', without being a 'spiralling whinge session'
- a forum for practical, professional development (this feature was particularly valued)
- a forum to network colleagues to skills, knowledge and persons (with those skills) across the school. This aspect of support also provided assurance to struggling colleagues early in the school year through careful networking with other colleagues by age, gender and experience.

The outcomes were consistently positive in areas such as stress reduction (especially anxiety), increased confidence in teaching and increased confidence in peer-networking across the school. Teachers noted that this meeting of needs came directly out of the first year peer-support groups.[44]

The groups met regularly in Term One, then had ad-hoc meetings during the year to evaluate progress in light of their aims. The groups often found it helpful to write up their expectations to assist incoming teachers in the following year.[45]

Feedback, appraisal and colleague support

One of the findings of the report *Teacher Stress in Victoria* (1989) noted that:

> 'Many respondents were concerned about themselves, how well they were doing, the development of their careers, and the regard in which they were held by others' (p. 29).

One of the eight recommendations made (about appraisal) in the report *Teacher Stress in Victoria* (1989, p. 29) was that the management team in each school be 'required' to talk with each teacher 'at least once a year' to 'provide feedback' about his/her work. While many schools have, since then, adopted what seems to be this very basic principle, the most recent formal expression of appraisal in Victorian schools is the PRP – the 'Professional Recognition Programme for teachers' (1996).[46] It was a Department of Education initiative and is (now) an integral part of a school's appraisal structure and professional recognition process. The extent to which it effectively and supportively enables professional appraisal is a moot point.

Addressing as it does sensitive features of a teacher's professional life and practice, part of the problem of the PRP is that as a major, formal appraisal process it is not an elective process; it is mandated by the Department of Education to schools. While addressing a twice-yearly 'form' of 'professional recognition', it does not seem to really address the ongoing nature of, and importance of, feedback as a form of formative appraisal.

Public servants need public accountability and this is a key feature of external appraisal (Ingvarson and Chadbourne, 1994);[47] teachers, however, have a natural tendency to be suspicious, perhaps even subtly unco-operative, about external and summative forms of appraisal.

As Hargreaves (1993) acknowledges, appraisal schemes (as distinct from appraisal per se) tend to invoke suspicion from teachers.

'Appraisal schemes are being imposed by central government in England and Wales on a suspicious profession, which not without good reason believes that, for the government, appraisal is an instrument of accountability and a means of disciplining weak teachers and/or introducing performance-related pay rather than a form of professional development' (p. 2).

Even though the shift (in the literature) appears to be moving away from summative approaches to appraisal that tend towards checklisting, monitoring and evaluating a teacher's performance, there will always be some element in 'appraisal' that relates to summative notions of 'appraising' of self and others in the teaching management role.[48]

As Kyriacou (1987) notes:

' ... perhaps the clearest benefit of teacher appraisal is the potential contribution it can make to foster the better flow of communication and support between teachers, and to offer in-service and professional development to all teachers on a regular basis ... perhaps the biggest change is that [if] it is introduced badly it can undermine the good which is already occurring' (p. 143).

As always with the 'appraisal issue' in schools there is the tension between 'summative' appraisal (those evaluative criteria, and processes, that lead to personnel and promotion decisions) and 'formative' appraisal (emphasising self-appraisal, professional development and professional growth). In this distinction, as Royce-Sadler (1989) observes, formative assessment, feedback and self- (and other) monitoring are all directly associated (p. 119).

Redman and MacKay (1994) note that it is important:

'... to recognise appraisal as a continuous and developmental process, one that can lead a school to reassess the types of skills and competencies it requires; to reconsider the definitions of teachers' and students' work and to review the supportive context required for both' (in Ingvarson and Chadbourne, 1994, pp. 238–9).

'It is an inescapable phenomenon, not necessarily to be deplored or to induce neurosis' (*Teacher Appraisal: A study,* 1996, p. 16).[49]

Feedback and appraisal

The distinction between feedback and appraisal, as such, is important for colleague support. Shulman (1986) makes the point that appraisal is a way of valuing teacher knowledge from within, and by, teachers. Teachers are often harder on themselves than an outside body – in that sense we hardly need an inspector 'checking up on us'.

In a 'collegial culture', feedback is a way of supportively 'affirming people in the team' making sure that they get the ongoing information essential to 'keep their efforts on track' (Goleman, 1996, p. 151). Royce-Sadler notes that feedback is a key element in formative assessment (1989, p. 120). Ingvarson and Chadbourne (1994) note that feedback, for on-learning, should be a 'key feature of a learning environment'.[50] Feedback is, then, an ongoing process of learning, evaluation and professional development. In this sense it is formative and not used as a direct means of assessing for tenure, promotion or pay and conditions.

- Feedback is actually part of the learning process and best accepted when there is an expressed need in the recipient, when the process has a degree of 'election' and 'choice' by the engaging recipient of feedback (Rogers, 2000), and where the feedback can be utilised in an ongoing way with respect to professional practice (Fullan, 1991, 1993; Johnson, 1972). Imposed or unsolicited feedback is generally unwelcome as many colleagues noted in my own study on colleague support (Rogers, 1999).
- When giving feedback it is most helpful when those giving feedback focus on their descriptive response, or reaction, to a colleague's behaviour rather than giving value judgments (Johnson, 1972). Descriptive feedback describes present and potential *behaviours*.
- Feedback can focus on the mutual needs of both the giver and receiver, though the primary focus is on the receiver.
- In giving feedback it is important to allow space for the colleague who receives it to respond, ask questions, to extend and develop the feedback given. It is easy for a 'more knowledgeable', 'more skilled' colleague, to swamp the 'less-skilled' with too much (of even positive, helpful) feedback. It is important to clarify, with the recipient, if they understand and see the implications of the feedback being given in a *context dependent sense* (for example, a post-classroom observation): 'Were you aware ...?', 'Did you notice ...?' (be specific), 'Were you conscious of ...?' (be specific), 'Did you hear yourself say ...?' (be specific).
- Supportively focus (where possible) on those things that the recipient can do something about; this implies clarity of focus with the feedback and ongoing colleague support. The focus ought to be on what the recipients can do to modify, fine-tune, alter or change their practice or behaviour. The focus is not (at least

directly) on changing their 'personality' but in what they can make things better, or different, relative to their aims and goals (Johnson, 1972; Rogers, 2000).

Feedback and encouragement

'Feedback', says Johnson (1992), can be both 'self-confirmatory', as well as 'goal confirmatory', increasing one's self-awareness and 'scope for reflection, understanding, focus, direction and change' (Rogers, 2000). This is most likely in a climate of acceptance and trust, and where the feedback is focused on specific issues and behaviours rather than a judgement on person(s) or personalities. All teachers, at some stage, receive incidental feedback (positive and 'negative') and encouragement – even from their students. In a consciously supportive school, team leaders, faculty heads and principals need to make a conscious effort to go beyond the incidental to acknowledge and affirm colleagues' efforts concerning life and work in the school. It can be disheartening when a teacher spends hours on a report, a program, a drama activity, a sports activity and not even receive a 'thanks', let alone an *acknowledged awareness* that the one giving feedback 'knows' what the report, program or activity actually entailed.

Of course, such encouragement needs to be valued and genuine. Countless colleagues have noted how they do not value feedback if it is 'routine', given by 'someone who really didn't know what effort, energy, I put in', 'or who wasn't even there ...' (Rogers, 1999).

> 'Hardly any positive reinforcement is given to many people who really feel their efforts and time are not respected. I spent hours setting up that excursion, and not a word of "well done" from the principal or vice-principal ...' (secondary teacher, ibid.).

> 'Apart from one or two people who seem to have gone out of their way to show kindness, as a 'first year' I've felt really isolated here' (secondary teacher, ibid.).

Feedback is more effective for personal and professional growth when it is descriptive (that is, 'I noticed *this* ...') rather than global (that is, 'that was a wonderful lesson ...'). This understanding ties in with the concept of shared aims, goals and practice 'to which feedback is related' (Breheney et al. 1996; Elton, 1989; Rogers, 2000).

Appraisal through colleague mentoring

The concept of 'colleague mentoring' as a means of enabling professional appraisal is reasonably well established as a useful, productive, concept – at least in the literature; less so in practice, particularly in secondary schools.

Colleague mentoring has its most practised focus in work with beginning teachers. Hargreaves (1993, p. 7) points out that the impact of trained mentors in a secondary school setting can be dramatic.

'Mentors work collaboratively with novices, and in school-based forms of initial teacher training, two students are assigned to the same school and often collaborate together. Not only is mentoring said to provide a much higher quality of support and guidance for the trainee on teaching practice, but it also helps to provide far better support to new teachers during their first few years in the profession, a period during which, the evidence unequivocally shows.'

Hargreaves goes on to point out that such collaborative mentoring practice often leads to a more general collegially collaborative practice within the school (see also Bernard, 1990; Rogers, 1996, 2000).

In my own work with schools, this is the common form of mentoring that occurs, when a more experienced teacher (with skills and expertise relative to the mentoring requirement) is electively paired with a colleague who seeks to develop skills with his/her colleague in a set area (teaching practice, method practice or behaviour management). In this sense the mentoring also takes on a 'coaching' role. This form of mentoring is developed more fully in Chapter 5.

The 'mentor' and 'mentee'[51] are often part of a small group of colleagues (a peer-support group), also engaged in peer-support mentoring or at least peer-observation and feedback. In peer-observation and feedback the roles of each teacher are 'mutually equivalent' in that they share common goals, visit each other's classes regularly, and give mutual feedback within stated aims and objectives. This is what Hoyle (1989) has termed 'collaboration professionalisation' (in Hargreaves, 1993).

In the mentoring role, the 'mentor' is often a more experienced (often senior) teacher who is able to work, with the 'mentee', in a climate of trustworthiness and mutual respect and giving accepting and non-judgmental feedback on a regular basis (Little, 1985, 1990; Rogers, 1996, 1997, 2000). This is to be distinguished from 'appraisal' because it is ongoing, based in elective mutuality and deemed supportive by the 'mentee'. As Bernard (1990) notes: 'Mentoring as a type of social support offers the person who is suited to this kind of relationship a definitive advantage in learning how to cope with the pressures of work' (p. 256).

Smyth (1983) calls this approach: 'Disarmingly simple but supportive of collegial growth, enabling teachers to become an active and conscious agent [sic] in the determination of his/her own practice ... it fits with the view that teachers learn about teaching from each other' (pp. 28–9).[52]

This certainly fits my own experience of peer-observation and peer-mentoring. I have observed, many times, the 'collegial hope' when non-judgmental, professionally focused, support like this is offered, received and utilised. This is not a one-off piece of advice (though that can have its place) but an ongoing supportive process based in mutual, professional, trust.[53] As one school notes, in its staff documentation on peer (colleague) support, mentoring has to be based on an 'elective', 'trusting', 'professional relationship' linked to 'goal setting in teaching and behaviour management skill development, and review':

> 'Teachers are at various points in their development of classroom management skills. This form of peer support would be an agreement between two or more members of staff to exchange visits to their classrooms for the purpose of observing the class. This would then be followed with a discussion on their repertoire of skills used and ways they could be expanded and improved, especially for particular students. In effect, this is a form of appraisal for improvement, not for performance' (La Trobe Valley Secondary College *Staff Handbook* 1996).

Trust and distrust in colleague relationships

Trust is most appropriate when there is a reasonable confidence the other person will behave, and relate, in ways that are beneficial, inclusive and fair – not exploiting others, especially the more vulnerable. I have seen first-year teachers, for example, given (knowingly, determinedly) particularly hard-to-manage classes simply because they were 'new', 'young' and vulnerable in the sense they 'would not know the score'. Thankfully this practice does not happen in supportive schools.

Trustworthiness is developed, and maintained, over time and while a single act (perhaps an ill-thought comment, joke or words of misunderstanding) may dent that trust, it can be regained. Again, I have observed in this research study that trust (based in mutual regard) appears to be a school-wide 'protocol' related to a conscious, school-wide, sense of collegiality.

Inherent in any understanding of trust (in social and professional relationships) is that of distrust. A feature of relational dynamics in any workplace (probably any relationship) is distrust that can arise from misperception, poor communication, misunderstanding (arising from poor communication), or even deliberate behaviours that seek to enhance one's own role, position or esteem at the expense of others. As Johnson (1972) notes:

> 'Distrust is difficult to change because it leads to the perception that despite the other person's attempt to "make-up", betrayal will occur in the future. This is more common where the 'betrayal' is not quickly resolved by the person or by others arising in any mediation' (p. 71).

In his article on school restructuring, Hargreaves (1994) speaks of a 'fundamental dilemma' in educational reform: that of 'trust in persons *and* trust in processes' (p. 47). Quoting Nias (in Nias, Southworth and Yeomans, 1989) he suggests we need to be careful we do not make trust into a 'black box … an abstract word packed with individual meanings' (p. 59).[54] He suggests that 'trust has two dimensions – predictability and goals' (ibid.). When interviewing colleagues in this study, and addressing the issue of colleague trust, the issue of predictability and consistency was frequently mentioned both in 'relational' terms and 'relational-structural' terms.[55]

Trust and patience are needed to build supportive relationships; trust is the creative human feature rather than the controlling feature. For trust to exist, 'people must find one another highly predictable and share, substantially, the same aims'. (p. 81) adding 'we might say that trust is a process of personal and predictable mutuality.' As Johnson, (1972, p. 73) points out, '*Never* trusting and *always* trusting are inappropriate.'

Trust, then, can be invested in both persons or processes, in the qualities of (and conduct of) individuals or the expertise and 'performance' of 'abstract systems'. It is important, argues Hargreaves (1994), that if there is an over-reliance of trust in persons at the expense of 'systems' when key individuals or leaders leave a school then a reliance on trust in persons (alone) could cause significant instability. This deceptively basic point has significant implications for school cultures and the 'systems' within them, as they are affected by (and affecting) colleague support. A school could – based on the kind of supportive individuals it has working in it – become a collegially supportive culture only to lose its supportive ethos when particular individuals leave. If the trust, by individuals, in a school is overly invested in its current individuals, without some 'embedded' supportive structures, the school's supportive culture could well change given new leadership. Even innovative schools spearheaded by charismatic leaders often reverted to mediocrity when they left (Hargreaves, 1994, p. 59).

Colleague collaboration is dependent on the kind of trust present in how individuals in a given school characteristically operate and co-operate. Such trust can enhance professional and personal meaning in the workplace when the focus on the mutual trust is a complementary commitment to shared expertise. This cannot, of course, be merely 'mandated'; it can be modelled, offered and encouraged.[56]

It is also important to affirm that trust, in the sense of trust in both persons and processes, is related to meeting needs. People in a social-professional setting have needs that are met (within a school context) relative to the kind, and degree, of trust its members exhibit. In more consciously whole-school colleague cultures I have noted both a dyadic-trust dependence as well as a more school-wide trust based in dependable 'structure' (or forms) such as workable whole-school policy;[57] discipline back-up procedures; parallel and shared planning in teams; and collaboration in staff planning across teams and in staff meetings (Rogers, 1995, 1999).

In her writing about a whole-school approach for student welfare and behaviour management in her school, Breheney (in Breheny et al., 1996) notes that when she and her staff team began to genuinely collaborate with a formerly disinterested and at times hostile local community there was, in time, significant and positive change in their school culture. By inviting and conveying trust she (and her staff team) were able (over time) to break down a number of preconceived ideas held by the community about schools, authority, punishment, and the rights and responsibilities of all stakeholders in the school. It is in the light of this kind of collaborative trust that the concept of *consciously supportive schools* is explored in Chapter 3.

End notes

1 In their engagingly practical book, Fullan and Hargreaves (1991) suggest, 'The problem of isolation is a deep-seated one. Architecture often supports it. The timetable reinforces it. Overload sustains it. History legitimises it' (p. 6). A point reinforced several times in the *Elton Report* (1989).

2 I would challenge the use of 'willingly' – at least from my own experience as a teacher. I do, however, sense and sympathise (as I believe Andy Miller does) with the 'tone' of what he seeks to say here.

3 This point was made directly by a number of colleagues I interviewed, though they were at some pains to point out that there was a difference between unsolicited advice-giving and 'invitationally sought' advice (Rogers, 1999).

4 From her experience of working in schools with students with severe emotional and behavioural disorders.

5 Seligman (1991) (Pennsylvania State University) has long studied 'learned helplessness' and 'learned optimism'. He has noted that: 'when there is a *preoccupation* with our own successes and failures and where there is a lack of commitment to the commons [sic] there is an increase in depression, poor health and lives without meaning' (p. 288).

6 See also Lortie (1975).

7 This theme of isolation was referred to in both the formal and unstructured dialogues with colleagues in my own research study (Rogers, 1999).

8 The psychiatrist Scott-Peck (1993) quoting Bolles (1986) suggests that humans are 'the comparing creatures'. 'By virtue of our awareness of self we are endlessly comparing ourselves with others ...' (p. 22). This, to me, rings true from my experience in the teaching world.

9 Scott-Peck (1993) quotes Jung's term of 'shadow' in a way I found relevant to the concept of 'mirror':

'Carl Jung used the term "shadow" to designate that part of our mind containing those things we would rather not own up to: traits that we are not only trying to hide from others but also from ourselves, that we are continually trying to sweep under the rug of consciousness.' (ibid.)

Scott-Peck, intriguingly, goes on to explore the concept of groups having a collective 'shadow'.

10 A point explored later in mentoring (Chapter 5). However, even in a peer-support group, for example, 'positive mirrors' can help compare and contrast without implied negative judgement.

11 Where staff feel reluctant to share concerns about their daily role there may well be an increased psychological vulnerability (at primary level) created by the 'need to relate', and 'belong', being subsumed *within* the adult–minor(s) relationship where some teachers compensate by, overly self-disclosing to students who cannot, effectively, meet the teacher's social–emotional needs.

12 A key finding in this research study was the value ascribed to immediate 'middle-management (team leaders) when support was uncritically 'offered', 'invited' and 'given'.

13 My preferred term is 'colleague support' (Introduction, p. xiii). Social support suggests (even implies) a wider *social* base than one's school-based colleagues. That wider social base for support was not the purview of my research study.

14 In a *Time* essay entitled, 'The burnout of almost everyone', a cartoon likeness illustrates a dishevelled man, arms outstretched, with a smoking wick in place of his head. The essayist Lance Morrow adds, 'most of the world's work is done by people who don't feel well'. (*Time*, 21 September, p. 90).

15 See also *Monitoring of Staff Opinions*, Office of Review, Education Victoria (1998), Melbourne.

16 This has been a major focus, and feature, of whole-school approaches to behaviour management. See Rogers (1995, 2000).

17 See also Bernard and Joyce (1984), Diamond (1996) and Fullan (1993). See also Seligman (1991) pp. 109–11, on 'pessimistic explanatory styles' as they relate to individuals and groups.

18 The 'incidental' aspects of colleague support are consistently, and frequently, cited as a valued expression of support (Rogers, 1992, 1999. See p. 76f).

19 Dunham's term for social (or collegial) support.

20 In Nelson (1987) p. xiv.

21 One of the understandings clearly demonstrated in this research (Rogers, 1999) was the high value colleagues give to what I have termed 'structural support'; institutional 'processes, procedures, policy' or 'ways of doing things' that can give some sense of certainty in difficult times so that both 'persons' and 'processes' meet (in a morally supportive sense) to enable colleague-coping.

22 See also the section on basic needs later in this chapter and in Chapters 4 and 5.

23 See Morgan (1991), O'Brien (1998) and Rogers (1996, 1998).

24 The typical questions often asked are 'Why do people affiliate?' 'What kinds of affiliation and affiliative behaviours are common?' 'What kind of behaviours or personalities are more likely to affiliate?' Personality styles are outside the scope of this study, though clearly some teachers will, and do, act as 'loners' with a seemingly minimal desire (or need) to affiliate, or to have expressed need for 'support'.

25 Some of my older colleagues described this as the 'Dunkirk Spirit'.

26 One of the reasons that 'isolationist ecologies' occur at the professional level (according to Miller, 1996) is a lack of commonly agreed 'technical language [sic] with which many teachers do their work' (p. 200).

27 Where teachers – in some schools – often feel 'solely' responsible for the welfare and learning of their pupils.

28 See Kyriacou (1981) pp. 40–50. Hearn (1974) notes 'needs are regarded as learned der-

ivations of the socialisation process which intone visceral sentiments deep within each individual. While some needs may be similar to psychological drives, it is the higher socio-psychological needs described by Maslow and others that are associated with alienation' (p. 132).

29 Scott-Peck is an American psychiatrist well known for his writing on individuals and community.

30 See also Cornett (1986), Hargreaves (1993), Walker and Adelman (1996). See also the place of humour in colleague coping, pp. 84–6.

31 Tauber (1995) exploring power, as both need and behaviour, says:

'That although exerting power is a basic human need, it carries a cultural taint that does not seem to extend to other human psychological needs such as loving and belonging. Regardless of the cultural prejudices, the seeking of power itself is neither good nor bad'.

He explores the bases of 'social power', distinguishing between 'coercive power' on the one hand and those more socially proactive expressions of power such as 'referent power', 'expert power', 'legitimate power' (where right and role coalesce) and 'reward power' (pp. 20-2).

32 An etymology of whingeing might well be the combination of the words 'whining' and 'cringing'(!)

33 A point noted in the report, *Teacher Stress in Victoria* (1989). Under the heading: 'Teaching staff factions and conflict' was the sub-heading – 'Hell is other teachers'. Almost all respondents mentioned this is related to 'incompetence, laziness, abuse of the system and lack of peer support' (p. 29). See also McLeod, 1987 pp. 10–12.

34 Communication in a supportive colleague culture can range from the incidental whingeing and 'off-loading' and 're-framing' to those brief communication exchanges that give verification and assurance that 'one is on the right track'. In a supportive culture the dyadic expressions and the more developed communication that focuses on professional issues, needs and concerns are present across the school.

35 This aspect of collaborative culture is consistent with the finding in this study on the management of differences and dissension in 'less' and 'more' supportive colleague culture. (See particularly Chapter 4, p. 96 and Chapter 5, p. 125).

36 In the Rogers (1999) study the concept of 'being valued' is frequently cited and valued by respondents as a key feature of colleague support. Indeed, a fundamental tenet of positive self- (and group) esteem is that when people feel valued (affirmed through practical, moral, professional, non-judgmental support), they feel better, learn better and are more motivated to work better. See also Coopersmith (1967); Elton (1989), Johnson and Johnson (1989), Powell (1976) and Rogers (1996, 1998).

37 In my own consultancy I have noted that some schools see the issue of teacher reflection and professional development as separate from continuous learning. Professional development is sometimes seen as segmented, separate from, a teacher's day-to-day needs and work, rather than arising from personal and shared reflection and feedback.

38 'A law unto oneself' (the literal meaning of the word).

39 See Little (1990) and Lortie (1975).

40 While this sounds like a 'tall-order' (and it is), the commitment by a leader to even the basic consideration of individual needs is a crucial feature of supporting the individual colleague *within the team* (Rogers, 1996). Lane et al. (1967) have argued that it is not the presence but also the absence of conflict that constitutes the surprising, even the abnormal … conflict is a normal adjunct of power relationship and provides a form of cohesiveness' (p. 42). This conflict may embrace role conflict, positional conflict, even the basic 'bad-day syndrome'.

41 Bernard (1990), too, notes that:

> '… teachers found this type of support made them feel that they were not alone in having problems and reactions, helped put problems in perspective, took the pressure off feeling responsible for a total class, helped reduce feelings of inadequacy and frustration, increased feelings of self-esteem and led to a sense of relaxation' (p. 229).

42 Johnson and Johnson (1989) note, 'For such a system to be successful it must be directed to the needs of staff in the complex contexts in which they work' (p. 18).

43 This does not mean, necessarily, 'a team' per se. The peer-support group can give a base from which from which dyadic-support networking can generate (Rogers, 1997). Kohn (1986) states, 'Study after study shows that nothing succeeds like co-operation' (p. 22). Quoting motivational research, he suggests that 'Co-operation establishes (and motivates) the knowledge that others are depending on you' (p. 28).

44 Macleod (1987) notes that such groupings have both a stress-relieving and a stress-coping function when first-year teachers can relate supportively with more experienced teachers (p. 17).

45 The program is still run in many schools (along the lines noted here).

46 'Professional attributes and roles are recognised through professional performance standards that take into account the complexities of teaching practice and school culture, and the developmental processes that characterise all teachers' progression from a beginning teacher to a highly skilled professional' (p. 29). *Guidelines For the PRP, 1996* (Department of Education, Victoria).

47 Kogan (1989) in Carr (1989) and Kyriacou (1987). Sometimes school leadership will also see appraisal as both an accountability and management task (Kyriacou, 1987, p. 139).

48 'There is a clear consensus in education that teacher evaluation is a complex process. It is based upon criteria of unknown validity, utilising methods and means of questionable reliability, performed by persons who often do not have the skill, time or will to do the job adequately, and directed to conflicting purposes. All of this is performed in an atmosphere of anxiety and distrust. In order to sustain credibility, teacher evaluation must develop clear purposes, methods and procedures consistent with these purposes and must show a healthy amount of scepticism concerning the validity of any narrowly structured method for judging the total and effectiveness of a teacher.' (Fedivebel, 1980, in *Teacher Appraisal: A study.* Suffolk Education Department (DFES) 1996, p. 16.)

49 There will no doubt always be an inevitable tension, as Ingvarson and Chadbourne (1994) note, between 'political–democratic' and 'professional' forms of authority and accountability in any profession (p. 38). Accountability assumes the requirement to answer to the broader social community (Kogan in Carr, 1989 p. 136).

50 Developing and maintaining an ongoing portfolio – in part documentation and in part collegially shared feedback. See Wolf, 1994, in Ingvarson and Chadbourne, 1994.

51 Terms we jokingly used 'in-house' as it were.

52 'A more formal arrangement for availing yourself of peer support can be found in teacher peer support groups. Support groups consist of a number of teachers who desire not only to advance their professional skills, but also to have an opportunity to discuss and share current teaching practices and specific school-related problems such as classroom discipline. Members of the group help each other to acquire new skills, as well as giving and receiving support in implementing new practices and solving problems. Peer support groups tend to be topic- and goal-focused with the emphasis on doing rather than talking; ideas are modelled rather than described' (Bernard, 1990, p. 297. See also Rogers, 1996, 2000).

53 Trust is a crucial, reciprocal, feature of such relationships. Trust exists in relationships, not in someone's personality, occurring between people not within people (see Johnson, 1972).

54 Hargreaves (1994) argues that 'the value of trust in collaboration working relationships is so widely acknowledged and understood that we rarely probe more than superficially into its meaning and nature' (p. 59).

55 Trust is explored, later, in terms of reciprocity within and between people *in* systems and *within* systems. This is a point made particularly by school leaders in this study (Rogers, 1999).

56 Like many of the critical features of interactive and professional life the critical human features that enable that life to function well cannot be mandated.

57 Particularly in the area of behaviour management and discipline.

CHAPTER 3

TOWARDS A TYPOLOGY OF COLLEAGUE SUPPORT –
whole-school approaches, change and growth

Schools are not buildings, curriculums and machines. Schools are relationships among people. It is the interaction patterns among people, among students, between students and teachers, among teachers, between teachers and administrators and among adminis-trators that determine how effective schools are.

Johnson and Johnson (1989, p. 101)

Colleague support can, and does, range from moral empathy, and a sense of con-nectedness[1] to one another to focused professional support that can enable both professional reflection and ideas-generation through to mentoring support.

While there are still strong vestiges of individualism in the teaching profession, the changes and challenges that have beset education and schools have seen teachers begin to move to a more focused and conscious collegiality that has seen expression in meaningful teaming and professional collegiality.

According to Hargreaves (1997) there has been an increasing 'culture of collab-oration' in schools since the 1980s.

> 'Not all teachers are being drawn to their colleagues. Many remain ignorant about or indifferent to the possibilities of collaboration, and some cling tightly to their classroom autonomy while others try to force collaboration upon them. While there is no solid evi-dence about just how many teachers are working collaboratively there are case studies and interview-based inquiries that point to collaborative practices and testify to its growing importance in the landscape of the teacher' (p. 95).

Nowhere is this collegial collaboration more focused than in the move towards whole-school practice – particularly in the area of behaviour management (Rogers, 1995).

Whole-school approaches for the enabling of colleague support

In the report *Teacher Stress in Victoria* the authors note an:

'... absence of shared beliefs, or culture, within a school about fit and proper student behaviour, [which] was perhaps, a symptomatic feature affecting the stress that comes from discipline and management concerns' (pp. 43–4).

This is consistent with in-school practice as noted by Breheney et al. (1996); Farrel (1991); Lowe and Istance (1989); Rogers (1995) and Axworthy et al. (1989). The report *Teacher Stress in Victoria* continues:

'... in Victoria, the Whole-School Program appears to be highly successful in mitigating the factors that have been implicated as causes of stress. There is also much conventional (but not uncontroversial) wisdom, based on both formal studies and experience, about policies which are likely to be effective in lessening classroom stress' (pp. 43–4).

A whole-school approach is fundamentally the school's best efforts to collaboratively and collegially engage and develop common aims, beliefs, practices and action plans in the daily behaviour management role: Brown at al. (1984); Axworthy et al. (1986); Rogers (1995); Rutter et al. (1979).[2] A key feature of a supportive culture was identified by Rutter et al. (1979) as occurring when the staff had a 'shared sense of purpose' reflected in key (characteristic) staff behaviours at the academic level, curriculum-delivery level, as well as at the behaviour management and school discipline level.

A central tenet in the development of whole-school approaches to behaviour management is that of 'problem-ownership' by the school of what it *could* change in terms of management and discipline in a school (see Appendix 2). In terms of professional change, and 'needs-based' change within the school (or even imposed change from without), a 'whole-school' program is predicated on participants accepting that the only long-term way they can impact a problem is by taking responsibility for those factors over which they have control at the local school setting. This is an important (and challenging) aspect to consider when utilising 'outside' consultancy within the school; to encourage and constructively convince colleagues that there is sufficient expertise 'within' the school to produce workable solutions relevant to *their* concerns and needs. As Axworthy et al. (1989) note:

'... this knowledge is not so obvious to those in the school. One of the tasks of the (external) consultant is to engage existing expertise of school-based participants ... by respecting (their) personal experiences ... so that teachers (themselves) are able to determine what is useful. Telling or advising is counterproductive as it produces both resistance and dependence ...' (pp. 69–70).

This 'shared sense of purpose' is not merely incidental, it is built on the kind of teamwork, decision-making, action plans and policy framework developed by staff with their senior colleagues (Elton, 1989; Rogers, 1995). In building a 'working cohesion' based in school-wide collegiality, Jones (1984, in Watkins and Wagner, 1987) notes that such coherence and purposefulness allows differences among staff but not active divisions, and suggests that a mark of such allowance of difference will be observed in the modelling by senior staff (see also p. 96f).

Hart (1992) notes that goal congruence (a set of objectives easily understood and shared by all staff) is also a strong predictor of staff morale in a school. This finding is also linked, strongly, to participative decision-making, effective school policies and supportive leadership and feedback.

In some schools, however, staff noted how in their school experience a school could maintain (even in printed policy) that it was a 'supportive school' (in a given area like behaviour management, discipline and student welfare), yet in practice be a long way from what it 'espoused' (Rogers, 1999).[3] Within whole-school approaches 'to anything' (curriculum, planning, behaviour management) it is what occurs in collegially supportive *practice* that appears to be the crucial factor. In whole-school policy this is a key issue – 'how is what we say we do, reflected in what we actually, and characteristically, do'.

Hamilton (1986) – in his studies on discipline and behaviour in schools – notes that a whole-school approach to behaviour management needs a collegially supportive approach based in common aims, and practice arising from collaborative needs-analysis. The benefits of such an approach he notes are:

- a reduction in 'levels of stress' in the 'pilot' schools (as measured by a Teacher Occupational Stress Questionnaire) compared with teachers in the 'control' schools[4]
- teachers in the 'pilot' schools (also) rated their experience of students' misbehaviour as lower than those teachers in the control school
- the pilot schools (also) developed a clear expression of norms, aims and practices in student welfare and behaviour management (in Axworthy et al., 1989).[5]

This is consistent with research by Wilson and Corcoran (1988), who note that 'shared goals and high expectations create strong collective identity' when such is based on 'regular opportunities for interaction and sharing with colleagues that promote (a) collective identity' (p. 96).

Structural support

Much of the support cited in the literature on support in schools focuses on how schools develop policy and practice to provide both 'structure', policy and 'forms' within which, and from which, people are able to give professional and moral support (Bernard, 1990; Howard and Arnez, 1982; Rogers, 1995, 1996, 1999).

Hargreaves (1994) asserts that trust in processes alone, or people alone, can be counterproductive to support (pp. 54–9). It is the interrelationship between the 'structures' (and processes) and how people engage and utilise them that creates an enabling, supportive, trust.[6]

A more pedestrian form of structure(s) that conveys both professional, and personal, value, to a colleague, and assists in reducing occupational stress is noted by Carl Glickman (1991) and Bernard (1990) as those resources and materials that one needs in day-to-day teaching. Basic aspects such as physical space and structure that can affect a sense of support are noted as occurring where:

- teachers have adequate personal planning and organisational space
- all teachers have their own desk, chair and stationery
- rooms have adequate heating/lighting/ventilation
- teachers have adequate relaxation areas such a staff common room
- decent tea/coffee facilities are available to all staff
- a telephone is provided where teachers can talk in private
- teachers and students are not subjected to excessive noise levels
- there are private rooms available for teachers to conduct interviews
- there is an efficient system for paging/getting messages to staff, rather than an *all too frequent* loudspeaker system in each classroom ['Will room 17 please send the swimming money now!', 'Will Adam B. and Jason D. come to the office immediately!', 'All teachers are asked to …'.]
- teachers have easy access to equipment such as photocopiers, audio-visual equipment, computers, stationery and library books
- meetings are held in rooms where everybody can be seen and be comfortable
- classes, where possible, are held in appropriate rooms close to all necessary equipment (and close to colleague support)
- all graffiti is regularly removed from classroom and equipment
- vandalised equipment is replaced or removed as soon as possible
- a school beautification campaign is conducted
- staff rooms are redecorated with colourful posters, plants etc., particularly secondary school classrooms
- staff rooms are regularly cleaned and kept tidy (Bernard, 1990, pp. 334–5).

The list, clearly, could go on.

Stress-auditing

My colleagues and I have developed a basic, but important form of stress-auditing to enable staff to outline what (and where) structural and *relational* stressors exist and are most common, especially those that affect crisis-management areas in the school (p. 168f).[7]

Change and colleague support – its effect on reciprocal coping

As noted in Chapter 1, schools in Victoria have been the recipients of significant and ongoing change in the past decade. This aspect of stress arising from imposed change was frequently referred to by colleagues in both survey and interview responses as the issue of change, and the reciprocal effect of colleague support was addressed (Rogers, 1999).

Fullan (1993) epigrammatically suggests that, 'productive educational change roams somewhere between over-control and chaos' (p. 19).

Hargreaves (1993) notes, interestingly, that 'externally imposed change is driving [sic] primary teachers to rely on colleagues and to co-ordinate with them to an unusual extent' (p. 3). This has certainly been my experience as a consultant; to see change in shared planning and teaming (across all levels in a school) is a significant collegial and structural change over the past eight to ten years. This aspect of collegiality affects, particularly, how a school interprets imposed changes (imposed from without) and reworks them for the benefit of the school. Purposeful teaming can often 'buffer' the potentially stressful impact of change by colleagues using their *shared* experience, expertise and ideas to manage and re-work the changes for the 'local' situation. In this way the school copes with change by finding a balance between external demands regarding change imperatives, internal school needs and current structures and collegial needs (the needs of individuals).

Even mandated change is not merely an event; it is a process within which the individual school needs to be the 'centre' (Hopkins, 1991); this means that even external reforms need to be sensitive to the situation in individual schools. Implementation by mandate (by external *fiat*) is never enough. The school itself has to find both meaning and purpose (even moral purpose) in the change(s) and the change process for it to be 'taken in' and 'taken-on' by staff.

The goal in managing change, says Fullan (1991) is to:

'Get into the habit of experiencing and thinking about educational change processes as an overlapping series of dynamically complex phenomena. As we develop a non-linear system language, new thinking about change occurs' (p. 21).

This, again, has been my experience of working with schools who are effectively managing imposed change in a stress-reducing way. A key feature of the management of change is how schools leadership empower their staff to cope – as a collegial team – as distinct from seeing (and acting) themselves as a dependent factor in the change process (Antonovosky, 1979); Johnson (1996).[8]

Any change process needs to include colleague support if change is to be owned at the local school level.[9] Huberman and Miles (1984) note that where the 'top-down' change is effected, 'large-scale, change-bearing innovations lived or died by the amount and quality of assistance their users received once the change process was under way' (in Stoll, 1998, p. 2). When adequate support is given to staff, and exercised by staff, this enables the capacity to take charge of change regardless of its source (Stoll and Fink, 1996, p. 43). I have seen this 'capacity to change' countless times in schools when:

- the emphasis is on organic, rather than mechanical, processes; especially when 'unpredictability' is inherent in the changes
- when school leaderships, with their staff, actively take charge of change, creatively accommodating external ideas within the school's own context and needs
- by emphasising action *and* meaning, construing *and* action, effective change is more likely to occur within a system.[10] This is best developed by collegial discussion about change that clarifies purpose and action and sets up supportive, collaborative, structures to cope with, and implement, those changes.

    Johnson (1996) suggests that in this sense, when teachers see a purpose (meaning) in change (even when a significant part of it is imposed), they can meet that striving for life-long learning and renewal; what Johnson describes as a school being a 'learning community'. Such a community manages change by staying 'in control' at 'the local level while linking with the wider environment'. A key feature of 'staying in control' is considering staff understanding of, and learning about, the change content and processes as a key factor in the 'effectiveness of change'.[11] All of this, however, means that the school is 'leading the change from within and thus maintaining quality of change' (Johnson, 1996, p. 48).

- teacher improvement, as well as changes in student outcomes, cannot be merely mandated by bureaucratic control (Hargreaves, 1994, p. 56). 'Successful schools ... adapt mandates to fit [their] vision[s], colonising external educational reforms' (Stoll, 1998, op. cit.). If teachers are not supportively empowered, and where necessary equipped, the changes are ineffectual; even if mandated.
- Change becomes more 'comprehensive in scope' when 'significant' (rather than superficial) redistribution of existing power relationships occur among principals, teachers, parents and students:

    'At the heart of these is a fundamental choice between restructuring as bureaucratic control, where teachers are controlled and regulated to implement the mandates of others, and restructuring a professional empowerment, where teachers are supported, encouraged and provided with newly structured opportunities to make improvements of their own, in partnership with parents, principals and students' (Hargreaves, 1994, p. 57).

When those 'existing power relationships' are affected by change – especially significant change – it follows that change and conflict are not antithetical as power relationships adjust to new demands, new ideas, different strategy and practice (Gretzels et al., 1968; Dunette, 1986; Hoy and Miskel, 1978; Fullan and Hargreaves, 1991; Fullan, 1993; Stoll, 1998). In this sense 'conflict' is not necessarily a bad thing; it often calls attention to existing problems, but it can also arouse feelings of interest, curiosity and enhanced task motivation. Within this more positive frame of understanding is the shared need to work through reassessment of resources, power and people within shared goals.[12] The issue of managing conflict, change and growth is developed more fully in Chapter 6.

Collaboration and collegiality – supportive cultures

The OECD report *Schools and Quality* (Lowe and Istance, 1989) indicated that collaborative planning and shared decision-making and 'collegial work' (in a framework of experimentation and evaluation) is a key characteristic of an 'effective' school.[13] Fullan (1993) asserts that:

> 'The real world demands collaboration – the collective solving of problem. Evidence [also] suggests than an individual's personal learning is enhanced by collaborative effort, the act of sharing ideas, having to put one's views clearly to others of finding defensible compromises ... is itself educative' (p. 46).[14]

Collaboration is a determining feature of colleague support and supportive school cultures as they engage, manage and utilise change imperatives. Constructive collaboration occurs when attitude and actions of staff work to:

- move from an isolationist teaching practice to reduce an unnecessary sense of 'powerlessness' and move towards purposeful, professional, efficacy. Effective collaboration occurs when there is a collaborative culture that 'empowers' teachers by 'reducing the uncertainty that must otherwise be faced in isolation'
- merge insights from differing perspectives when addressing common problems, issues or concerns
- increase the *integrative* solutions when the concerns are too important to be compromised (Thomas and Kilman, 1989)
- accept, and work through, the hard (even uncomfortable) feelings that interpersonal relationships bring to problem analysis and problem resolution

- collaborate within a climate where people are willing to learn by testing their own assumptions and understandings of other's views. As O'Brien (1998) notes:

  'A supportive school will offer other staff opportunities to talk about their feelings and to express their opinions even if they challenge the school's structure' (p. 110)

- gain commitment 'by incorporating other's concerns into a consensual decision' (Thomas and Kilman 1989, p. 12).Change and supportive (collegial) collaboration occurs more effectively when collaborative school communities do not have a 'dependent relationship' to externally imposed change that isolation and uncertainty tend to encourage (Nias et al., 1989)

- teachers develop the collective confidence to respond to change critically, selecting and adapting those elements that will aid improvement in their own work context and rejecting those that will not. In such a process both the individual and the group are inherently and simultaneously valued; individuals are valued, so is interdependence (Rogers, 1998).

Towards a typology of school-wide colleague support

A typology is an attempt to portray, in summary form, key features or aspects of complex reality. When that reality involves how people supportively relate to one another I looked for distinct features or patterns that could fairly characterise a colleague culture in terms of how its individuals, and groups, supported one another. What salient features could one note about colleague support in a range of schools? As you read through this section you might want to compare, contrast, your own school in light of the general findings represented in the typology noted below on pp. 64–7.

A typology, in the sense used here, describes salient features or distinguishing characteristics, that are representative (but not exhaustive) of a case.[15] This typology drawn from grounded research has, among its signal features, the degree of consciousness demonstrated in a school regarding nature and utility of colleague support. To illustrate the 'degree' and 'movement' of a school's consciousness about support, I have shown the typology on a visual continuum from 'less' to 'more' conscious; this is a representational device (see Figure 3.1, p. 66). This 'typology' is also used, later (in Chapters 6 and 7), to inform and complement a school's review of how their colleague culture operates in terms of a school-wide consciousness of support.

School cultures, and the collegial behaviour affecting school cultures, can be typified in various ways that help describe and understand an individual school. As this research study developed, I began to posit, develop and refine a 'typology of support' that seemed to represent the meanings and practices of colleague support I was observing in the schools studied.

In developing a 'typology of colleague support', I have drawn on the work of several researchers: Joyce et al. (1981), Stoll (1997), Rosenholtz (1989), Gossen and Anderson (1995) and particularly Purkey and Novak (1984), as well as my own research (Rogers, 1999).

Joyce and his colleagues (1981) outline three 'school types':

- The 'energising school' describes a school that has a shared sense of purpose; the interdependency among its colleagues energises that shared purpose.
- The 'maintenance school' begins its 'journey' with shared purpose and some collegial energy and yet, in time, becomes a school culture exhibiting collegial autonomy and collegial independence. The initial energy of shared purpose is no longer the real day-to-day practice.
- The 'depressing and fragmented school' describes a school that has lost its aim and purpose; a school culture no longer expressed in interdependency and collaboration.

In a study of over 70 elementary schools, Rosenholtz (1989) used broad typologies of 'stuck' and 'moving' schools. The key characteristic of such schools (noted, similarly by Stoll, 1997) are that 'stuck' schools were not fully supportive of change and improvement in their professional life and practice, and often exhibited 'uncertainty' and 'isolation'. She further describes 'stuck' schools as 'learning impoverished' and 'moving' schools as 'learning enriched'. As Fullan and Hargreaves (1991) note:

> 'Most teachers and principals become so professionally estranged in their workplace isolation that they neglect each other. They do not often compliment, support and acknowledge each other's positive efforts. Indeed, strong norms of self-reliance may even evoke adverse reaction to a teacher's successful performance' (p. 39).

Fullan (1993) adds a cautionary note when describing school cultures. His own, broad, typology of 'sharing' and 'non-sharing' cultures is a case in point suggesting that a 'dynamic systems perspective leads to a view of culture as emergent' (p. 36), rather than uniformly 'static' or 'fixed'. I observe this same 'emergence' as I see some schools 'moving' from 'less conscious' to 'more conscious' colleague cultures. I have used the term 'culture' here in the sense of describing the *characteristic* features of a school's beliefs, attitudes and behaviour. Fullan and Hargreaves (1991) suggest, 'In simple terms culture is "the way we do things here!"' (p. 37). A 'culture' is not — normally — a fixed or static entity — it evolves or develops in relationship to many factors, not the least being the imperatives of external changes. Fullan and Hargreaves (1991) suggest that we need to see systems, within a culture, as both 'dynamic' and 'emergent'; 'some degree of multiple cultures is essential for questioning the status quo in the face of continually changing and contentious issues in the environment' (pp. 26–37). Like the research on stress noted earlier, the degree to which a school believes, and acts, as if it is 'at effect' or 'at cause' (in Bernard, 1990) with respect to imposed change will also affect how a school, as a community of individuals, believes it can live, work, support each other and effectively manage change.[16]

Stoll (1997) proposes typology of school culture based on 'movement' and 'relative inertia':

- *The moving school* is effective in terms of how the people in it are 'actively working together to respond to their changing context'. Practices are reflected on and examined, and structures and support systems put into place to enable a partnership in aims, goals and communal will.
- *The cruising school* is effective but 'declining'; it tends to 'camouflage' its struggle so that outsiders may not see its real shape only its 'form'. Stoll suggests that such a school may 'lack the capacity and will to change' no less than the 'sinking school' (p. 9).
- *The strolling school* is neither particularly effective nor ineffective. Its 'ill-defined' (and 'often-conflicting') aims inhibit improvement and change management.
- *The struggling school* is ineffective but improving. It has a residual 'willingness' to improve but it is characterised by 'unproductive thrashing' (there is the willingness to 'try anything' that will make the difference).
- *The sinking school* (ineffective and declining) is a failing school. Isolation, counterproductive self-reliance, blame and loss of faith inhibit change (Stoll, 1997, pp. 8–10).

Rather than seeing a school typology simply as only 'best–worst case scenario', Stoll places them into a 'cultural typology' that sees all 'types' in movement or decline.

Stoll argues that 'school cultures influence readiness for change' (p. 7). She then outlines ten major factors relevant to that cultural readiness. These include shared goals; the active belief that everyone can and 'must' make a difference collegially; emphasises 'joint work' as the strongest expression of collegiality[17] (for example, team-teaching, mentoring, peer-coaching, planning, improvement, life-long learning and risk-taking); support expressed beyond work-related interdependence to personal availability; kindness and caring where, in short, people make time for one another,[18] mutual respect expressed in the attitude that 'everyone has something to offer' (p. 12); openness ('We can discuss our differences'), and celebration and humour ('We feel good about ourselves').

These last four features, also outlined by Gossen (1995), were notably, and characteristically, present in schools I have termed 'consciously supportive' (see p. 66).

Gossen and Anderson (1995) have outlined a typology of schools along three descriptive frames:

- *The conventional school*: here the motif of power is hierarchical rather than shared collegially. Teachers tend to work autonomously and there tends to be a 'closed-door' mentality.
- *The congenial school* is often seen as a social, friendly, school. 'Belonging' is important yet conflict is seen as adverse to its culture; when a difficult decision arises in staff meetings issues are 'tabled' or 'silence' ensues (gossip, side talk, small committees make important decisions for the group rather than genuine collaboration).
- *The collegial school* is not afraid to engage dialogue with vigour, even disagreement. While staff maintain 'belonging' as a collegial ideal, they deepen it through sharing ideas *and* differences. Staff examine practices based on shared values, beliefs and best knowledge.[19] Most of all they are open to paradigm shifts through a broad commitment to ongoing teaming.

Anyone who is a teacher can observe features, from each of these schools, in their retrospective employment histories. I can, and I still, ask why? What makes the difference in collegiality in those schools? Are those differences transferable to other schools?

Purkey and Novak (1984) present a typology of 'school functioning' that emphasises the importance of how the 'people in the process' operate (pp. 16–20), as well as how features of school organisation and structure operate. No system or technology can substitute for human relationships. Within this central underpinning the authors outline their typology based on characteristic 'levels of intention'. These 'levels' describe the salient, 'invitational', features in interactive and relational collegial behaviour.

Level One – 'Intentionally disinviting'

As noted in Chapter 1, key features of broadly supportive and broadly unsupportive schools lie on a similar continuum to that noted by Purkey and Novak – displaying professional isolation, personal and professional 'protectiveness'. Where the 'intentionally disinviting' school is overly concerned about failure, selective, or defensive, communication networks, ad-hoc (even confrontational) forms of problem-solving occur. Like Purkey and Novak I would agree that few schools are 'intentionally disinviting' (at least for any extended period of time). 'Disinviting' features in a school culture and behaviour are more likely related to situational crises, situational frustration, poor facilities, the seemingly relentless impact of stressful transitional changes (imposed from without) and lack of collaborative practice. The authors believe that 'disinviting behaviour' needs to be challenged to invite the human potential in the school.

Level Two –'Unintentionally disinviting'

The policies and practices, the people (and even places) are characterised by 'a lack of consciousness' about what is in the school that is 'disinviting'. It may be as basic (for example) as a staff room having non-invitational aesthetics (poor tea/coffee-making, seating facilities), a cramped photocopier room, difficulty in getting adequate and necessary resources through to unchallenged sexism or racism and unchallenged comments about who is doing the 'real education' here.[20] Insensitivity to others' feelings, not developing and extending positive communication that can address needs all significantly contribute to such 'disinviting' features in such a school.

Level Three – 'Unintentionally inviting'

This 'level' is particularly interesting because the authors note that the school culture is, broadly, 'inviting' but 'seem[s] to have stumbled into particular ways of functioning that are usually effective, but they have a difficult time explaining why'. Being unaware of the behavioural dynamics that operate to currently sustain such an 'invitational' school climate can create difficulties in consistency of vision and direction, especially when the school faces new changes or challenges its current cultural dynamic may be unprepared for.

In one of the schools I researched, several staff noted that if a new principal came to their school and promoted a different approach to collaboration and teaming 'it might well change things here'. That qualifying 'if' became (as a result of the interview process itself) a topic of discussion. What they have now sought to do in this particular school is 'consciously' to acknowledge and affirm what they believe, and seek to do, that enhances colleague support in the hope this will maintain, and sustain, the supportive culture beyond the current group of teachers and leadership in the school.

As Purkey and Novak (1984) argue, if the educators are 'unable to identify' the reasons for ... 'success' or 'failure' ... or lack a 'consistent stance', or 'dependability', or 'the knowledge' that if 'whatever it is that makes us invitational' now should change, or even, stop, how would we start it up again? This raised for me the concept of 'collegial consciousness' about the culture colleagues have developed within a given school and has led me to ask how can such a 'culture' be monitored, affirmed and (at times) celebrated?

Level Four – 'Intentionally inviting'

The degree of dependability, reliability and consistency of policy and practice and the kinds of behaviours that teachers characteristically engage in (and value and endorse) is summarised by Purkey and Novak as:

> '… artfully inviting educators (to) think in a special language of "doing with" rather than "doing to". They have developed the ability to approach even the most difficult situation in a professionally inviting manner' (1984, p. 20).

I have particularly focused on Purkey and Novak's 'typology' because it seems to me that aspects and degrees of 'invitational' social cultures are also related to 'aspects of consciousness' that reflect how colleague support operates within a school culture. In its professional and relational life, in its precept and practice; indeed, the concept of an 'invitational culture' is not dissimilar to a 'supportive culture'.

All these typologies give valuable insight (and potentially practical entry points) to a discussion on colleague support as it is understood in a given school. Each of the writers referred to mentions, at some point, the importance of 'colleague support' without necessarily using the term. What I have sought to do is draw on, and from, their expertise to develop colleague support as the integrating feature of a supportive culture and express the typical features along a supportive continuum. The defining protocols, and practices, are developed within this typology in Chapter 4.

Towards a typology of colleague support: Consciousness of support

The proposed typology – 'consciousness of support' – outlines and typifies features and understandings of colleague support in a school culture (Rogers, 1999) (see Figure 3.1, p. 66). Four 'levels' of 'consciousness' are proposed with an intervening transitional 'level'. These 'levels', within the typology, describe features and indicate movement from a 'less' to 'more' consciously supportive colleague culture. (Conversely, they could describe movement from a 'more' to 'less' consciously supportive cultures.)

Unconsciously unsupportive

This typifies a culture that is unaware ('unconscious') of its characteristically unsupportive colleague behaviour and practices. Isolationist practice is more typically the 'norm' – but conscious reflection on such a 'norm' is not really occurring. Emotional support, and mutual-sharing may occur in small dyadic pockets but structural support in terms of teams and teaming, school-wide collaboration and policy is 'paper-policy' rather than collegial practice. This sort of school culture is,

I believe, more the exception these days (thankfully). Where such schools do exist they are very difficult places to teach in. At a recent in-service I conducted, several teachers (all from one secondary school) commented that in their current school they felt as if it was *'dog eat dog'* [sic]. *'People here have been worried about getting stabbed in the back if you ask for support. We're all so _____ tired. It's also the Department of Education on our back ...'* The rest of the unstructured dialogue was a fairly depressing whinge. These colleagues felt as they had limited control with the unsupportive administration in the school, adding *'We're in survival mode'*. A more disturbing term heard, in this depressing dialogue, was *'snake pit'*, which was used to describe the school 'culture'. These are very disturbing examples of an unconsciously unsupportive colleague culture – with pockets of 'frustrated consciousness'(!).

Consciously unsupportive

This is a more common description of some schools. In such a school, individuals, even groups, are often aware – even painfully aware – of those aspects of school life, organisation and practice that symbolise and contribute to a lack of colleague support as it affects their core purposes as a school. Moral support exists in such schools (it has to), but it is often as small dyadic pockets and in transitional ad-hoc engagements.

Schools that have gone through significant change – such as forced amalgamation[21] – mean that teachers have to work through some natural anxiety, denial, disorientation and frustration.[22] If these natural reactions and 'stages' are not worked through, the school can become what Stoll (1981) calls a 'stuck' school; not really moving. To use Joyce's (1981) term, they have 'disparate' (even dissipated) 'unharnessed energy'. They are not moving beyond natural frustration to collaborative reflection and action geared to necessary change.

These schools – I have worked with many – often use such 'consciousness' to address, and re-address, aspects of their school culture, pursuing a common needs-analysis, combined with an active willingness to pursue – and support – necessary changes.

Transitional culture

This aspect of the typology explores how a school begins to make explicit, and to reassess, what its core values and needs are, and how it might go about effecting change to a more consciously supportive culture. In Purkey and Novak's (1984) term the individuals are beginning to 'consciously invite' their culture to exhibit mutual regard for colleague needs. Professional sharing, and even planning, become more typical as colleagues move from an isolationist mentality and practice to collaboration in planning, professional development and interdependency in teaching and management practice.

Consciously supportive

Colleagues here are aware of where they have come from and what it is about their colleague culture that has affected change towards the culture 'as is'. Colleagues can articulate what it is they believe in, and practice, about colleague support. In success, in struggle and failure colleagues feel they are in a culture where they are more likely not only to detect problems at an earlier stage, but will acknowledge the normative nature of fallibility and uncertainty, and work (more supportively) to cope with natural fallibility, failure and change to meet their individual and common needs.

The colleague culture, its structures and the emphasis on collegial relationships, endorses and seeks to affirm an 'ecology of support'. Such an 'ecology' consciously affirms the needs of all in its school community: teaching staff, casual relief teachers, support staff and non-teaching staff.[23] I have, for example, seen the montage of school staff photos on the display board in school foyers and noticed – in some schools – a notable absence of teacher aides, cleaners, grounds-persons ...

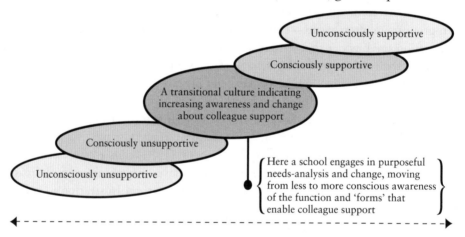

Figure 3.1   *Proposed typology: consciousness of colleague support*

Unconsciously supportive

At its most common, this typology describes the embedded nature of collegiality; where beliefs and practices are so much the norm that colleagues *'just relate this way'* (as one group of primary teachers acknowledged). *'It {colleague support} is quite conscious at times, yet, at times, it's just the way we are. It occurs because this place* **is that way'** (interviewee's emphasis). In the interviews I asked my colleague(s) to extend the unifying expressions like *'we do things that way'.* Teachers went on to speak about a *'united staff', 'common values', 'stability of staff', 'shared planning'.* In one school a teacher used an interesting term to describe empowerment of staff – *'positive* power'

– *'whenever an individual is thanked so is the team – this is what I mean by positive power ...'* In this way my colleagues were beginning to re-conceptualise, and verbalise, what *'just the way we are'* meant to them.

This feature of the 'typology' can also indicate a school whose culture is so typically, even naturally, supportive that its staff are 'unaware' (until pressed) of what it is they do, what they believe and do, that makes their school so 'unconsciously' supportive.

However, some highly supportive colleague cultures can change, even regress to less supportive cultures as new conditions or circumstances arise: notably when new senior staff – say a principal – arrive to take up leadership positions in a school. It is important that a school culture retains some 'consciousness', some awareness, of what it is its members believe, hold and practise about colleague support. This includes affirmation and even celebration – as well as review – that can all help endorse and strengthen the best features of the school's colleague culture.

Fullan (1993) notes 'that changing formal structures is not the same as changing norms, habits, skills and beliefs'. He quotes an interesting study by Wehlage et al. (1992) that demonstrates that for teachers who were accustomed to working in separate classrooms and who had little or no experience within the school of co-operating with others, simply providing time to meet ' ... was no guarantee that teachers would know how to work together in ways likely to result in more engaging curriculum and improved student performance' (in Fullan, 1993, p. 49). As one principal noted (Rogers, 1999) it took three patient and (at time) frustrating years *'for the kind of attitudes and norms to change from "closed-door" to "open-door" and from "individual" to "shared planning"*. Restructuring is clearly not the same as 'reculturing'.

A school's culture can aid or hinder effective change. When I studied school cultures in terms of how colleagues supported each other and the difference such support made, I observed significant differences regarding the 'consciousness' of support in a given school. As I compared and contrasted school cultures I noticed that certain features, practices and behaviours affected the degree of, and nature of, colleague support in a given school. That support had a marked effect on the quality of professional interaction, problem-solving, daily coping (particularly with change) and a sense of whole-school commitment to shared values and practices across teaching and management responsibilities.

End notes

1   To borrow a phrase of Tim Costello's (*The Age*, 18 October, p. 25). Costello makes an interesting point when he notes that the 'father' of *laissez faire* capitalism (Adam Smith) argued for a basic principle of 'interdependency' of 'the market' on 'social, relational and communal concerns'.

2 The report *Teacher Stress in Victoria* (1989) notes that 'an absence of *shared* beliefs (or culture) within the school about fit and proper student and teacher behaviours and differences in underlying views about discipline practices in the same school' contributed to teacher stress (my emphasis) (p. 43). See also Knutton and Mycroft (1986) who note that stress and conflict are reflected in the degree to which school ethos is based in a consensual model.

3 Argyris and Schon (1978) developed the terms 'espoused theory' and 'theory in use' to refer to the 'overt' and 'covert' cultural expression of a school's way of doing things.

4 'The aims of the Whole-School Approach are to reduce job stress and increase job satisfaction through improvements in individual, group and organisational functioning. One of its underlying assumptions is that teachers' job stress can be reduced and job satisfaction can be increased if a school has as part of its staff policy, ways and means to increase teacher achievement, sense of affiliation, and increase in decision-making influence. In taking on the approach, a school agrees to incorporate the following elements in a staff welfare policy' (Bernard, 1990, p. 325).

5 The schools in this study (on the effects of a whole-school approach) were compared to schools (in similar socioeconomic environments) that had not developed a 'whole-school' approach.

6 Some of the common 'structures' and 'processes' noted in my own research (Rogers, 1999) that enabled support were:
   • productive and purposeful teaming
   • effective communication pathways
   • whole-school behaviour policy and practice
   • effective crisis management procedures in a discipline/'control' context.
   It is also important to note the relationship between 'structures' and 'forms' of colleague support, *and* the culture and relationships that occur within structures and 'organisations'.

7 See Chapter 7 especially for a development of this concept. A recent policy initiative from Education Victoria (the Occupational Health and Safety Unit, Department of Education) encourages schools to develop a school-wide plan to address organisational, structural (physical environment) and social health (1999).

8 In his book *Change Forces*, Fullan (1993) speaks of 'change as a journey, not a blueprint ... change is non-linear, loaded with uncertainty, and sometimes perverse' (p. 24). He has a rather nice example where a group who had likened change 'to a planned journey into uncharted waters in a leaky boat with a mutinous crew' (pp. 24–5).

9 See also in Bernard (1990) the description of an individual or group perceiving themselves to be 'at cause' or 'at effect' in terms of taking control of external stressors.

10 Miller (1996) (quoting Dallos, 1991) notes: 'Change involves a shift at both levels – action and construing – we need to be wary when there is only evidence of movement in one area and not the other. It is easy enough to talk about things in a different way and to act in a different way, at least for a while. However, in order for change to be sustained, shifts in both areas are necessary' (p. 108).

11 Guskey (1986) argues that 'change is a learning process for teachers that is developmental and primarily experimentally based' (p. 7). This is particularly true when

addressing change(s) in teaching and management practices (Rogers, 2000).

12 It would be nice to 'wax poetic' about collaborative rationality being the working tool in such conflict resolution and decision-making, but reality attests that everything from 'group think' to '*formal* procedures' sometimes dethrone workable rationality. Bargaining, accommodation, compromises and tactical power plays can all emerge. Nadler et al. (1979) aptly calls this 'the political context of conflict'. As Miller (1996) notes 'organisationals are extremely well practiced in defensive routines' (p. 92).

13 A theme well developed in the literature: Johnson and Johnson (1989); Bernard (1990); Fullan (1991, 1993); Hargreaves (1991); Stoll (1998).

14 He cites McLaughlin (1992) who addresses collaboration in three ways as 'collaborative *skills*', '*attitudes*' and '*behaviours*'. Collaborative colleagues are:
  • people who can *communicate, think and continue to learn* throughout their lives
  • people who can demonstrate *positive attitudes and behaviours, responsibility and adaptability*
  • people who can work *with others* (Fullan, 1993, p. 45).

15 Reber (1985) reminds of the importance of 'type fallacy' in psychology where a researcher limits the variables of a 'type' so they are 'encapsulating categories in totally distinct ways' (p. 796).

16 Fullan (1993) notes that 'moving schools' (as typified by Rosenholtz, 1989) are also 'learning schools' characterised by 'learning enriched habits' … 'accustomed to dealing with the unknown' (p. 17). I would add *because* they are supportively engaged in this aspect of their learning culture, they are actively learning with, and from, each other.

17 This is a crucial point emphasised by Hamilton (1989) in his research on whole-school approaches to behaviour management (in Axworthy et al., 1989). See also Nias et al., 1989.

18 Here Stoll has drawn on Little's (1990) work. I would argue though with the qualifier 'strongest'; if there was, to my mind, a universal finding in my own research it is this, it is the '*indispensable variable*', the variable of 'mutual regard'.

19 This description is probably closest to what I have chosen to term the *consciously supportive colleague culture*.

20 I have been in many schools where some faculties covertly disparage subject areas like LOTE (Languages Other Than English) or 'home economics', implying that the 'real education' occurs in the 'core subjects'.

21 As in those secondary schools that were subject to a process of mandated, or 'semi-negotiated', amalgamation of former high schools with former technical schools into a 'new' post-primary school.

22 I have witnessed these emotions in individuals, and groups, not dissimilar to those stages of grief well known in the counselling literature. See, for example, Kubler-Ross (1971).

23 Breheney et al. (1996) note this important aspect of the school-wide colleague culture that 'non-teaching' staff are included in the school's support culture.

CHAPTER 4

UNDERSTANDING COLLEAGUE SUPPORT IN YOUR SCHOOL

'One necessary condition for its meaning is the attachment to something larger than you are.'
'Concepts like "meaning", "hope", "identity" and "coping ability" in failure and struggle actually need the longer term setting, the commons' [sic].

Seligman (1991, pp. 283, 287)

'It's a belief that we matter. If you feel accepted (by your colleagues) and if people believe and know you're trying to do your best then (for me) I can be myself even if I fall in a heap [sic] they're not going to criticise you. From those "things" other "things" flow – you're learning from them.'

(Primary school teacher cited in Rogers, 1999.)

Introduction

My aim throughout my research was to better understand how teachers rate, perceive, exercise and benefit from colleague support. I wanted both to observe, and research, colleague support as grounded in, and grounded from, my colleagues' experiences in the schools I studied and worked with.[1] What emerged, as 'grounded', is a theory-in-use in the sense that the study has highlighted:

- common, shared, meanings of colleague support, often highlighting what is highly valued about support in a given school
- major expressions and themes of colleague support as evidenced in schools
- common, and unifying, 'protocols' of colleague support that give value and core meaning to what colleagues understand as support. A 'protocol' – in this sense – is a stable, even defining, feature of colleague support in a school

- that colleague support meets fundamental coping needs as well as professional needs; depending on the 'form' such colleague support takes
- how colleague support affects professional development, feedback and appraisal
- how colleague support affects, and is affected by, change processes in schools
- how colleague support affects areas such as struggling teachers and casual (relief) teachers.

The 'grounded understandings' of this research study are based on a wide, ongoing dialogue that has evidenced – 'as theory' – several key understandings that give both meaning, adaptive utility and facility, to the concept and practice of colleague support in schools.[2] This 'dialogue' has been more than the wide survey data and the formal interviews themselves; it addresses those 'natural properties' (that) cannot simply be expressed in quantitative terms alone.

A notable feature of the grounded understandings I have developed from the research indicates that a 'whole-school consciousness' of support is a key factor in the wider utility of colleague support within a given school, particularly in areas such as teaming, shared-planning and school-wide policy and practice. The 'typology of colleague support' (see p. 64f) links the 'protocols of support' (p. 88f.), the fundamental 'dimensions of support' (p. xiv), the ascribed values given to aspects of support, and the degree and nature of the 'consciousness' of colleague support within a school as it develops supportive structures, processes and policies and how it copes with change (see Chapter 6).

This study has also demonstrated – with respect to change management and coping with change (natural, normative and mandated change) – that collegial behaviours such as shared planning, collaborative practices and purposeful teaming are confirming of these aspects of organisation and culture as they are defined as supportive within this study. The key, qualifying, feature of *whole-school* commitment to an ecology of colleague support is that it is consciously affirmed, encouraged and practised.

Consciousness of colleague support: an emerging typology

In Chapter 3 I proposed a typology of support built around the increasing degree of consciousness a school culture holds and normatively exhibits about colleague support.

In Figure 4.1 below I have sought to present a 'typology' that indicates the relationship between protocols of colleague support, the school-based processes and structures that enable colleague support, and how the transitional culture between unsupportive and supportive cultures can enable a more consciously supportive colleague culture to develop and sustain colleague needs.

The development from 'less' to 'more' consciously supportive cultures in a school is developed through building and sharing a vision of what colleague support is, and can be, and the school owning and controlling the processes necessary to develop and maintain a supportive culture; this is what is meant by 'consciously supportive'.

In terms of this transitional culture and change, many school leaders noted that bringing about changes in this area is not always easy. Colleague support can hardly be 'mandated' as such. As several school leaders noted (Rogers, 1999):

> 'When I first came here there were 15 teachers, 15 doors shut and 15 work programs. I made a promise I'd do nothing for 12 months, but I couldn't **just** do it that way. Teachers were not "coping" in the classrooms but they didn't talk about their needs; especially regarding the children's behaviour. It seemed there were heaps [sic] of problems but **given time** staff didn't feel threatened to speak about it' (colleague's emphasis).

> 'It was important; to talk things out in **a non-threatening way**. Although we could not always find answers, they *knew* I'd listen without them being put down – doors opened. They listened as soon as they **knew** I was willing to listen ... you do what you can, but you can **be** there'.

> 'It's taken a lot of hard work to get changes into place. Take the grade team meeting (this is a key feature of the school's organisation and teaming and an oft-quoted school feature of colleague support) – the staff assisted in the shaping of grade team leader role; this was crucial to expectations, and expectation and ownership go together. There are times when things don't go as you would envisage, that's okay. We keep working at it here ...'

> 'The "trick" is trying to get change going because people **want it to happen without forcing them**. This isn't easy when you see the need for change and they (your staff) don't'.

This last quote highlights the frustrations of espoused aims and needs and that which is effectively practical. Knowing this colleague, I don't think his use of 'they' was intentionally dismissive, rather it was based in natural frustration.

A primary teacher comments on change and collaboration:

> 'The culture (here) has changed **over time**. There has been a lot of delegation – people have been given genuine responsibility. The old hierarchical structures have effectively gone. In the past I would not have thought of popping in to the principal's office to talk – I would have felt like a kid who'd done something wrong!' (colleague's emphasis).

Even the phrase 'popping in', my colleague agreed, indicated the much more relaxed, but not casual, degree of admission by staff of one's professional and coping needs in the school *now*.

The senior staff and the 'middle management',[3] even the teaching staff, at times (in many of the schools I worked with), have accepted the reality that the concept of *whole team* and *whole-school* when applied to any policy or practice may mean about 80% of staff at most; for most of the time (bad-days notwithstanding). Even the 20% of staff who appear unwilling, or 'recalcitrant' to change have days when they make an effort to work within the 'whole-school' framework. Whether they share the values and aims that drive such changes is another issue.

It is clear from this research study that 'consciously supportive' schools share common characteristics of colleague culture that contribute to, and shape, whole-school culture. These characteristics are:

- shared values communicated through a shared vision of what 'our' school stands for. Such a vision needs to be more than a 'school logo'; it is a meaningful expression of core beliefs that affect, influence and shape collegial behaviours
- shared beliefs and understandings of and about colleague support; these I have termed 'protocols of colleague support' (see p. 88f.)
- a commitment to, and a shared trust in, school-wide processes and practices as well as in each other.[4] (See below and also Appendix 3.)

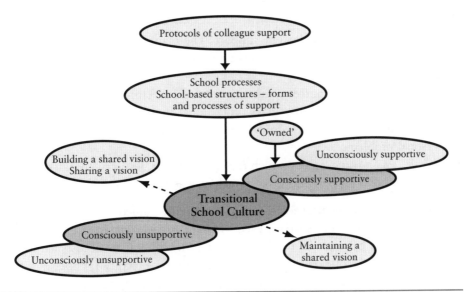

Figure 4.1   *An integrated typology of colleague support*

Hargreaves (1994) notes that there is a 'pervasive theme' that runs throughout the literature of shared leadership and collaborative cultures: what he terms 'the truism of trust'. The establishment of trust, it is argued, is essential to the building up of effective and meaningful collaborative work relationships; 'trust and rapport ... are the foundations for building collegiality in a school ...' (p. 58).

As the school, as a community, moves towards a more 'conscious' utility and practice of colleague support, the 'protocols' take on a more conscious viability and expression. Staff speak about colleague support beyond the dyadic, the transitional and the ad-hoc. There appears in staff documentation and policy aspects of support and staff welfare, as well as formative structures – and practices – put in place to enhance moral and professional support.

Of course it can be argued that a policy expression on colleague support may only represent 'espoused theory' rather than 'theory in use'. I have worked with schools who can chronicle a grand vision that seems to uphold (even affirm) aspects of collegiality such as 'mutual respect', 'consideration of others', 'staff welfare'; such loquacity, however, is not always reflected in characteristic staff treatment of one another or modelled by its senior staff.

Colleague support is concerned with meeting espoused needs rather than assumed needs.

Meeting needs in colleague support: function and form (see Figure 4.2)

Form follows function in colleague support. The main themes noted in Chapter 1 highlight how colleague support meets basic needs through:

- *sharing* 'of ideas', 'resources', 'management and teaching concerns' and 'generating shared plans'; this also gives professional confidence and assurance
- *coping support* ranging widely from 'whingeing' to the sharing of professional and personal problems
- *planning and teaming support*, which too can enable professional confidence, assurance and moral support and professional feedback.

What is frequently mentioned, though, and highly valued – is how colleagues' needs are met within such 'sharing' even when it is transitional in expression. These needs may be as basic as the need 'to belong', 'to affiliate', or needs such as 'fun' being met through collegial goodwill. As one colleague (typically) notes:

' ... it means people to talk to when you have problems with discipline or the whole range of things that can worry you ... of course it means sharing when things go right but you **really** need the sharing when "it" goes wrong. The one thing I really appreciate is people who are **willing** to share **and care**. It's all very well to share, you'll appreciate if you know they **care as well** ...' (in Rogers, 1999).

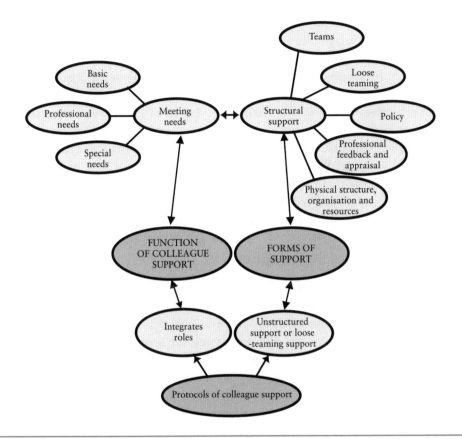

Figure 4.2   *Function and form in colleague support*

Many colleagues also indicated that 'fun', 'humour' and 'having a shared laugh' is also a 'coping mechanism'.

The need to affiliate is often expressed as reducing one's feeling of 'isolation' or 'not-being-the-only-one'; of knowing the 'we-*all*-make-mistakes' and that it is '*okay to fail*'. This is a frequently cited feature (by colleagues) of needs-meeting, that of knowing that '*all of us*', '*get it wrong*' or '*fail*' or '*screw up*' or '*forget*'.

The meeting of needs can be further, and significantly, enhanced through 'forms' and 'structures', such as school-wide collaborative policy and practice, purposeful teaming and supportive school-wide appraisal. The 'forms' of support vary with the degree of whole-school emphasis in consciously meeting basic needs. Any 'forms' or structures, are not, in themselves, the answer to colleague support but the 'forms' can, and do, enable support and the meeting of colleagues' needs. Such 'forms' also enable the meeting of needs because the culture of the school evidences the sorts of protocols of support noted later in this chapter: mutual regard and mutual respect, colleague watchfulness, communicating trust in people and processes, realistic acceptance of fallibility in self and others, a non-competitive collegial ethos and a realistic acceptance of the 'certainty of uncertainty'.

The most fundamental need, cited by colleagues, is the need to feel valued: 'I belong, I'm worthwhile here'. This fundamental human need does not change because a teacher is in a school setting; its degree of expression may change – naturally – but teachers frequently speak about the reciprocity of 'acceptance', 'mutual respect', 'dignity' and 'humanity'. It is as if staff have said, 'I am valuable, in part, because you "care for", "support", "encourage me", "you back me up", "trust me"; "you make provision for me by thinking about me in this way"'. The treatment variable (the way one treats others, not merely 'manages' others) seems to be an axial variable across the dimensions of support: moral, professional and structural.[5]

Transitional, dyadic, support

In every school I have taught in, in every school I have ever worked in, in every school I worked with during this research, 'dyadic support' was present. Even in the most unsupportive school cultures there are always a few people one can 'trust', 'off-load' with, gain 'assurance' and gain some support from. In less supportive schools this may be limiting; it may at times lead to 'cliques' or little in-groups; at its worst it may create that professional isolationism that severely limits the learning culture of teachers in a school.

Even in consciously supportive schools, however, this commonly cited expression of support often occurs at the dyadic level (rather than in multi-dyads or teams) with fellow teachers. As one colleague noted ' ... they're the ones that most understand the day-to-day trials and can better support me if necessary ...' This is not to say team leaders do not provide that level of support; clearly they do.

> The photocopy room seems to be a collegial transfer place ... people coming in and out, often passing each other with transitional, supportive, acknowledgment.
>
> I was photocopying some material and Paul came in. We chatted about this and that. I asked how he was going 'Oh you, know running around like a blue-arsed fly ...'
>
> 'What's that?' I nodded to the long, flat steel things wrapped in plastic in his hand. 'Oh they're blades for Greg (in woodwork) he's got a crook back at the moment so I got them sharpened for him ...' To me this demonstrated substantial colleague support and care while Paul (I'm sure) took it for 'normal'.
>
> David comes in. I'd finished my photocopying and Paul and I were still talking. Paul added (to David) 'won't be long'. Their brief, shared look of concern (about fitting 101

things into a teaching day) was obvious. 'It's the report ...' He crossed his fingers. 'Only got one hour, got to get it copied and off!' We had a chat about the 'utility' of this lengthy report but both acknowledged it was one of those necessary 'service' tasks.

This vignette is typical of common experiences whenever I was in the photocopy room in this school. Part whinge, part moral support, transitional – and always valued. (in Rogers, 1999)

Where such support is only, or *characteristically*, dyadic[6], and dependent on selectivity and the colleague comfort zone, it limits the wider school consciousness of how the constructive and positive features of dyadic colleague support can be more widely 'structured-in'.[7] Even when colleague support is consciously present in 'forms', 'structures', 'policies' and 'processes' – within a school culture – the 'ad hoc' and dyadic, the transitional and 'on-the-run', feature of colleague support will be the normative expression.

'Take Mary-Anne – she comes into my class once a week – just for a chat. It's not a formal thing; it's just that she shows interest in me and what I'm doing. **We don't even plan from it** – it's just that she often comes in. Being a senior teacher she knows what's going on and we talk about things. I notice it, it helps ...' I asked my colleague how it helped and she said, ' it was just *kind of assuring knowing she knew how things were here ...*' (colleague's emphasis). (op. cit. Rogers)

'Small' expressions of support?

The casual relief teachers I discussed the issue of support with, particularly noted the deceptively small 'things' like 'having a map of the school', 'having the support' of a 'teaching buddy', 'being introduced to staff at morning tea', or 'having their own photocopy number' ... The support, spoken of here, is often in those small things,[8] as noted in the protocol on 'bearing one another's burdens' (see p. 97f). One of my colleagues and I made a brief list of some of these typical 'small things' expressed in attitude and action:

- 'gave me a cuppa *on the way*'
- 'a quiet reminder, or assurance, in the corridor' (on the run!)
- 'the remembered birthday'
- 'the card on the desk when you've been away'
- 'I got a choccy in my pigeon hole!'
- 'We make the effort here to positively greet and acknowledge one another', 'even smile!'[9] (I noticed this general, unforced, behaviour even on the days when the smiles were weary. I could sense the 'Dunkirk Spirit'!)

- We 'back-each-other-up', 'we look out for each other' (This came through constantly in the interviews I had with colleagues in supportive schools. p. 97f.)
- 'We don't blame each other, we support each other'
- 'We make the effort to encourage one another'. This, I observed, meant 'noticing', 'acknowledging' and 'affirming' others' efforts and contributions. This 'noticing' was frequently observed in 'small' ways, such as flowers on the desk after someone returns from being unwell, the small gift or thank-you card, doing a small job for a colleague who is particularly hassled that day or week.
- 'We make time for one another …' 'When a colleague says, "have you got a minute?" it's often *literal*. We need to have "it" – that's why we work together. It's mostly incidental – but that's how colleague support works, isn't it? Like "time-out" – it works because we're comfortable with one another. On these sorts of issues it's like a toothache – it's no good saying "come and see me Friday afternoon" – we need to deal with it now. My colleague is physically close (next door). I could see today that this child was "off". Ten minutes he had next door (with my colleague) – he came back and apologised even; and that's all he needed and so did I' (colleague's emphasis).

Now, I asked, was this all accidental? The result of those particular 'kink of personalities' resident in the school? Or had previous staff 'policy', and culture (even if unwritten), heightened these supportive behaviours? What features or processes in this school made it possible for the staff to more readily, more willingly, more consistently, offer, give and receive such colleague support? It is, in essence, *colleague watchfulness* based on colleague perspective-taking:

> 'Often it's the small things, the fact you've been consistent in following up on, say, a broken light, a needed item or resource. A policy issue about student behaviour even in small things about "bringing bags into class (!)" – because it may be a big issue for some teachers. **We're back to black dot white square!**' (colleague's emphasis, Rogers, 1999).

My colleague, here, was referring to a metaphor I had used at a staff workshop recently – we were comparing and contrasting the frustrating, annoying, even stressful aspects and features of our day-to-day teaching life, which we termed (using the metaphor), as being like a 'black dot' relative to a 'white square'. The 'white square' represented the positive, good, worthwhile, commendable, enjoyable aspects or outcomes of our work together. What we drew from this metaphor is that it is easy to *over-focus* on the negative and stressful aspects of our teaching life (the 'black dot') at the expense of the wider, bigger, more common (we hope) 'white square' features of our teaching life at school.

It's about realistic perspective-taking. If we over-focus on the 'black dot' – to the forgetful exclusion of the 'white square' – we will be more jaded than we need to be.

The deceptively 'small' features of colleague support increase the 'white square' as it were to give balance to the 'normative black dot'.

Collegial perspective-taking

In such 'dyadic', transitory, episodic expressions of support, colleagues noted that the opportunity to 'just talk things through', 'to discuss common needs', even just to 'off-load', 'sound-off'' and 'whinge' was needs-meeting *when* an ethos of non-judgment was normally present. As one colleague put it, 'What I want is non-judgmental support'. This 'qualifier' came out of a long discussion with a colleague who, when he had asked for help from a senior faculty colleague, felt he had merely been criticised not supported. '... It means listening, really listening, not necessarily giving you advice'. 'It also means being understood'.

Teachers frequently acknowledged that they didn't 'feel stupid ...' or 'feel a goose ...' if they asked the dumb questions about, for example, imposed changes or new program implementation. As one colleague reflected, 'When an older teacher asks a dumb question they *could* look more stupid than they should be as an older teacher. I mean a younger teacher, well you can understand them not knowing something ...' (This teacher was honest enough, in this school, to share her 'doubts' with younger teachers.)

In one of the high schools I worked in, a first-year teacher almost 'broke down' as she shared her struggle with a known 'hard' year 8 class. One of the senior staff admitted he too had found this class a real challenge. 'You too?' His admission was a filip to her perceived failure, it was also the beginning of a more confident process of support.

For some colleagues, listening, or being heard, is sometimes enough. They often said that realistically 'some things about the school (for example, the 'client group' of students) will probably never change':

> '... but when we acknowledge that it's okay to whinge about how difficult it can be here with these students, we feel better ... not pointing the finger at you (as if you can't cope) or judging you ... that's not support.'

The ability to share needs and concerns, and have the opportunity to share is acknowledged as both difficult and helpful. Whether it is a transitory whinge (the easiest), or sharing a specific concern, need or problem, with a view to longer term support; what was valued highly as colleague support is the accepting of the 'mutual struggle' and 'common fallibility' and being understood within that struggle.

In a very long, and frank, interview one of my colleagues noted 'When you spill your guts it's a humbling experience, but it has helped. I've had a lot of personal problems as well this year'. He then added, ' ... along with report-writing, the appraisal process in our school, re-organising aspects of the faculty curriculum ... it's all compounded the stress ... it's not *just* me ... but guts-spilling has really helped ...' He named a senior teacher who had really helped by listening, he used phrases about her like ' ... she *valued* me ... she was a person I could confide in as a professional ...' (colleague's emphasis). At the end of the day my colleague was describing the underlying feature of colleague support that has a capacity for risk, when trust and self-disclosure is present, that brings fundamental human dignity in the very pressured time-frame of day-to-day teaching. How can one 'benchmark' this aspect of colleague support? (in Rogers, 1999)

Another colleague noted these aspects of moral support:

' ...it is important for someone to **listen**, to know someone is listening (some students can be hell, as you know). *It's important for someone to know* what I'm going through ...' (colleague's emphasis).

Again, here, the theme of how one is *treated* in sharing one's needs is important. The support given may contain professional advice but the humanising context is the moral support underlying it.

'You need to **feel you're being heard** – but we also need help to solve problems'.

'No favouritism, it can destroy a hard-working team. If I'm treated fairly and what I do is valued, I'll even go a bit further ... but if I'm mistreated, if they (admin.) are unfair, then I'll do just the basics ...'

Here my colleague compared the principal to a previous one who had his 'little coterie'. 'If you were with them it was okay. I'd do the minimum for him – I'd do "a" and "b" but not "c", "d", "e" and "f". You with me ...?' (I was).

Of course there are personality factors when people are interacting, whether at the level of 'off-loading', whingeing or professional-sharing. There are those who are more confident in themselves as people generally, as well as in their professional role and skills; these colleagues find it easier to approach others and talk through issues. There are those colleagues, though, who are lacking in personal (and professional) confidence – whose self-esteem has taken some bruising with, say, a 'hard class' who perceive that others may be judging them as 'weak' or 'ineffective'; these colleagues find it much harder to self-initiate colleague support. There are also those colleagues who *appear* to cope, who seem to need to be seen as 'effective', as 'coping', as 'strong' or 'tough', as 'having got-it-together', as 'not failing' – some of these teachers mask their needs and concerns. I have had many, many discussions with such colleagues. While these sorts of transitional discussions between colleagues, (especially informal discussions), do not always 'fix' the problem as it were, they can decrease the feeling of personal failure and increase the *shared* perspective confirming that the reality is wider than one's own perception.

Such discussion is also more than mere *whingeing*, although whingeing, in its various forms, is valued consistently by teachers as a coping mechanism – it is the discussion itself that is purposeful. This doesn't mean that all discussion has to be directed at action; some discussion is an extension of the whinge ('Oh, you too!'); a way of acknowledging even re-framing stressful events. For example, '… talking about highs and lows … look, you think that's bad let me tell you about …'. 'It's a chance to talk about things in a relaxed way'. 'We laugh a lot … humour is a top priority'. This colleague then added, '… give advice if wanted.' 'I'm not a shrink but I try to help out by listening and being there – if that's all I can do sometimes, I do it – it's the dependability of being there …'

As Shakespeare succinctly puts it in *Antony and Cleopatra*, 'Pour out the pack of matter to mine ear. The good and the bad together' (Act 2, scene 5).

Moral support

When staff spoke about moral support in these ways, several recurring points were made:

- That our job can be quite stressful for all of us at times. We *all* need a helping hand. This 'helping hand', this reciprocity of support, is a way of acknowledging the individual and affirming the individual in light of our common needs and responsibilities. As one colleague describes:

    'It's important to know I'm not the only one having problems with him …' [we were discussing, as I have with many colleagues, a particularly difficult student]. 'It tells me we *all* have some problems with _____ and we can talk about it. "How do you find him? What works and what doesn't work?" We bounce things off each other. As long as I've got support from my colleagues … you can't do things alone.'

    A beginning teacher added that this kind of sharing, 'gives (me) confidence that I'm doing much the same as my colleagues in behaviour management.'

- That we are *all* fallible; we all at times 'run late', 'make mistakes', 'forget to print the worksheets', are 'late with reports', 'get it wrong …' Accepting fallibility in one's self means acknowledging and accepting it in others. This does not mean we do not, and should not, address ongoing problems or concerns with teachers who

are characteristically struggling or failing. It does mean that our acceptance of fallibility in ourselves, and others, can humanise the necessary encounter and hopefully enable ongoing support for teachers who are struggling or who are not fulfilling preferred, and expected, management and teacher practice.
- There is nearly always something constructive that can be done to help improve things both in the short-term and in a longer-term sense.

Whingeing as a feature of colleague coping

One of the most basic 'coping strategies' noted by teachers was that of 'whingeing' ('sounding-off', 'moaning about ...', 'getting it off one's chest!'). It occurs daily in shared talk in staff rooms, in discussions, in teams. It can be both a 'coping mechanism', as well as an expression of affiliative bonding. It can be a way of transitorily coping with stress; an 'emotional release valve' as it were, but one that often *identifies* with common feelings, needs and concerns. Colleagues often noted they 'felt better' after a 'whinge with those they identified as sharing common ground.[10]

Whingeing, however, can be self-defeating, and group-defeating, where it characteristically ratifies the worst features, and experiences, of a school (p. 31). Communication exchanges that overly feature 'moaning' and 'complaining' and 'griping' often admit to an uncommitted collegial stance to problem analysis and collaborative practices.

When a school seeks to manage change there are natural dissenters: those who are uncertain, even anxious, and those who dissent because they may not care, or have strong beliefs, about why any changes should be made. While natural uncertainty and concerns in any school need addressing, what is more difficult to deal with are those who go out of their way to disturb, derail, or destroy any change process and change imperatives.

I have worked in schools where complaining, even dissenting, colleagues are invited into working groups to effect change in the very areas they often whinge about. It is not uncommon to hear them say they don't want to 'join' any such group. As one senior secondary colleague noted when discussing change-dynamics in his school:

'They were quite happy to say what should have been done, what we **should** do. They're "safe" while white-anting[11] – they can criticise and moan and complain and judge (or prejudge) from a distance because they're not accountable' (colleague's emphasis, Rogers, 1999).

I had further discussed with my colleague the effect of this behaviour on morale:

'Once they're **in** the process they're responsible because they're part of the process – they're now "formally" accountable; it changes their "safety position". Now they can't have the easy luxury of judgement that it should be "this" or "that" because they are part of the process of solution' (colleague's emphasis, ibid.).

The interpretation, perhaps fairly, placed on this 'whingeing behaviour' was that the colleagues in question felt 'safe' to whinge as long as they remained uncommitted to the school-wide process of change. As Bramson (1981, p. 58) points out, 'negative whingers can often create a climate where the other party to the whingeing becomes confirmatory and a "pattern" occurs creating negative impasse: "the blame lies elsewhere other than us!"'

With supporting colleagues who are in the 'habit' of negative whingeing it is important to get beyond the easy judgement and accusing tenor of the whinger. It is easy, too easy, to get trapped into counter-accusation to 'ram-home' the point that the whinger is his or her own worst enemy, which may well be true!

In any workable dialogue where we attempt to understand and support the more chronically whingeing colleague it can help to:

- Affirm the colleague's perceived struggle and frustration. This in turn affirms the fundamental 'humanity' that ought at least to coexist in a collegial culture. To do this requires some challenging, conscious, effort at times. We may not 'like' this particular colleague, we may be fed up with his or her whingeing behaviour, especially when it leads to collusive, destructive, whingeing. If we are a leader, however, we have a professional and moral obligation to address any *pattern* of such whingeing early before it becomes 'catalytic'.

- Avoid the easy temptation to move to immediate 'utility', immediate 'solution', 'blaming' or even 'mocking' our colleague (again a tempting exercise) with calls such as: 'Well, no wonder you've got problems, the way you teach!', 'Well, no wonder no-one takes *you* seriously, you miserable sod(!)' 'You *never* come up with *any* useful, constructive, suggestion or solution …'

  Listening to a colleague's complaint(s) is not necessarily agreeing with his or her perceptions, or constructions, of reality. It does not mean we agree he or she is 'right'. The listening is an important step in some workable understandings of our colleague's world!

- It is important, though, when we have given our colleague a fair hearing ('So, you seem to be saying?', 'Have I got that right?', 'Can you develop that?', 'I'm not sure what you mean by … ?'), and when we have got some understanding of the issue, the 'facts of the case' or, ongoing grievance, that we move to problem-solving.

  A senior colleague described how he acknowledges whingeing from his colleagues, often noting it validates their coping needs and also enhances the problem-solving process.

'Let them whinge! But get them focused on the issue. **You've got to hear that whinge**, it validates their perspective, how they see the problem. Normally, the colleague who whinges knows there's a problem or two! ... It's important to listen but you need to go beyond their generalising; for example, when they say so-and-so's class are all sh*ts, I say what about so-and-so? (I name a few students in that class.) You know what the kids are like here, Bill (here we had a tangential discussion on unemployment, parental negligence, even abuse ...). I try to help my colleague see the bigger picture. See, we're **all** fallible but not all, or **all the time** ...' (colleague's emphasis).

- Any problem-solving needs to focus on addressing colleagues' needs within their responsibilities. This is rarely a short-term process but it begins with acknowledgment, affirmation and helping the colleague to be a significant 'part of the solution'. If they choose not to work constructively to address the concerns at issue, they will need to be challenged within their core responsibilities and professional obligations.

An important 'key' here is early intervention, before a spiral of negative and defeatist communication sets in. Such 'early intervention' is most likely to be constructive if the school's climate is consciously supportive and colleagues affirm the protocols of mutual regard and 'colleague watchfulness' (see p. 97f. below).

The place of humour in colleague-coping

Many of my colleagues noted how fundamental – yet significant – humour is in the day-to-day life of the school, both with colleagues and students. I noticed on my many visits to supportive schools a common, almost residual, goodwill that often expressed itself in relaxed humour. Colleagues saw 'safe' and 'acceptable' kinds of humour as a means of 'helping us feel better about ourselves or some issue we're facing'; 'it just helps us feel good' or 'at least feel better' and it 'defuses tension'. 'Sometimes humour can help. Light humour related to our difficult day-to-day situations can help some of 'em to come out of their pedantic shell ... shared laughter is important ...'

Dr Robert Moodie, in an article on managing stress in the workplace, advocates the application of humour to promote both mental and psychological health. Whether there is clinical, evidential, proof that humour is correlated with increasing health and stress reduction is a moot point – claims are made. There is the suggestion that endorphins are released into the blood stream when one is in a humorous mood, or laughing, giving a temporary, pleasant sensation (a temporary illusion?).[12]

Koestler (1964) (in Cornett, 1986, p. 26) notes that humour is the only domain of creativity where a stimulus produces a massive and sharply defined response at the level of psychological reflexes.

In the 1860s Freud suggested that humour develops as a means of coping with stressful situations or anxiety-arousing circumstances.

I think both Moodie, and even Freud, mean we feel better when we laugh at, or about, difficult situations, circumstances or even others whose company we may find stressful at times. (As Mark Twain once wrote, 'Everything is funny as long as it's happening to someone else.')

The forms of humour exhibited and enjoyed in schools range from the in-house jokes, wit (dry or otherwise), repartee, the appropriate *bon mot*, verbal incongruency, irony, farce, even satire (I've seen many a little-acted drama by staff to illustrate and relieve tension when addressing quite serious issues). Even the shared look that says, 'You-feel-like-that-too?' and a smile or wink can give a transitional feeling of shared identity. During a mentoring visit to a secondary school a few years back, someone noticed my cartoon-motif tie. From there it was a short step to every second male modelling their socks with pictorial motifs. (We stopped there – no full Monty!) Soon a larger group had joined in. It was a brief moment of shared morale, unforced and transitorily valued. It perhaps met what Glasser (1992) calls one's 'need for fun'.

A colleague notes the almost accepted 'role' of one of the staff at her school who is seen as a bit of a court jester:

> 'She's really funny, she keeps us sane. It's usually [she] who kicks "it" off. She'll write a ditty or two; she's a fantastic poet ... always makes us laugh. If it wasn't for her it might be a bit more serious I don't know ...' (Rogers, 1999).

My colleagues in this study frequently said humour, in the day-to-day ups and downs, gave them a 'coping edge', a feeling of 'temporary uplift';[13] the sense of feeling better 'when we have a laugh'. Even our cognitive frame of reference can be enhanced when we see something in a more humorous light as we defuse normative tension and, perhaps, refocus to a less stressful way of looking at things.

When staff communicate in more formal group settings, humour can motivate and arouse interest as well as defuse residual tension; there is also the sense of shared identity. Cornett (1986, p. 11) notes that the emotionally positive experience of laughing together creates a group feeling, giving the members a sense of security and self-confidence.

This is similar to Walker and Adelman's (1976) findings that humour can both 'promote positive relationships' and 'imply or engage group solidarity' (in Robertson, 1996, p. 138). In this sense, humour can be creative as well as relieve tension. Goleman (1996) in his work on emotional intelligence develops this point:

> 'Laughing, like elation, seems to help people think more broadly and associate more freely, noticing relationships that might have eluded them otherwise ... One study found that people who had just watched a video of television bloopers were better at solving a puzzle long used by psychologists to test creative thinking' (p. 85).

Humour can help when revisiting disturbing or painful experiences in a school's history. I was conducting an afternoon workshop in a primary school, and after the tea break two members of staff, complete with guitar, sang a comic song about the principal's recent *contretemps* with an abusive, aggressive, mother who had yelled, accusingly, and pronounced threats and dire protestations in full hearing of all and sundry.

The singing duo had cleverly put together the account (now in-house 'folklore') complete with chorus and at the close of the performance presented Laurie with a copy in the form of a scroll of the song.

In this example humour helped to revisit and re-interpret an experience which, at the time, was quite stressful for the principal. In the sense of a 'buffering effect' on stress it was quite appropriate, timely and effective.

The incident, revisited in comic song, helped all the staff to cohere, to reframe and defuse the natural frustrations staff have about *some* of the parents at the school.

The laughter, itself, was supportive to Laurie (the principal) and a way of saying that *'while this situation is stressful we understand – this is our way of letting off safe, healthy, steam (psychological steam) about it and not letting it deter, or detract, us from what we know we do well here.'* (in Rogers, 1999)

The psychiatrist Paul Tournier (1970) says:

> 'The vocation of the humorist seems to me to be eminently beneficent ... he is able to get some valuable truth across much more directly and more delicately than the moralist' (p. 144).

Perhaps it is that when we feel better we 'do better'. When possible embarrassment, tension or even a weighty matter is on the agenda, humour can enable the individual and the group to temporarily refocus.

I can recall a tense staff discussion we were having on discipline in schools, now that corporal punishment had been abolished, and how ' ... we all needed to rethink our discipline in light of these changes ...' In the course of the discussion some of those staff who saw this as a threat, and perhaps saw less support from the principal for 'punishment' regimes in the foreseeable future, were demonstrating some disaffectation for the then Department of Education imperative. At one stage in the 'discussion' our principal, making heavy weather of the staff meeting, said something like, 'Well, since capital punishment in schools has been abolished ...' He did not get much further; everybody was now laughing. It was apparent, as soon as the principal caught up with what he had *actually* said and reiterated, he had meant 'corporal' not' capital', but much of the residual tension had been defused. It marked a change in the communal sense of shared frustration, shared need and shared understanding.

Nash (1968) suggests that humour can also help a person, 'to some extent deal with (his) repressed emotions' (p. 335); this may well be true of 'the group' as well.

Malicious humour

There are staff who distort humour into sarcasm: the hurtful jest, the 'loaded comment' or even malice. Sarcasm is a distortion of humour by those whose intent is to primarily exercise some social power over the person to whom the sarcasm is directed; it is the intention that is the key feature. Skilful use of the *bon mot*, repartee or witticism can highlight cynicism, frustration or even engage bonhomie without intent to hurt others. In these cases the humour is often directed as much at the speaker or the situation as at any 'victim' as such.[14] Sarcasm, however, has the in-built tendency, when used frequently, to 'boomerang' by creating a competitive and reactive environment among staff. Whereas humour can create an 'identification with others', regular use of sarcasm is most often divisive among others.

It is often the most cynical who resort to easy targets through such 'humour' – it is to be resisted and challenged rather than accepted (or worse tolerated). Manning Clark (1991) notes:-

'I started my career as a teacher believing a joke could also be a parable, a professional metaphor for our times. Sarcasm and foolishness could be the prelude to an epiphany. Behind the mask of the fool there was a man searching for the answers. I was wearing the mask of a man who wanted to shout "no" to much around him. In time I would discard the sarcasm. Why tear the flesh as a prologue to the truth?' (p. 121).

Louis Kronenberger (1954) writing on humour, points out:

'Humour simultaneously wounds and heals, indicts and pardons, diminishes and enlarges; it constitutes inner growth at the expense of outer gain, and those who possess and honestly practice it will make themselves more through a willingness to make themselves less' (in Cornett, 1986, p. 32).

Wilower (in Burford, 1996) suggests that maybe there is a particular 'brand' of humour present in educational administration in educational subcultures that can turn what could be considered a personal attack on the administration into a less threatening and amusing incident when expressed in meetings (with members of the subculture). Such humour seems to evoke shared ordeals, common meanings and social support. When one is even temporarily more relaxed the mind is temporarily more open to another point of view.

In his book *Man's Search For Meaning,* the psychiatrist Victor Frankyl (1963) describes his experiences in the concentration camps of Dachau and Auschwitz. His recollections contain all the horror, terror and worst abuses of human to human – yet he also chronicles the incredible power of human love, affirmation, dignity and support also present amid such horror. Surprisingly, he mentions the effect of humour on personal and social coping and the difference, even a small difference, it could make in personal and communal suffering. He speaks of seeing things in a 'humorous light', not as a denial of reality but a way of coping with reality (p. 69).

> 'To discover there was any semblance of art in a concentration camp must be surprise enough for an outsider, but he may be even more astonished to hear that one could find a sense of humour there as well; of course, only the faint trace of one, and then only for a few second or minutes. Humour was another of the soul's weapons in the fight for self-preservation. It is well known that humour, more than anything else in the human make-up, can afford an aloofness and an ability to rise above any situation, even if only for a few seconds' (p. 54).

Wood in Burford (1987) has concluded that humour and laughter play(ed) a major role in 'coping strategies' of teachers and students alike (pp. 29–54). I have noticed in the schools I worked with in this study, the general 'feel' of a school when relaxed humour and laughter is present. It is not directly quantifiable as such, but one 'knows it is there' and knows it makes a difference.

A school environment can at times be a quite stressful place to work and live in for a third of one's day. I know my colleagues valued the temporary respite from such stress, as well as the reframing that sometimes comes when humour was present.[15] As one colleague noted, 'We don't feel as bad, as often, for as long.'

The protocols of colleague support

As noted earlier, colleagues frequently noted certain underlying aspects or features of colleague support that occur in supportive schools. These 'aspects' cross the dimensions of 'moral', 'professional' and 'structural' support; I have termed these central, characteristic features, or aspects, of colleague support as 'protocols'.[16] These protocols have descriptive and enabling features; they also appear as expressions of meaning when addressed to the 'ecology of support'. They can embrace dyadic as well as whole-school expressions of support. At their conceptual heart is the acknowledgment of our shared humanity, whether addressing the issue of incidental sharing, lesson-planning, stress and coping or organisational change.

These protocols offer both presuppositional understandings of colleague support and confirmatory understandings of how support is expressed and utilised in a school community. The protocols are not so much the 'route' to colleague support as they are the 'enabling' conditions for a culture of support. They are not, by themselves, 'the ecology': they describe the ecology of support as they illustrate the *function* of colleague support. A collegially supportive culture needs 'form' and 'structure', but without the protocols there is only 'form' and 'structure', not necessarily colleague support.

No 'one' protocol stands alone as pertinent to, or descriptive of, a consciously supportive colleague culture; each protocol stands in relationship to the others as dynamic features of a school culture.

The most repeated expression when describing and attenuating colleague support, for example, is that of 'mutual respect' and 'respectful treatment' – the way one is normally treated by one's colleagues. Such a 'protocol' is noted by colleagues as foundational, even axiomatic; whether in professional-sharing, giving advice, shared planning or appraisal. The way one treats, and is treated by, others can acknowledge, affirm and support our shared humanity as well as our shared professionalism.[17]

Key words, phrases and themes related to such a universal concept like respect are noted by my colleagues in countless phrases such as: 'acceptance of others', 'trust', 'consciousness of others', 'take time for others', 'willingness to ...', 'show others you care', 'follow through', 'all chip in ...', 'giving breathing space', 'we share (time, resources, help ...)', 'identify with ...' As one grade leader (primary) notes: ' ... people's openness here is what it [colleague support] is about is that people are conscious of other people ... of treating others as persons not *just* as colleagues' (colleague's emphasis).

What is interesting to note in my colleague's comment is that she invests the term 'colleague' with a meaning that contains, but extends, the concept of 'professional' within the personal – and consciously so. Whatever professional support is given in the school, staff also value highly the 'moral' aspects expressed in mutual respect. 'I can't imagine people not teaching without *that* kind of support – teaching is a hard enough job without not being willing to support each other' (colleague's emphasis).

In this sense the 'protocol' of mutual respect arising from mutual regard becomes a pervasive, stable feature describing a characteristic quality of colleague support. For example, when supporting struggling colleagues, whatever support is offered – whether in advice, action-plans or mentoring – it will be how they feel 'they are treated', how 'their failure and fallibility is acknowledged', and how they feel others are 'watching out for them' that determines – at least for them – the nature, and quality, of colleague *support*.

Protocols and shared values

No protocol of support is value-free, whether the colleague support is loosely coupled or expressed within a more whole-school structure. Colleagues express certain values redolent in concepts of colleague support. These values are expressed as:

- mutual regard (with respect to the personal and professional)
- tolerance of others' differences[18] (this is often associated with compassion, empathy)
- a sensitivity to others' needs[19]
- commitment to equality and justice
- commitment to collaboration rather than individualism
- the acceptance of 'fallibility' and the certainty of 'uncertainty'.

Shared values are those values that, fundamentally, bind us to others: socially and professionally. They define and shape meaning and give a sense of social coherence. When enunciated – whole-school – they can further enable a shared consensus about a school's collegial life.[20]

The protocols

Mutual respect: the treatment variable

As noted earlier, purely on citation frequency this aspect of colleague support rates highest. More than that, however, colleagues spoke about 'the way they are (or have been) treated' as the crucial factor in how the respect and support of others is perceived, accepted and valued.[21] As one colleague noted, ' ... it's seeing people; not just their job.' Another colleague in a different school echoes this crucial feature of respect:

> 'It also relates to the way we give acceptance and *respect* for what we *all* do here. It's really a *belief in people*. They are dedicated here ...' (colleague's emphasis).

Typical words and phrases colleague respondents cited that define, describe and qualify colleague support (noted in interviews and surveys) were: 'trust', 'ability to trust', 'openness'/'honesty in communication', 'respect' (giving/receiving), 'no pressure'/'confidentiality', 'give time to one another', 'loyalty', 'feedback without fear', 'positive', 'encouraging', 'availability', 'accepted', 'acknowledged', 'willingness', 'equality', 'sharing of workload/time', 'caring', 'empathetic' and 'cohesion'.

Mutual respect at its most basic is, at least, civility and at its more thoughtful it is:

- faith in the abilities of others
- interest in the point of view of others (as well as one's own)
- the willingness to go out of one's way, at times, for others; particularly in their struggles and failures.

It is, fundamentally, the acceptance of our shared humanity in a common goal and common purposes. It also means that when addressing failure and struggle in others that they are treated with consideration of their feelings, within ethical probity, without pettiness or unreasonable criticism. Such consideration also means 'tuning-in' to how they might feel about 'their failure', their struggle:

> 'I was treated from the first as a professional. I was shown how the school works but trusted to do my job – it's a nice balance. I was made to feel welcome not left out at all. They also noted, and acknowledged, what I'd done best at my last school ... and how it could fit in here. They were reassuring in all that. My team leader, Pam, has given me respect and acknowledged my worth; I needed that ... it has helped me feel good about myself as a person as well as a teacher' (primary school teacher in her first year, in Rogers, 1999).

This, again, illustrates the importance of how professional, situational and personal needs of colleague support combine, and how the kind of respectful treatment one receives can increase both personal assurance and coping, and professional assurance and coping. In more 'consciously supportive' school cultures the degree to which professional concerns are effectively addressed seems to relate to the characteristic 'climate of acceptance' and the treatment one receives.[22]

> 'I remember at ... [school unnamed] when I first started as woodwork teacher. I came into the staff room, my first day, and this senior teacher came over to me – I'd sat down – and she'd said, pointing, in a supercilious way, to some chairs in the far corner of the staff room: "The woodwork teachers sit over there ..."' (in Rogers, 1999).
>
> David and I had been discussing staff room 'socialisation patterns', as it were: where staff sat, how chairs were placed around the large staff room, what people might be feeling in terms of moving into an apparent coterie of several teachers whose seats face each other in a kind of social bloc; separate from the rest. The discussion was good natured as we relived different first-year experiences, the most ludicrous being when I'd reached for a cup in a staff room, on my first day at a new school, and a teacher pettily challenged me with, '... that's *my* cup!'

Case example

During one of the interviews for this research, Frank, a colleague, and I were interrupted several times in his office as teachers knocked on the door to come in to check the 'extras' (classes over and above one's normal timetable loading. All teachers, in all schools, face their 'extras'!). Frank is an affable, good-humoured, colleague. After briefly reassuring and clarifying with several colleagues about which classes and where, he turned to me, and apologising, added, 'Okay, they've got the info already on extras, but it's better if they *know*, and that means some face-to-face communication with me. I don't have a closed door, here' (colleague's emphasis).

'Today I had this meeting! And I'd got an extra myself so I said to Andrew, "look I've got a problem ..." Andrew replied, "I'll take your class, but only if you buy me a coffee!"' (Head of Department, Secondary).

Later that day I passed these two teachers chatting in the co-ordinator's office and I dropped in for a chat. I noticed Frank had his cappuccino coffee; I winked. 'Bribery?' I asked; we had a good laugh. I've observed Frank in many difficult situations over the last two years of working in this school; I've watched the way he talks to people, follows-up on issues, gives brief reassurances. When I asked him how he initiated support to colleagues he said, 'You *notice*; you take some notice. I know it sounds banal but it isn't, I'm willing to give support.' I assured him it wasn't banal.

Respect also includes professional as well as normative civility when working with colleagues one dislikes, disagrees with or even 'despises':

'It is important to remember that even if you despise "x" or "y" you can still be professional with them – it doesn't happen often – and it took me a while to realise this but it is important' (secondary teacher) (Rogers, 1999, op. cit.).

In another secondary school, a colleague commented on a feature of relational peer behaviour in less supportive schools:

'Some teachers here need to improve how they work with others – in being more empathetic, more professional in the relationships in the sense of their interpersonal skills. They're offhand, they get what they want by being pushy or uncivil ...' (ibid.).

Civility as respect

When we're busy, tired, stressed; when we feel unsupported by some of our peers' (senior teachers) fundamental respect, even civility can go. I have seen such an ethos in (what I have chosen to call) 'unconsciously unsupportive schools': schools where even school leadership exhibit cursory, intemperate, insouciant, off-hand, mean-spirited, sarcastic, insensitive collegial behaviour. These schools tend to be schools where there is little constructive collegiality. Here I am not talking about 'bad-day syndrome'; all of us get tired, 'run off our feet', 'stretched to the limit' on some days. We sometimes 'snap', speak irritably, 'forget', 'miscue' – that is understandable and forgivable.

Basic civility, in any social or professional setting, is not some kind of elitist code of social manners or behaviour; it is basic courtesy and basic respect; hopefully, it is more than that. Civility enables general social coping, it enhances social coping when we are pleasant and considerate; it makes our 'daily grind' a little more bearable, even enjoyable.

I've noticed colleagues who push in on tuck-shop queues (without even a 'Sorry, folks, I'm on playground duty do you mind ...?'), who leave a significant mess for other teachers to clean up after them, who are characteristically lazy, who chatter and natter audibly while the principal is trying to conduct a staff meeting (if such behaviour were to occur in their own classrooms, those same teachers would be 'on to it like a tonne of bricks', but they perceive themselves as allowed to behave with impunity).

While this sounds like 'small beer', if unchecked and characteristic it can create a tone of dismissive selfishness ('Well, why should I bother ...!!'). Civility moderates that easy selfishness that can arise when we forget what it means to be a community; the reciprocity of respect. 'Do unto others as you would they do unto you ...' (and we have the best Teacher for that ...).

Acceptance of – but not acquiescence to – fallibility in self and others

The acceptance of fallibility in oneself and others is an acceptance of our fundamental humanity: from the 'bad-day syndrome' of tiredness (last-minute-ness!), forgetfulness and mistakes to 'Murphy's Law'.[23] This 'protocol' is related to 'appropriate' flexibility, it is realistic about the 'constraints of time' and acknowledges the need for compromise at times.[24]

Like the protocol noted below – 'the certainty of uncertainty' – the acceptance of fallibility can lend a realism and perspective to grand plans, put 'some perspective back into things' (as my colleagues said), and even 'lend some grace to the daily grind'. As one colleague acknowledges:

'... this, the tolerance of fallibility [sic] goes without saying. You have to bite your tongue at times; at other times it's better to sit and talk it out. We differ, yes, but it's sort of "healthy differing" if you know what I mean ...?' (in Rogers, 1999).

This protocol also works against the sort of demanding perfectionism that can create significant stress in school communities.[25] I've seen senior staff make demands on reality, that reality cannot or will not bear. It is important to remember that not every colleague is a 'high flyer'; not all colleagues have the same experience, knowledge, commitment, abilities and skills. While this is patently obvious it can be temporarily 'forgotten' by more 'successful', 'competent', 'effective' colleagues when advising or supporting less experienced, less competent colleagues.

However, where there is *characteristic* laziness, indifference, insensitivity, 'white-anting' in colleague behaviour this will need to be supportively addressed within the school's shared values and practices. Within a whole-school perspective of shared values, aims and practices, the addressing of 'poor' or 'ineffective' performance is made somewhat clearer, not necessarily easier. 'Acceptance of fallibility' means acceptance of the person without denying the need, at times, to address their behaviour and support them in their struggle, their failure and even in their consciously irresponsible unprofessionalism. It is seeing a colleague's failure and struggle, not seeing them *as a* failure. In a supportive school, failure is genuinely seen as a learning experience if, and when, colleagues are supported through their failure.

> 'Some teachers you have to be jovial with, low key – and relaxed; others more assertive (depending on the issue and the person). People are different and you need to change your approach. *But* the way you treat and approach them, and speak with them is important. While there are limits to flexibility, **fairness is fundamental** even with the lazy whingers. Being amicable, having basic civility, even with the occasional teacher who will p-ss you off ... You know they haven't left any work for an "extra" or a casual relief teacher but – I try to keep a **working relationship** with them ... You're trying to increase their ownership of the issue at stake ...' (head of department, colleague's emphasis) (Rogers, 1999, op. cit.).

> ' ... we learn from our mistakes – by not being too easily critical or judgmental. Yes, we whinge, but we learn from it. It's open-door and shared resources **including our mistakes** – *I feel I'm not running the school by myself* ...'(primary principal, colleague's emphasis) (ibid.).

> 'I don't have to pretend to be something I'm not here. I'm not seen as a failure by "them" when things don't go too well. I don't have to know everything or I get behind' (primary teacher) (ibid.).

'Acceptance of fallibility' also recognises (as in 'the acceptance of uncertainty' – see below) that there are many situations over which we have no control, particularly a student's background, that often contribute to the normative stresses of teaching and classroom management in many schools.[26] In the more supportive schools I work with this 'protocol' is, in part, liberating. It frees us from unnecessary self-blame and, in part, from undue anxiety that we cannot directly or easily change 'this child' or 'all the circumstances' that contribute to his or her behaviour in school. Conversely, it also means that we avoid, too easily, making the child a 'victim' of his or her 'causative pathology' (of particular home background, structural poverty, parental unemployment, substance abuse etc.). There is a great deal school can do, day in day out, to support children with emotional and behavioural disorders, and learning needs, where such are adversely affected by non-school settings. (Rogers, 1994, 2000). For some children a supportive and caring school may offer a significantly 'safe', 'secure' and sane place for a third of their waking day.

One of the more annoying comments heard in schools is, 'I don't have a problem with ...' (a particular student, a subject area, new curriculum design or ...). Of course, the speaker may be telling the truth, but it doesn't help or support the colleague who really is struggling with Jason, Craig, Misty or 8D, 9C or 10E.[27]

What such a comment, or response, often does is see the hearer unhelpfully or unrealistically rate themselves against such a 'good' teacher perhaps engaging in unnecessary negative, and global, self-rating (I'm inadequate', 'I'm not a good teacher ...', 'I'll never get it right', 'I'll always struggle with this class ...').[28] Colleagues who hear such comments (as 'I never have problems with ...') may be less likely to accept support from someone who, in reality, could probably give valuable assistance, advice and support.

An extension to the protocol of 'acceptance of fallibility' is the balance offered through 'affirming no-blame support'. When colleagues were describing aspects of either 'advice' or 'sharing' or 'coping' support, there was the frequent qualification of being given support 'without blame'. It was a caveat added by colleagues to highlight the difference in the acceptance of support and ascribed value given to support. As one colleague highlights: '... they look out for you – literally. They notice, they try to balance the offer of support with the need for space [sic].'

Failure

When failure becomes typically characteristic of a teacher's practice it is important that some senior staff supportively intervene. Some people do not learn from failure; they repeat patterns of thinking and behaviour that work against the aims and objectives of positive teaching and management. Learning from failure is meaningful only if a person actually *learns* from it.

A teacher frequently says 'shh', 'shh', 'shh' 35 to 40 times a lesson to settle an overly loud class. This pattern of behaviour is so embedded the teacher is unaware it has a 'conditioning effect' on the group of students. This 'pattern of behaviour', when combined with other features of ineffective or less effective management, is actually habituating student noise and inattention.

Teachers will benefit from support to:

- know what it is that is ineffective, or inappropriate, in their teaching/management practice
- know how such 'practice' is working against core aims and objectives of teacher/management at the classroom level. Assisting teachers to be consciously – and professionally – reflective is often a crucial and difficult first step in change in practice. Any feedback based on classroom observation and reflective discussion should centre on teacher behaviour, not personality, and refocus to teachable skills in order to reframe behaviour to re-engage aims and objectives.
- *Meaningful* change can occur – in such a context – only if colleagues see a need, if they are willing to embrace professional feedback and reflections about cur-

rent 'practice', are given skills and approaches to effect change (they need to know the necessary skills and *how* to utilise them) and ongoing support through feedback and encouragement is provided.

Noel Coward once said, 'The secret of success is the ability to survive failure.' We might also add, '... and learn from it.'

- know what to change and why and how. A trusted mentor/coaching relationship can often be a necessary and effective means to that end (see Chapter 5).

Acceptance of differences in others

A school community has a wide range of personality styles and professional expressions in teaching. There are colleagues who prefer a more 'individual' style than those who prefer a more collegial teaching style.[29] There are those who are more ebullient when sharing and teaching and those who are more reticent, less 'outgoing' but no less effective. This is important when addressing the issue of differences in ideas, approaches, opinions and teaching/management practice.

Colleagues frequently noted that in more collegially supportive schools their differences were accepted; even acknowledged. Differences of opinion, and practice, even healthy conflict, is a part of a school's social and organisational fabric.

Acceptance of difference does not mean acquiescence to those who actively and purposefully dissent and divide. It is important that difference does not easily, or necessarily, become division or dissension; it certainly does not have to. There are many natural differences in a distribution of personalities that make up a school staff: differences of personality, temperament, even approach to life itself let alone their profession. There is, of course, a difference between 'dissenting' voices in a school, or even a team, and allowing for and learning from such differences. Active dissent or 'white-anting' is another matter (see p. 82).[30]

In some of the schools I noticed a small, and quite vocal, number of teachers who seemed, too often, to exhibit a destructive 'dissenting voice' rather than a willingness to work for new, workable, positions *across* perceived, or real, divisions; new positions that could focus not only on the problems (or division itself) or the accompanying rhetoric, but the deeper aspects of our role and relational life at school that affects us all. Divisive rhetoric can so easily mask, or hide, the areas of potential agreement that may have to include appropriate compromise at times.[31]

It is easy to stereotype, for example, that which we dislike in ourselves and then project blame on to others when we see the same behaviour in them, or accuse others of similar behaviours as those we often exhibit. Jesus taught that we need to be careful we don't easily judge others ... 'Why do you, then, look at the speck in your brother's eye and pay no attention to the log in your own eye? ... Take the log out of your own eye first, and then you will be able to see and take the speck out of your brother's eye ...' (Matthew 7: 3–5; Jesus had a nice touch of humour in this image ...). It is so easy to blur, even sever, the identity between 'I' and 'them', '*we*' and 'they'; to treat another within a label such that having labelled another one can treat the other within the deceptive safety of the label.[32] It is important for school leadership to acknowledge differences in values, beliefs and practice if a school is to move towards a sense of realistic cohesion in its policy and practice.

Guiness (1973) has observed that as soon as we lessen the sense of humanness or 'personalness' in others, it is much easier to 'dispose' of others and their views in an argument.[33] Within a group, or team, in a school the dissenting voice can so easily dismiss others, even in subtle ways: the over-emphatic non-verbal sigh, the folded arms, leaning back in calculated disinterest, 'you're-wasting-my-time', the loud and calculated rustling of a work program by a teacher during a staff meeting ...

In a group it is not easy to treat the active dissenter with conscious civility; we may be often tempted to take the easy cheap shot, the sarcastic barb, in preference to some assertive leadership. When we treat the dissenting voice – the active or passive voice – as *the* outsider it is easy to stereotype or scapegoat it, to mock or simply dismiss it. Labels are easy, even understandably natural, when a colleague's behaviour is characteristically lazy, indifferent, cavalier, arrogant, insensitive or rude.

When building a team from a group it is important that solidarity does not mean that members of the group easily suppress what they don't like in themselves and then project it on to those outside the immediate group. It also means we do not create 'acquiescent collegial clones' as it were.[34]

In managing disparate personalities senior colleagues often commented on their singular lack of training in this area:

> 'Our middle managers should be trained in management skills ... it's not that they're incompetent but they're not trained for it ... like dealing with problems of conflict management ... there are skills that some don't have but need' (Rogers, 1999).

Responsibility within the team needs to include both the 'group' and the individuals who carry out the shared decision-making. It is easy for an individual to deny accountability and responsibility because 'the group' made the decision to do 'x' or 'y'. ('Don't blame me, it wasn't "my" decision.')

Colleague watchfulness: 'Bearing one another's burdens'

One of my colleagues used the term 'bearing on another's burdens'[35] to describe his understanding of moral support; 'looking out for one another'. Like the protocol of 'mutual regard', it carries the idea of 'watchfulness', 'looking out for one another', 'acting for the common good', 'collegial awareness' and 'being here for one another'.

'It means being aware of how people are coping; you observe, listen, acknowledge and sometimes it's giving approval. Some people don't see ... the antennae aren't there ... it means being sensitive to and conscious of others ...' (primary teacher) (Rogers, 1999, op. cit.).

It can include the most deceptively basic expressions such as, 'You look sh_thouse today!' or the more erudite, 'You look a little wan and disconsolate!' This is the recognition of 'one's bad day' – colleagues often gave this not uncommon example. As a more widely conscious protocol it is the awareness of the need to increase the safety margins around stress and coping by using 'purposeful teaming and communication', and addressing early the areas of need and stress, particularly with teachers who are struggling (see p. 144f. below).

Such a 'protocol' – like that of mutual respect – carries a meaning of active effort exercised for another. It includes related meanings such as 'reliance on others' and 'dependability' and 'being sensitive to the needs of colleagues'. As one colleague said, 'I know most people here would cover me if needed' (he meant in terms of 'covering a class' – if running late – or supporting him in a crisis situation in terms of 'back-up').

One notable example of this was noted by several senior staff members (uninvited) who noted, at length, that colleagues would cover an unsupervised class if a teacher was running late: I actually did this on a number of occasions in some of the schools I was working with as a researcher. On one occasion I covered a class for up to 10 minutes. One teacher, in particular, who had been hostile to any kind of surveying of colleague support was running late for her class. Passing an unsupervised year 8 class one day (noisily unsupervised) I went in, 'settled' them down, discussed what sorts of things they were studying in that class. After nearly 10 minutes she came in 'puffing' and thanked me – as I 'handed' over the class she asked if I would stay. I had a meeting to go to (I was after all a visiting teacher!). I stayed a little longer as she reclaimed her teaching breath! Later she came up to me in the staff room, thanked me and was much more open to discussing the nature of colleague support as a viable, and useful, topic for 'research'.

'Someone cares enough to notice you've been having a bad day or a hard time of it and is prepared to bail you out – it's called survival!' My colleague (a senior teacher) then discussed the normative stress of 'day-to-day-teaching' and the human side of it all ... She went on to describe a recent incident where a colleague went out of his way to give assistance with physically moving materials from one classroom to another when she was in a hurry ...

'No one asked him, he just knew we needed a hand. I know he knew we'd do the same for him. Teachers do exercise a lot of give and take here but admin. don't always see it and goodwill can get eroded.'

She added another example of 'reciprocal-watchfulness':

> '... say when you're running late for a class and they [a colleague] let your class in and you settle them down, or if you see a colleague is struggling with a kid, you sometimes have a chat later; share some common concerns with them. It takes ages but it really helps ...' (in Rogers, 1999).

> 'I really appreciate daily organisers who deliberately **do not** give you an extra the day after you return from an absence because it is obvious you need time to recuperate' (secondary teacher) (ibid.).

Trust is often noted as the integrating feature of such watchfulness 'if you stuff up, your friends will cover for you or they'll do something as when you yourself can't do it.' There is, in this, a reciprocity of goodwill. It is not 'structured'; it can't be. While it can be aided by 'structure' and 'form', such 'watchfulness' is dependent on a culture where there is enough reciprocal trust for colleagues to more readily exercise such mutual regard.

I have witnessed senior colleagues walking past a class that is clearly out-of-control and not offering immediate tactful support. Instead, they frown through the corridor window, or, as bad, barge into the classroom and 'yell the class down' and leave their colleague with the throwaway line '... that's how you deal with them ...' In contrast, a senior teacher notes:

> 'I see a big part of my job here as trying to open (and keep open) closed doors – to make sure the doors didn't stay shut [sic]. I didn't want them [my colleagues] to shut the doors and keep their problems inside' (primary principal) (Rogers, 1999, op. cit.).

Such 'supportive watchfulness' can – for the giver – be taxing at times, but I frequently note that in a consciously supportive colleague culture one sees colleagues looking out for one another, whether it's the covering of a class, an 'extra' or simply copying a worksheet on behalf of another teacher. As one colleague put it, 'There isn't in our school "a keep-it-to-yourself mentality", or a negative watchfulness that is critical rather than supportive'.[36]

Colleague 'watchfulness' can occur in the many ad-hoc and transitional settings in a school day through to a conscious awareness by the leadership about what is really going on and being aware of, and sensitive to the needs of their colleagues. In every school this aspect of 'making time for others', 'being aware of others' needs' was highly valued. As several colleagues noted when acknowledging such watchfulness in their deputy principal – 'He listens, he's around and he communicates with us directly, not like ...' (here they contrasted a previous principal's selective, preferential communication style).

In a collegial culture, diversity and concord are not opposites. Where the values of mutual regard are widely 'held', 'observed' and 'modelled', especially by senior staff, collaboration and interdependency become collegial norms.

Communicating trust in both people and processes

People let you down sometimes, so do structures and the 'best laid-plans of ...'. A school culture whose primary expression and evidence of support are dyadic, transitional and context-dependent will probably see far less school-wide consciousness of colleague support. In less supportive schools, trust is much more conditional, preferential, transitional; limited and perhaps limiting. Not that such trust is different in kind when invested in others, rather that such trust is not developed across structures as well as within dyadic expressions of support.

In those schools I studied where there was a high, school-wide consciousness of support, there was also a higher degree of shared trust – relationally and professionally.

It is important to place trust in people *and* processes; not merely in people alone.[37] Thoughtful procedures, plans and policies, while subject to human constraints and fallibility, are also vehicles for human action. Such 'processes', or 'forms', can give a sense of shared purpose, of dependable organisational 'structure', of back-up support.[38] Of course, such processes need to be broadly and characteristically worthy of trust: time, assurance and usage will give such confirmation or (disconfirmation). There is also risk with trust; I receive another; I identify with another; I extend my goodwill to another in the hope it will be accepted in good faith, honoured, even reciprocated. 'Trust needs also to be exercised, to be enjoyed – and that's the potential risk. But we say to the kids that they learn by "risking" – that's an acceptable "risk"' (senior teacher).

Trust implies an interdependency; a reciprocal interdependency. It also implies a common basis, and framework, within which it can operate. This framework can be purely personal and of course it can include the larger, school-wide structures, or processes, of support.

Trust

My colleagues noted that trust is often expressed in basic aspects of relational behaviour such as:

- Acceptance of others as being in the same fundamental professional and human situation and therefore having the same *fundamental* needs.

  'For me it's the emotional support; of all that I seek it's that. When I'm frustrated or angry about something, or just tired – or fed up – the opportunity to sound off about things ... there are colleagues who'll give me a shoulder to cry on; who'll give me that opportunity.' [This colleague qualified this by obviating the need in such cases for 'rapport-tested rapport' [sic] (primary teacher) (in Rogers, 1999).

- As a fundamental, interdependent reliance on others (in contrast to overly protective self-reliance). This feature of trust is most evident in purposeful teaming.
- Assurance that the other(s) will 'support', 'back you up', 'listen', 'understand' (because of the 'acceptance that we're in the same boat').
- Trust is also linked to professional growth; we trust our colleagues' perceptions, pedagogical understanding (based in common, extensive, experience) and knowledge, skills and abilities (that are transferable). We trust their wisdom and common sense.
- Trust expressed as enabling one's confidence through encouragement and feedback. Even where teachers have, at times, to be approached and spoken to, or supportively confronted about inappropriate professional practice or behaviour this, too, can be addressed in a professional way that does its best not to destroy fundamental professional trust.

There are, naturally, levels of trust in a school community from ideas-sharing and generation, to having a mentor/coach relationship through to personal disclosure where private (and professional) confidences are risked. I have spoken with many colleagues who regretted even professional self-disclosure with some colleagues. It is not easy to rebuild trust with an individual, a team, even a whole-school staff once trust is broken and people feel 'let down'.

Without basic professional trust it is difficult for a school to work collegially. When staff have 'shared aims' and 'structures' that are dependable, such as purposeful teams, workable policies, shared planning and supportive feedback, professional trust is enhanced.

The 'risk' of trust is often rewarded. I have seen leaders who have been able to 'stir up', 'motivate' and develop skills and abilities in their team; allow, accommodate and refocus failure with encouragement and support, and in doing so build up the professional growth of their staff. It is those features of trust I noticed mostly in 'consciously supportive schools'.

Affirming (and maintaining) a non-competitive collegial ethos

'If anybody's got a problem ... we all chip in and give our opinions and we're supportive of that teacher, and we share that we've had problems too ...'

'You feel you're not the only one in that situation, that others have gone through the same situation as you have ...'

'We all know we're feeling the same. If you feel you're alone it's more stressful.'

'The fact that everyone is struggling together is helpful. You're not alone ...' (Primary teachers) (in Rogers, 1999).

When staff are competitive about their teaching practice, when they are highly comparing (by default or by design), when they over-promote *their* practice at the expense of others, when they suggest that there is only one way to do things ('their way'), such attitudes and behaviours breed unnecessary comparing (even competitive) behaviour.

As noted earlier, a collegially supportive ethos can entertain and celebrate differences in pedagogy and teaching methodology and management practice *within core values, shared aims and common, shared, core practice* (Rogers, 1995).

In less supportive schools, staff described unhealthy competitive behaviours that actually worked against other colleagues, that saw colleagues working 'alone', content to do '*their* best, *their* way, in *their* class(es) ...' Others were unabashed about competitive self-interest: 'Watch your back, here ...' as a colleague said in one such school. 'You get support here, but at a remembered price [sic] ... At the periodic review one is reminded about the support one has been given with a particular class. What I've learned is to basically say little, keep my head down and do what I think I do best – teach with my kids, in my classes ...'.

This dispiriting case example comes from a teacher who is a hard-working, committed colleague whose teaching practice is well received by his students and their parents. He happened to be working in a school whose leadership was fragmented, and any *esprit de corps* was largely dyadic or focused in selective groups or cliques.

Contrast this example with the colleague feedback from teachers in a 'consciously supportive' primary school (cited in Rogers, 1999):

- 'People here can share without fear of repercussions; to speak openly and voice opinions ...'
- 'No one here knocks you on the head when an idea or suggestion is presented; they'll listen and trial it.'
- 'There's never that thing of saying "sink or swim" here.'
- 'No one judges your not being able to get new programs straight away.'
- 'No one puts anyone down here, though we do have a lot of fun ... you feel you can be honest without being judged and you can give advice without going into solution mode all the time.'

Several others also noted that a non-competitive environment also works against 'individualism':

'If anybody's got a problem, we all chip in and give our opinions and we're supportive of that teacher and we share that we've had problems too ... You feel you're not the only one in that situation, that others have gone through the same situation as you have ... I've never heard staff grizzle about other staff ... (I'm not saying they don't but I haven't heard it ...)' (Rogers, 1999, op. cit.).

"We all know we're **feeling the same** sorts of concerns. If you feel you're alone it's more stressful' (ibid.).

This shared identity, and affective solidarity, is also expressed in the *'non-cliquey'* [sic] nature of the staff. 'There's a lack of cliques here … I've been here six years and it's never been evident. It's peculiar to this place … It's probably in part to do with us being a small school … we became aware of one another's problems very quickly' (senior primary teacher).

We also discussed how quickly too one's needs can become apparent not just because it is a smaller school, but because the school has developed a 'climate' of openness; not prying, but affirming and practising interdependency and 'colleague watchfulness'.

A non-competitive ethos embraces:

- A collaborative, and participative, approach to planning, problem-solving and decision-making. While affirming leadership and lines of role-authority, a collaborative culture listens and learns from each other; from teaching *and* non-teaching staff. This is crucial when addressing external, or 'in-house', change.

- A non-critical, non-judgmental, response when sharing common concerns, or giving feedback (for example, 'Oh, I don't have any problems with that class … or that student …'). This does not mean that staff will not naturally disagree, have differing opinions, will not challenge other colleagues' ideas or teaching/management behaviour. What it does mean is that such disagreements are explored within a spirit of professional communication. It further means that any referent anchor keeps the core values and mission of the school in focus.

- Commitment to face-to-face communication – again – most notably present in purposeful teaming (see Chapter 5). It is also present in a leadership's reasonable attempts to inform, and share, 'face-to-face' wherever possible and avoid an over-reliance on memos or e-mail. I've worked in many supportive schools where the day begins with a staff briefing that brings some shared clarity and focus to the day. Even basic forms of communication such as this can assist in a sense of shared knowing and purpose. Staff also value the moral support that comes from the face-to-face communication (often dyadic) that can give transitional assurance ('Yes, you're on the right track there …'), or immediate coping support, ('Look, I'll cover that for you …') and the most basic or transitional whinge that can defuse some of the residual tension in managing *that* class, *that* student (' … that 8D, they drive me up the wall sometimes!').

- Most of all, a non-competitive ethos is delineated through a teaching staff who are 'purpose-driven', not merely 'task-driven'. This feature of colleague support is strongest when the aspect of teaming and teams is functional, purposeful and ongoing; and when the team's existence has meaning not just for meeting their professional obligations and the needs of the individuals in the team, but for the school's purpose and mission (See p. 123f).

The certainty of uncertainty

This seemingly paradoxical protocol can be a creative underpinning to a school culture rather than a self-limiting factor. Ann Riches (1998) notes, 'the greatest failure of Australian managers is not recognising they don't have all the answers' (in Bouchon, 1999, p. 23). In the complex nature of school organisations a healthy respect for uncertainty can, I believe, give a sense of perspective to the flow and pace of day-to-day teaching, as well as positively affecting the stress level of the collegial community, particularly when facing the demands of change.[39]

The demand for fixed, stable and totally certain answers, at least in the organisational sense, can be a stressful exercise, especially when governmental policy of mandated change means the goalposts move with increasing frequency these days.

Such a protocol also does not delimit the need for structure, planning, policy and the creative attempt at reasonable consistency (in a fallible world), what it does do is reduce the unrealistic and stressful striving for simplistic perfection.[40]

I was discussing this issue, at a more basic level, with some colleagues at a secondary staff meeting. The shared talk centred on how this 'protocol' helped 'keep perspective' and, at times, 'keep reality in mind';

> 'You think you've got it all sorted with a student, or a class, then you "slip" or they "slip" and you're in the poo again! It's not that there's no certainty, there is, relatively speaking. It's more that when there's an off day, for no apparent reason, like with the year 7s – well it brings you back to reality.'

Another colleague bravely asserted that acknowledgment of obvious uncertainty can also, like the acceptance of fallibility, 'bring you back to earth a bit if you've been, you know, a bit cocky about classroom teaching, or how you can manage that class well ...'. (This from a senior teacher.)

Colleague support cannot be mandated

McLaughlin (1990) notes a widely held axiom in education: 'we cannot mandate what matters to effective practice' (p. 15). Fullan (1993)[41] adds, 'the more complex the change the less you can force it' (p. 21).

As Stoll (1998) has observed, when exploring change processes and school cultures, '... real improvement comes from within' (p. 14), and here is the anomaly: colleagues acknowledge they want, need and benefit from support, yet a school administration cannot simply mandate that such support will operate in their school. This does not negate external direction, or policy initiative, it means that what colleagues say they value and need concerning colleague support cannot be simply built by policy, structure or *fiat*. Commitment to an 'ecology of support' depends on how a community of individuals chooses to operate and is encouraged to operate in terms of mutual regard and colleague support. Two colleagues comment on this aspect of colleague support:

> 'You can't actually structure colleague support – as such – you *can*, *though*, promote it by *providing* a climate through structures and the kind of environment you have in a school' (team leader, colleague's emphasis) (in Rogers, 1999).

> ' … can't really mandate, nor can you make people want support … especially re difficult classes, behaviour management, lesson delivery, teaching style. You can have structures to assist such likelihood but forcing it won't work' (senior teacher) (ibid.).

Choices that enhance colleague support are more likely to occur when the school culture values, endorses, encourages and models collegiality within a belief and practice of positive mutual regard. The *expressed values* and *characteristic protocols* of colleague support are, thus, as important as any structures developed by school leadership that seek to meet the need for colleague support. The building of colleague support as a 'conscious ecology' is addressed in Chapters 5, 6 and 7.

End notes

1 Grounded theory, in the sense used in this study, should be seen as 'understanding' about a given area of research or 'making theoretical sense' of much diversity in [the] data, such that from this 'the analyst is forced to develop ideas at a level of generality higher in conceptual abstraction' Glaser and Strauss (1967, p. 144). In this sense the research outcome, as shared here, is not a *single* grounded theory but rather a grounded understanding pertinent to colleague support in school contexts (Rogers, 1999).

2 It is dialogue that allows the negotiation of meanings through which the self in relation to other selves and to one's cultural communities is constituted. See also Walsh (1972, pp. 17–20) and Eisner (1979 pp. 346–8). Knowledge of human beings involves the understanding of qualities which cannot be described through the *exclusive* use of numbers. As qualitative researchers direct their attention to the meanings given to events by participants, they come to understand more than what a list of descriptions or a table of statistics could support.

3 The commonly used 'vogue' term for year level co-ordinators and heads of department these days. This is a distinction for the sake of emphasis about role only, all-year level co-ordinators and heads of departments teach too (!)

4 Trust and mutuality go together; as one colleague notes 'I don't have to pretend here.' As it relates to teamwork such lack of pretence allows openness to others in the team

without fear of criticism or judgment. See protocols of support within this chapter.

5 It is also frequently cited by teachers as important that school leaders model such *professional* respect.

6 As Middlebrook (1974) notes 'The two-person group (dyad) is important to note; a great deal of social interaction takes place on a one-to-one basis. A study by James (1951) with a several thousand sample size (observed interaction involving five or more people) suggesting that the majority of social interactions may be dyadic' (pp. 412–16).

7 Purkey and Smith (1983) when listing the variables of school effectiveness note 'collaborative planning' and 'collegial relationships' as 'process variables' within 'whole-school' effectiveness (in Breheney et al., 1996, pp. 8–10).

8 'It may be just a little tiny thing, but it could well be an important tiny little thing' as one colleague adroitly observed.

9 'A smile's a smile, wherever you go – at least in terms of the psychological changes it creates in people.' In a study on psychological patterns and responses that accompany facial expression, Paul Ekman (at California University) notes that, 'It isn't just the look on the face but the feelings inside that people share ... emotional expression signal to other members of the species what's going on and what may be about to occur' (1989, *Psychology Today*).

10 A colleague reminded me about the humanity of the transitional whinge: '... we have to remember the human side of colleague support and teaching; that teaching is your job *not you*. The whinge (or the moan) helps to bring that out.'

11 'White-anting' is a term familiar to those in the hotter, northern, parts of Australia who have houses built on tall, timber stumps: to give a cool flow of air through the underneath area of the house. If white ants start seriously boring into these stumps, the foundation can become unstable and the house starts to tilt and ...

12 *The Age*, Newspaper, 22 August 1998, Section F. p. 2.

13 See Lazarus (1981) and Lazarus and Folkman (1984).

14 Koestler, too, notes 'that the jester is brother to the sage' (in Cornett, 1986, p. 9).

15 Hargreaves (1993) links 'good humour' with a key feature of group life and collaborative cultures in school (p. 4). Little (1985), in her work on collegial relationships, makes the point that ' 'goodwill and humour' can often defuse those 'tense moments in giving feedback ...' in collegial mentoring (p. 36).

16 Protocol (from *protokollon* Gk.) comes from the term used to describe the 'first leaf' glued to a manuscript. In its more popular form it describes diplomatic, professional, etiquette or 'norm' by agreement.

17 Fullan and Hargreaves (1991) note:

'What characterises cultures of collaboration, are not formal organisation, meetings or bureaucratic procedures. Nor are cultures of collaboration mounted for specific projects and events. Rather, they consist of pervasive qualities, attitudes and behaviours that run through staff relationships on a moment-by-moment, day-by-day basis. Help, support, trust and openness are at the heart of these relationships. Beneath that, there is a commitment to valuing people as individuals and valuing groups to which people belong' (p. 48).

18 Also expressed as protocols themselves (common to each supportive school I researched) are 'acceptance of fallibility' and 'respectful inter-personal treatment of one another'. Such tolerance does not equate to indifference but rather the understanding of differences. Where, however, those differences are actively working against the school's mission then they need to be firmly, and professionally, addressed.

19 Schopenhauer, the nineteenth-century German philosopher, when addressing fundamental humanity in its shared struggle notes:

'… from this point of view one might indeed consider that the appropriate form of address between man and man ought to be, not *monsieur*, sir, but fellow sufferer, *compagnon de misères*. However strange this may sound it corresponds to the nature of the case, makes us see other men in a true light and reminds us of what are the most necessary of all things: tolerance, patience, forbearance and charity, which each of us needs and each of us therefore owes' (in *Essays and Aphorisms*, Penguin, p. 50).

20 As Aitken (1996) argues: 'Identifying your core values individually and collectively as a school community helps articulate why you are a teacher, why a school exists, who you are, what you stand for, what is most important to you and what your vision is' (p. 9).

21 As noted in the Elton Report (1989) 'perhaps the most important characteristic of schools with a positive atmosphere is that pupils, teachers and other staff feel that they are known and valued members of the school community' (p. 90).

22 As Kilman suggests in organisations needing to be more adaptable, flexible and responsive to modern times, one of the norms often listed are: *treat everyone with respect and as a potential source of valuable insight and expertise.*

23 Or O'Casey's Law: *Murphy was an optimist.*

24 Nehru once suggested that 'compromise that represents a step toward attaining a desirable objective may be good; compromise that results in abandoning an objective *or* substituting an inferior principle may be bad'. The most efficient groups, however, will not resort to compromise without first attempting to find an integrated solution (in Lane et al., 1967, p. 30).

25 Bernard (1990) speaks of the stress created in schools by 'negative self and other rating …' It can include the 'mirroring' of our self in others where we judge self (or others) too quickly as we mirror our incompetence (and fallibility) in others' competence; and vice versa. 'Do *they* really have no problem classes?' (Rogers, 1999).

26 There are many factors we have no control over at all in the teaching profession: a student's family functionality (or dysfunctionality); structural poverty; mobility; family health/diet regime; family housing etc. See Howell (1993), Rutter et al. (1979) and Rogers (1994, 1997).

27 A colleague and friend, Tim O'Brien (1998), describes the scene where a teacher has had a hard time with a difficult student, comes into the staff room for a caffeine fix, bravely (and professionally) shares his struggle: 'in the hope that empathy or advice will ensue. The response given is the verbal equivalent of a swift kick in the groin: 'He's alright with me' … He suggests that we should ban 'the singular and plural versions of this morale-wrecking phrase from our school (p. 90).

28 As Seligman (1991) notes when people start to characteristically globalise ('I *always*', 'I'll *never* be able to ...') they are more likely to be candidates for stress and poor coping behaviour.

29 Hargreaves (1994) makes a helpful distinction here: 'Not all individualistic teachers are weak teachers. A few are strong, even excellent classroom practitioners. They may be eccentric, prima donna-ish, difficult to work with as colleagues, but skilled in their own classrooms more or less. The idiosyncratic excellence of such teachers should not be punished in pursuit of the collegial norm' (p. 58).

30 Simons (1998) describes non-collaborative leadership styles as 'those who tend to guard their power base, dislike ambiguity, show discomfort with people's feelings, and emotions, shy away from exposing personal values or motivations, be suspicious of others – particularly those who are different – exercise power through rank and reject anything that threatens their position ... in contrast to leadership styles that allow for "the unsettling business of change"' (p. 27).

31 O'Brien (1989) notes that in his school, when addressing differences, and individual stances 'on pedagogy or philosophy or curriculum content' that their focus in teams was 'on problem solving; the group operating within its agreed aims, to support each other in their practice' (p. 117).

32 This issue of 'severed identity' as it relates to our fundamental humanity is powerfully addressed in the seminal work of Martin Buber (1958) in his work *I and Thou*.

33 Taped lectures: *The Social and Cultural Forces Influencing Christians in the Late 20th Century/New Boundaries of Western Consciousness* (1983 10/10/1983) (IVF Publications, London).

34 People in a team should be able to argue without destroying the team. This in fact may be a strength of the team when:

> 'New norms that directly pertain to complex and difficult problems include: bringing uncomfortable issues out into the open; persist in drawing attention to problems even if others seem reluctant to consider the implications of what you are saying; listen to other members' viewpoints even if you disagree with them; encourage zany and bizarre perspectives to insure that nothing important and possible has been overlooked; make people aware when a topic that should generate a heated debate has not' (Kilmann, 1985, p. 66).

35 A description used by the apostle Paul in the New Testament. It carries, apparently, both a physical and moral meaning as well as a spiritual meaning (Galatians, 6: 2).

36 Described by Aristotle as where a person 'secures advantages for himself, he keeps a critical eye on his neighbour to prevent him from gaining them ...' This, of course, is the opposite of 'concord'. Aristotle: *Ethics* (p. 271). In those more unconsciously unsupportive schools this might be expressed as 'negative power' (Fullan, 1991). 'People at all levels of the education systems have power most often *not* to do things. Negative politics from below means constantly resisting changes; from above it means attempting to improve reform through *fiat* (p. 347).

37 A point well made by Hargreaves (1994); 'Trust can be invested in persons or in processes – in the qualities and conduct of individuals, or in the expertise and per-

formance of abstract systems. It can be an outcome of meaningful face-to-face relationships or a condition of their existence' (p. 39).

38 As Shaw (1987) develops this concept he notes that: 'trust-based relationships presuppose a broad measure of shared goals within the institution, so that there is ample scope for social rather than economically calculated exchanges. From the point of view of school management, "goodwill", which assumes a readiness to undertake unspecified obligations, is much preferable to contracts, where attempts are made to impose particular obligations – low trust is made more explicit, non-reciprocal exchanges are demanded, and a power conflict atmosphere draws a step nearer' (p. 783).

39 Saul (1990) gives a salient reminder here, 'The virtue of uncertainty is not a comfortable idea, but then a citizen-based democracy is built on participation, which is the very expression of permanent discomfort. The corporatist system depends on the citizen's desire for inner comfort. Equilibrium is dependent upon our recognition of reality, which is the acceptance of permanent psychic discomfort. And the acceptance of psychic discomfort is the acceptance of consciousness' (1996, p. 195).

40 'I consider it a dangerous misconception of mental hygiene to assume that what man needs in the first place is equilibrium or, as it is called in biology, 'homeostasis'; i.e. a tensionless state. What man actually needs is not a tensionless state but rather the struggling and striving for some goal worthy of him. What he needs is not the discharge of tension at any cost, but the call of a potential meaning waiting to be fulfilled by him' (Frankyl, 1963, p. 166).

41 A concept explored by Fullan (1991, 1993), Hargreaves (1993) and Hopkins (1991). Fullan and Hargreaves (1991) point out that, 'many staff initiatives take the form of something that is done to teachers rather than with them, still less by them' (p. 17).

CHAPTER 5

BUILDING COLLEAGUE SUPPORT IN YOUR SCHOOL

'I like my isolation within easy reach of other people, wide open spaces set me on edge.'
Roger McGough (1993, p. 66)

'People and processes are important; it is feasible that a new principal could still tacitly support the process of collaborative decision-making, collaborative teaming (for each grade team), a whole-school approach to discipline and welfare (all key features of our school structure here), but without the heart.'
(School principal, cited in Rogers, 1999)

Mutual obligation within an ecology of support

A key feature, perhaps the main feature, of school-wide 'consciousness of support' is highlighted in the observable, conscious difference between mutual obligation as a personal construct and mutual obligation as a characteristic school-wide expression of school values and practice. As one of my colleagues notes, in contrasting her past school with her current school: 'The difference here is, I *could rely on anyone not just a particular colleague at a particular time*; or if the mood was okay ...' (colleague's emphasis).

A primary teacher with two decades of experience notes that the key concerns *all* teachers faced with the management of challenging students, for example, is a consciously shared 'problem': 'Everyone here looks after the kids, so if you've got a problem or a discipline issue with a student it's not just your problem *it's everyone's'* (colleague's emphasis).

> 'If you couldn't talk things out it would add to the stress, for example, with issues like problem children. This is better for me *and* the children when I've got support.'

'It's essential, that it makes us feel worthwhile – it gives the confidence to go ahead if you've been reassured … especially when you're struggling' (secondary teacher, in Rogers, 1999).

The 'personal construct' of colleague support is always rated, and valued, highly by colleagues, in most schools I have worked in; particularly at a dyadic level.

In consciously supportive schools, however, the 'consciousness of colleague support' moves from a 'personal construct' to a 'social construct' in key areas such as:

- *purposeful teaming*, with emphasis on professional planning and coping strategies, as well as aspects of social coping such as managing stress by directly talking things though with one's colleagues in the team; not just to relieve normative stress but work for shared, 'owned', solutions in the longer term
- *a consistent, school-wide, policy framework and practice* particularly in the naturally stressful area of behaviour management and discipline (see Appendix 2)
- *back-up support in discipline situations*, notably use of short-term 'time-out' practices and conflict-resolution processes with difficult students, classes and parents that can enable and support teachers and students in both crisis management and follow-up
- *professional feedback* and professional development as teachers consciously take time to reflect on their teaching, pedagogy, management and discipline.

The fundamental protocols of colleague support noted earlier (see Chapter 4) enable a school-wide ethos of mutual regard, even 'obligation', such that staff are more likely to give support when:

- they are treated with 'mutual and professional respect'; a respect that allows for fallibility in self and in others
- there is 'no (intentional) blame' directed to them when they seek support; there is no 'implied judgement' or 'criticism'
- 'structures', 'forms', 'processes' and 'organised expressions' of support are developed to enhance and encourage collegiality.

The concept of 'mutual obligation' – when it is a school-wide value *and* practice – highlights how congruent colleague support is between what a school espouses and what it actually, and normatively, does.[1]

Structural support

'Structural' support refers to those organisational and physical 'forms' or 'structures' that give support to teachers. As noted in Chapter 2, policy imperatives, programs, plans, organisational structure, time-tabling, physical spaces and places, even decent tea/coffee-making facilities are all expressions of 'structural support'.

'Structures', 'forms' and 'processes' can provide the means whereby the school can consciously address colleague support beyond 'natural goodwill', 'colleague watchfulness' and 'mutual regard'. In the less supportive schools that had begun to address colleague support in a more conscious way, there was a corresponding emphasis on 'structural support' as the *visible expression* of such mutual regard. School leadership, in such schools, were beginning to seriously address the viability and utility of its organisational behaviour, its policies, even its physical structures in terms of whether they were meeting colleague needs. A critical factor in attempting to more realistically 'meet' such needs occurred when the senior staff collaboratively engaged with all staff to assess, and seek to address, espoused needs and more consciously model collegial behaviour themselves.

Normative 'physical' structures that are 'organisational', in form, can enable the smooth running aspects of daily school life. As noted earlier, such 'apparently mundane' structural support ranges from adequate furniture and cupboard space, to decent work/planning areas, access to filing space, even fixing flickering lights and reasonable opportunity for phone usage. Many schools, as part of their ongoing support of staff, now run staff 'audits' in this area to assess areas of need as they relate to *unnecessary* 'structural stress'. Staff feel valued when these 'deceptively mundane' issues are taken seriously (see Chapter 6, p. 168f).

Policy structures outline due process and practice that can support collaborative collegiality. The most referred policy noted by colleagues was that of a whole-school approach to behaviour management and school discipline.[2] Special 'structural' aspects of support such as 'time-out plans' and 'crisis management plans' for disruptive classes, too, are built into whole-school policy provisions. Such a whole-school policy will need to have school-wide preferred practices for behaviour management and discipline. Such a school-wide policy will also need clear plans to carry those practices into the daily reality of the classroom, outside the classroom (general duty-of-care) and special plans for students who present with behaviour disorders (see Appendix 2).

'Structures' – as processes – can enable collaboration, shared planning and problem-solving for both management and teaching issues. The most cited and valued 'structure' for this was purposeful teaming, this is discussed later in this chapter.

Colleagues have emphasised that these 'structures' or 'organised expressions' of support can be supportive when they give assured 'back-up' and 'encouragement', enable 'confidence and assurance' and 'professional direction and affirmation'. In this sense more formal, stable 'structures' become needs-meeting for staff.

Challenging classes and support

'Structural support' (a case example)

As I walked past Mary's classroom I could hear and see significant student unrest: loud calling out, several boys 'testosteronically bonding' with 'just-mucking-around-punches', students wandering around the classroom and hassling other students … In the three or four seconds I walked past, I could see through the corridor windows Mary's frazzled look. It was an 'extra'; a 'cover' class.

A number of staff (at this 'very challenging school') had previously discussed the issue of 'crisis management', adopting a policy option that a colleague might come in to a very disruptive class and *diplomatically* offer direct support. The key word being diplomatically: not barging in and yelling at the class thus diminishing their colleague's self-esteem and teaching 'status', even if such an approach would shut the class up!

We had discussed the option of the 'passing' colleague, or even a colleague teaching 'next door' knocking on the door and asking if they could, for example, 'borrow a couple of students'. The other option we canvassed was that a passing colleague could cue their stressed colleague in the classroom with the words, 'There's a message for you at the office'. This was meant to be code for 'leave now, I'll take over till the bell goes. Then we'll talk through things to see if we can work on longer-term solutions later.' This approach was, again, to be carried out with dignity to the colleague 'under fire' (based on a passing 'risk assessment').

I knocked on Mary's door. 'Ms Smith, can I borrow a couple of students, please?' The brief, pained, look said it all, 'Yes, of course, Mr Rogers.' I withdrew two of the most 'likely' lads, for a walk up the corridor and a chat about their behaviour. A little later I 'withdrew' two more (all 'power-brokers' in that classroom). I found a spare classroom and had a mini-lesson with them until the bell went for that period. Later Mary and I had a chat about the event; she was more than happy that I had taken the professional initiative to direct the students from the room. We also commiserated that these students were not the easiest to manage at any time. That shared admission was also affirming. We then set about some longer-term 'structural' and 'professional' support (see p. 115f below).

A number of schools use this form of 'structural support' as a kind of 'collegial safety-valve' to decrease the likelihood of self-defeating 'chaos' or teacher/student slanging matches. Where there is *thoughtful follow-up* (beyond such immediate support), staff note that this 'cue' is a means of giving assurance of support – in advance as it were – as well as reducing the immediate stress.[3]

Of course, it needs clear agreement with colleagues beforehand within the understanding that there is no imputation of blame to the colleague concerned;

problems analysis and action planning need to follow such usage.

Another option is a colleague-based 'time-out plan', using a pre-arranged cue-card sent with a trustworthy student to a senior colleague who is able to come to the classroom in question, and support their colleague by escorting a 'troublesome' or 'hostile' student(s) away to 'time-out' provision. Such support, naturally, requires trust and reciprocal goodwill.[4] Colleagues value highly the kind of back-up they receive in 'crisis' situations. While 'structures' are important, so is the underlying moral support, as immediate needs are met, as well as longer-term professional concerns being addressed.

Teachers frequently noted the difference that such back-up support gave as they contrasted other schools where some teachers were anxious to ask for support lest they be seen as 'weak', 'insecure' or 'ineffective' or a 'teacher who couldn't cope'; and there's the absurd anomaly again – perhaps they cannot cope, or not cope as effectively, without 'no-blame' support. The qualifiers used by teachers when describing such support addressed the need to 'feel supported', 'not blamed', 'treated respectfully' and 'treated professionally'.

One of my primary school colleagues had a particularly dysfunctional grade 1 child in her class. His behaviour included frequent aggression to other children, biting, hitting, kicking, pushing, etc.

Debbie, with her colleagues, set up an individual behaviour plan with this child that included time-out support for her and the child. Over many weeks with patience, effort and goodwill the child's self-esteem and behaviour 'improved enormously – the class helped, too, to encourage Tony. One of the key things for me as a teacher has been to know that I have got the support and back up of the other members of the staff. At different times during Tony's story probably all of our staff have had to deal with Tony in different situations, shared the load with me, brainstormed new ideas or supported the other children. It has been essential to know that Tony is dealt with consistently across the school by each person and *for me to know that I was not alone in the situation*' (colleague's emphasis).

Other colleagues make this point over and over again: 'There needs to be a level of trust and respect when you support others.' 'This means in part being prepared to listen to a colleague (say, when a particular child is annoying you!) and being available and approachable, even when the pressure is on – [and] that's hard.'

'[Colleague support] means, here is a group of people who *together* do the best they can to improve the lot for their [sic] children and their professional life. [It is also seen in] the *way* teachers help and support themselves as well as their children.'

The overwhelming impression I gained was that such support in crisis management situations was not asked for as an end in itself, but as a means to the end that longer term problem-solving, and professional, support options could enable the teacher in question to work through the antecedents and issues that may have led to the 'crisis' in question. Where a colleague 'feels comfortable' in asking for support, as early as possible, then it is more likely that not only will workable solutions be forthcoming but the supportive climate enables workable solutions.

I have worked in some schools where the management of very challenging students creates significant, daily stress for teachers, but such stress is not always acknowledged by senior staff – it would if they had a regular teaching allocation with such students and classes!

In one such school I was invited in as the 'outside expert', as it were (a term I dislike and one I eschew). I was asked to set up 'some year 8 mentoring'. I was, initially, 'naive' to the internal politics of this particular school.

I quickly got the 'message' that the principal felt the staff were 'over-rating' their concerns about management and behaviour with this year 8 group. I began to work with a couple of very challenging classes with some extremely disruptive, 'power-broking' students. I very quickly saw, *and* felt, what my colleagues were feeling in terms of significant noise levels, 'catalytic' and fractious behaviour (including a boy literally hanging off the internal rafters of the classroom, like a monkey – and there's me, I'd forgotten to buy bananas!). The group dynamics of this class were making any effective, long-term teaching and learning very difficult.

A related problem was that the staff felt marginalised by this principal; they believed he did not take their concerns seriously, that the 'ring-leaders' were 'getting away with it all ...' The year-advisor felt as if he was the 'meat in the sandwich', as it were.

Having taught a number of sessions with those classes, across several learning areas, I was able to report my concerns to the principal and suggest a *collaborative approach* to the year 8 management issue to allow a genuine sharing of concerns about student behaviour (without any blame about 'teacher-effectiveness'). Because I had 'been there with them', I, too, as the so-called expert, was able to share my genuine concerns, my perspectives and (later) suggestions.

We felt better as we all acknowledged the common challenges and stresses of the classes in question and of several students in particular. The principal, to his eventual credit, listened and took on board *our* shared perceptions and allowed us to develop, with him, a collaborative plan that:

- saw an immediate regrouping of students across year 8
- a focused, year-level 'time-out' plan for the support, and short-term supervision

of 'catalytic' and 'extreme' attention-seeking students

- a reappraisal of *core* routines for classroom management and learning (even basics such as seating plans and student groupings within a given class …)
- development of a year-level behaviour agreement that focused on fundamental rights such as 'the right to feel safe' in our classroom, the 'right to basic respect' and 'fair treatment', and the 'right to learn' and the 'right to teach' (without disruption and distraction). We discussed with the students the principle of behaviour ownership in social settings: 'We all share the same place here, the same time together, the same furniture and resources; we're all here for the same basic reasons in this learning community. We also all share the same basic feelings and needs, all of us … To work well in this learning community, to get along well with each other, we need to genuinely consider what our rights and responsibilities are.' This behaviour agreement was based in teacher direction and guided collaboration with the students.

We realised, quickly, that most of the students actually wanted a 'fresh start'.[5] The behaviour agreement acknowledged and affirmed the students' perceived concerns and developed a year-level approach, with them, to harness that latent goodwill of the majority. It is easy for a class as a group to become habituated into poor behaviour, self-defeating behaviour and poor learning practice. A 'fresh-start plan' gives the teacher and students the opportunity to 're-habituate' what is necessary for a classroom group to be a 'learning community'.

We also set up long-term 'case-management' for the extremely disruptive students. A senior staff member set up *individual* behaviour management plans with the students in question. These 'management plans' were used by all year 8 teachers to enable consistency of ongoing management and support for those students identified as 'at risk'. These plans emphasised teaching students the core 'academic survival skills' and the fundamental 'social survival skills' to enable class learning and relationships to work for their benefit, as well as their peers and teachers.[6] (A couple of students were redirected to 'out-of-school' programs as it was patently clear that normal schooling was not able to serve, or address, these students' needs.)

Colleagues were encouraged to further develop their management practice through collegial mentoring (see p. 135f below). This mentoring was based in colleagues reflecting on and sharing effective practices beyond the whingeing we had all engaged in. By sharing effective practice we were becoming more professionally positive (and realistic) about where we could work on changes in our management and discipline, as well as the changes we were expecting and encouraging in our students. The key feature of this mentoring involved coaching in behaviour management and discipline skills, and re-appraising aspects of teaching skill where appropriate (Rogers, 2000).

This mentoring was based in collegial need for professional reflection *and* development; there was no suggestion given or received of 'superior'/'inferior' roles. The most challenging aspect of such mentoring is the giving of supportive, descriptive feedback to enable reflection on one's characteristic teaching and management behaviour. We always emphasised that the feedback was:

- to raise personal awareness of teaching, behaviour management and discipline practice that was working against our fundamental aims of classrooms as learning communities
- descriptive; for example, 'Were you aware of ...?', 'Did you hear yourself say ...?', 'Were you conscious of ...?', 'What were you seeking to achieve when ...?' Such feedback was *heightening* self-reflection with a view to considered, and specific, change in one's practice (see also Chapter 2 and p. 132f.)
- shared in a supportive form and manner with an emphasis – team wide – on professional development
- focused on achievable skills of management, discipline and teaching.

Lastly, we had periodic reviews of our shared progress with the classes in question to both encourage our efforts and fine-tune our concerns.

A safe working environment

A school leadership, with its staff, has a fundamental responsibility to ensure the welfare of its community. The fundamental rights to a safe working environment (physical and psychological safety), as well as catering, as much as one can, for the well-being of the community needs to be a conscious, school-wide responsibility.

Some aspects of social and psychological safety can be established and managed in policy and practice. For example, no teacher should have to endure psychological harassment from individual students or even substantial groups of students. I have, in the past decade, come across teachers who have in effect been bullied by students; in and out of classroom settings. This bullying is psychological (rarely physical) and in less supportive schools, teachers will not report such harassment because of anxiety that other teachers, notably senior staff, may think them 'weak' disciplinarians or that they 'can't cope', or they are ineffective or, worse, incompetent.

Notwithstanding any contributing factors such as teacher personality (characteristic non-assertive behaviour), or ineffective teaching and management practice, no teacher should have to suffer regular, intentional harassment in professional silence. This sort of degrading survivalism exists in some collegially unsupportive schools (it exists 'unconsciously', or even with tacit consciousness).

In supportive schools such student behaviour is addressed early, decisively, within a context of accountability (and appropriate mediation) to the students in question. Students engaged in such behaviour are called to account, with the teacher who is the recipient of such behaviour, and the issue of their harassing behaviour is addressed within the school's rights/responsibilities code and expectations. These 'accountability conferences' are conducted early in any cycle of harassment, and are subject to regular review.[7] This due 'process' is an expression of institutional policy-based colleague support. It is also based in the context of professional welfare that does not eschew appropriate responsibility of students *or* teachers. Such support, in consciously supportive schools, is given 'without strings attached'.

An aside on time constraints to colleague support

Schools are extremely busy places. Apart from formal meeting times, colleagues are constantly 'on the go'. Much of their communication is not extended face to face so much as *'face-to-face-on-the-run'* (as one colleague aptly described it). Colleagues frequently referred to 'time' as a 'limiting factor' and in terms of the 'quality of support' they would like to give their collegial peers. This is probably why the ad-hoc, dyadic, and 'transitional' support is so highly valued; 'the brief chat', 'the passed note', the 'corridor affirmation and assurance' ('look, I'll pigeon hole that stuff on directed numbers for your year 8 class …'). It is the noticeable effort made to keep in contact. At lunchtime many of my colleagues, if they are not on playground duty, are beavering away planning, marking, working on one of the several computers in the staff room, or chatting about a student, a class, a parent … Staff – universally – complained about the constraints of time, the daily interruptions, privations and demands *on* their time.[8]

In all the primary schools I worked with, staff, with their leadership colleagues, have worked consciously on their use of time; most noticeably discretionary time.[9] Staff, for example, had reworked their 'release time' across the school so that it was now more meaningfully used to plan together as well as problem-solve together and motivate each other. Staff in some larger schools had also set aside some time for cross grade peer-support groupings (not teams per se), using such teaming for appropriate consultation, planning and decision-making regarding common concerns and problems.

I approached a wan and disconsolate-looking colleague in the staff room with a 'trite' but unintentional social opener, 'How's it going, Frank?'

'Sh__house.' His wry smile said as much as his epigrammatic reply. 'What are you doing here today, did you have a class?'

(I sometimes team teach in this school as part of a peer-coaching 'program'). I brought up the almost-finished interview process I was conducting on colleague support.

He gave a tired look, and turned to Paul, who was working on the staff room computer and asked, 'What's that?'

'What's what?' Paul glanced at Frank and then me.

'**Colleague support**, what's that?' Frank had another wry smile.

Paul replied: 'It's when you come into my office and whinge about the extra I've given you and I say, "Calm down, it'll be all right", and I soothe you ...'

Paul is a wag; and he's right. That is colleague support, not the whole story but an important part of the teaching day.

The three of us continued for several minutes amplifying on the theme of 'transitional colleague support' within the strictures of time. Then the music came on for period 4.

Most colleagues in most schools acknowledged they were *able* to share a range of issues professionally, and share some issues of personal coping with most of their colleagues (*'up to 80% of staff'*). One interviewee noted:

> 'I'd like to do and say more in support but it's time! But I know it's highly unlikely we'll get more time, you know what a teacher's life is like! We don't often have time to really have a long talk, we're too busy with the day-after-day stuff' (Rogers, 1999).

> 'I also know that my colleagues have a workload like mine! Asking for support means extra work for them, yet I know I'd do the same the other way round' (ibid.).

> 'Trying to get **time** to talk to co-ordinators is very difficult, **but** it is changing; it's got to the point where they've started to make time' (ibid.).

'Ability to share' and 'willingness to share' (and be 'listened to', even 'upheld') are essential aspects of moral support; this was often qualified within the understanding of not wanting to create 'extra work' for a colleague. It was a tension, a natural tension, acknowledged from a common professional identity.

This was a key sub-theme when staff discussed time and support – that of natural tension between being 'able to approach others', and from that, 'having other's expertise, experience and information', and 'being able to go to people at the same level for a personal chat about children'. 'The expertise is often there, it's being able to access it; time is a big factor.'

In some of the secondary schools, year advisors have organised breakfast meetings on a regular basis as an 'extra' opportunity for sharing and planning. Colleagues noticed that this time allocation had made a difference to general stress levels as common 'off-loading' could be directed to shared solutions. Colleagues noted that this form of 'teaming' met both 'moral' and 'professional' needs. Fundamentally, the degree to which all staff believed they had some input into planned and 'discretionary' time seems to highlight how supportively they view such collegially shared time.

Staff meetings in collegially supportive schools are also managed differently; rather than the principal simply reporting to a whole staff, these staff times are focused on core issues relating to the school's ongoing mission allowing small-group collaboration to enhance collegial ownership. As one teacher notes: 'While the principal leads the decision-making, everything is tabled', 'the cards are on the table for all of us.'

The principal describes general staff-teaming, collaboration and decision-making as:

'I've fostered collaboration to move away from the notion that we *just* **assume** the principal runs everything. Now, I think, it's more collegial; we've bonded more, [sic] we've asked, "how can we make it [staff decision-making] better" and I give time [preface time] to consider how I can. Often I have to make a final decision but I've tried to give significant responsibility to staff to make decisions themselves, especially through, say, "global budgeting" and the Key Learning Area teams. It's about trust and professional value' (in Rogers, 1999).

Leadership in a collegially supportive culture

All staff commented on their leaders directly, or indirectly, as they supported individuals and teams across the school. Common indicators of supportive leadership were noted by staff as:

- They engage staff in developing vision and workable goals. In this, their approach to management and necessary and 'imposed' change is that the purpose, not only the tasks, of change need to be understood. In this sense a leader is more than a 'manager'.
- They are available; realistically available:
    'The **new** principal ... she listens to **all** sides. She's really fair. She doesn't just sit and say "yes". But she'll tell you why. She's supported a lot of my (and our faculty's) ideas – or at least she'll say "we'll give it a go". Nothing is too menial for [the principal], she can pick up the cues both professionally and personally, she'll take time for you, but she'll give you space if you're not ready ... she'll delegate ... If [staff]

make a bad decision she'll guide them back ... She delegates, yes ... but if you muck up, though, it can be fixed ... she'll talk up-front honestly with staff, but she'll keep confidences, too' (colleague's emphasis) (in Rogers, 1999).

- They enable their staff to be self-reflecting, as well as enabling perspective-taking of others, by giving a wide consultative base, including the information needed, and pursuing collaborative decision-making processes. One colleague noted that with their previous principal it was, 'as if he'd decided on our behalf, he'd already made the decision about what affected us. If we were not consulted to our face it was as if we were not capable of doing it.' Commenting on their current principal other colleagues added:

> 'She's brought us together more as a staff ... she's got us talking "privately", then together **and** she's got to know us as people, too. ... She didn't make radical changes straight away. It was through individual dialogue at first. She also discussed a range of issues with parents by forming a school advisory council ... and she takes them out to dinner once a year too ... I don't know how she keeps up' (colleague's emphasis) (ibid.).

In another (primary) school several teachers commented on their 'new' principal:

> 'We have a new principal ... in the second week she initiated a senior teachers' group (the three senior staff and her); she listened to us, I feel she acknowledged our expertise and **valued** it ... She learned *we're not cliquey here*' (colleague's emphasis) (ibid.).

When commenting on another principal they'd had, one of the teachers commented: 'We had a principal, she was too "direct".' She meant, by this, too direct in her communication style. 'I felt I couldn't really share with her. When I was using a particular language approach with my children she said, "I *don't* like that ... you *shouldn't* have used that language program."' She contrasted this approach with the current principal who was 'very democratic, always included staff in discussions about issues that affect all staff, plus the changes ... The present principal makes you feel like you're doing a good job.' A key feature of the present principal's approach is to have 'frequent and open communication' with the staff (though this is acknowledged, by all, as much easier in a small(er) school).

- They allow time for reflection on change requirements, as well as equipping staff to manage and monitor change. They also allow for differences to be aired and worked through in the process of change.
- They direct support to team relationships whenever possible and build team morale across the school. This includes ongoing acknowledgment of what staff are doing, and contributing to as well as acknowledging and supporting their

struggles; acknowledgment encourages commitment, contribution and effort within shared plans.

Staff at one of the primary schools noted that 'when an individual is acknowledged so, often, is the team'.

- They make some time to engage in 'face-to-face communication', to show personal interest and acknowledgment.
- They initiate and promote abilities and skills in others that they may not have seen in themselves, fostering a balance between individual responsibility and accountability and positive interdependence. Clarifying roles (task roles and team roles), giving team support and delegating trust and support to the team were noted significant features of leadership.[10]
- They invite and model trust and respect. As one principal described:

  'We must treat colleagues as human beings, not like "things"; treat them with respect when you've got to keep the task and their responsibility in front of them ... Don't double standard them!'[11] (Rogers, 1999, op.cit.).

  'No favouritism, it can destroy a hard-working team. If I'm treated fairly and what I do is valued I'll even go a bit further ... but if I'm mistreated, if they (admin.) are unfair, then I'll just do the basics ...'

  Here my colleague compared the present principal to a previous one who had his 'little coterie': 'If you were with them it was okay. I'd do the minimum for him – I'd do "a" and "b" but not "c", "d", "e" and "f". You with me?' (I was.) (Senior secondary teacher) (ibid.).

- A primary principal noted that it is also important to 'acknowledge one's own failure and shortcomings, especially the bad-day syndrome'. It is important to recognise one's own failings as a leader. It is so easy to see another's weakness, or failings, and not acknowledge one's own. A healthy acceptance of that reality plus the 'bad-day syndrome' helps keep some sense of perspective. This point intrigued me because it came up so often in interviews and discussions. While it is natural, even easy, to get frustrated with others' failings and shortcomings, our self-reflection as *leaders* will enable us to supportively 'confront' others (when it is needed) as we would like to be treated in a similar situation. It acknowledges and affirms the protocol of 'fallibility in self and others'.
- When giving feedback they give feedback *with support,* such that if negative issues have to be raised, then they are set in the context of support that works for the resolution of problems, and required support is offered for necessary change.

Few principals have all these qualities at all times. What is important in a school is that the leadership *team* evidence these features and characteristics of supportive leadership.[12] One of my senior secondary colleagues notes how important model-ling from senior staff is when creating and sustaining collegially supportive environments. 'We've had to model this from *all* senior staff – it has to be mod-elled from all senior staff if it's going to have meaning across the school *as* a school' (colleague's emphasis).

Teams and teaming

The research on supportive cultures in schools consistently confirms that the concept of teaming holds potential for colleague support. Teaming can enable the stimulation of ideas, mutual care, affirmation and encouragement, as well as the more professionally 'prosaic' needs, such as increased professional communication, organisation and shared-planning, problem-solving and the management of change. Of course, many of these 'needs' can be met at the transitional and dyadic levels of support in a school and often are; teams, however, can give a 'structure' or 'form' within which colleague needs can be addressed on a regular basis.

Having teams and *being* a team in this sense are quite different. The function of teaming – purposeful teaming – shares a number of characteristics across con-sciously supportive colleague cultures:

- a shared identity;[13] and shared values, particularly the value that each team-partner's contribution and perspective is valued
- a shared purpose about their existence as a team: their tasks and their common work. As noted by a colleague with reference to her grade team:

  'We're here for a purpose, not just a task. It is really important to have common values about the way we do things here. Obviously there is some variation; some finer points **but we believe the same things** about our teaching **here** and about the way we encourage our students and manage behaviour and student welfare' (in Rogers, 1999, colleague's emphasis).

- shared planning and 'shared work'; in consciously supportive colleague cultures, staff were often able to organise mutual time release for parallel planning in their grade or faculty teams. Such planning, teachers noted, saves time, increases confidence and assurance, and gives a forum for colleague feedback. It was clear that staff valued this aspect of teaming: the use of productive, meaningful, discretionary time, together.

Shared planning can also be stress-relieving, a 'coping mechanism' as one's col-leagues give assurance or reassurance: 'we' (as well, as 'I') are 'on the right track' ('at least the best track we can be on at the moment'). Such sharing can give characteristic re-framing when difficult and stressful events occur. Re-framing negative experience was often seen as a way of learning from mistakes, failure and 'bad events'. Re-framing, as a coping mechanism, can also be seen as a feature of a school's 'resilience', especially as it managed change.

Such teaming also supports 'professional risk'; by this my colleagues meant supported risk, or being prepared to 'try things out even if we fail'. This professional risk also arises from team-modelling as members of the team try out new ways of working in their classrooms.

A teacher, new to her school, makes the point that 'teaming', at both informal and formal levels, had really made a difference to her teaching practice, though not without some 'early discomfort':

> 'I hadn't worked this way before, or until 1994 when we developed grade teams here; now we plan and work as a team. I know **practically** the sharing of ideas will result in us both getting what we need to get done and include teacher feedback. This is especially important when we're planning units of work. It's also important in getting ideas started – sharing them develops the ideas better and, for example, when I've got an unhappy parent to talk with the team is there to back me up and to give me that moral support. This strengthens what we are doing' (colleague's emphasis) (Rogers, op.cit.).

Through 'experimentation' teams can also meet the needs for ongoing professional development.

A supportive team allows differences to be aired and worked through within the aims and objectives of the team (see also p. 96f.). As one team leader noted: 'It is not that we "never disagree, never argue, never dispute"; it is, if we, and when we, argue, dispute or have differences we do it *clean*, *fair* and *open*' (colleague's emphasis).

Two teachers in a primary school note features about their grade team:

> 'There's a lot of sharing across year levels, of course. There's the formal aspect as in the meetings ["key learning areas"], but most sharing is because people want to; it's not a feeling of I'm competing with the colleague next door. We talk through and share about the things that don't work as well as things that do' (Rogers, 1999, op. cit.).

> 'There's no back-biting here, we're not bitchy; in our school we can approach any of the staff members to give you support. [For] more personal things, of course, you'll seek out someone you can share with more personally. It's about approachability and assurance' (ibid.).

Some of these aspects of teaming can operate in temporary 'systems', 'groups', 'alliances' or 'loosely coupled teaming', as well as more stable ongoing teams.

Teams and teaming in less-supportive schools

One notable finding in this study relates to teaming and teams as they operate in less-supportive schools. 'Consciously unsupportive' schools obviously do have 'teaming' within their school but they are not *rated* as highly as the *informal teams* that operate within and across faculties in such schools (Rogers, 1999). While staff, obviously, plan together in faculty and year-level teams, they did not rate the 'formal' teaming process particularly supportive in the areas of moral support and personal coping support.

A lot of 'teaming', however, does occur outside of, or across, faculty teams.

'It's the people you establish with who are the most helpful … structural support, here, is not well handled. There's no system as such … but people will help out if you ask – plus, I wanted it, their help, I mean. If I hadn't asked maybe I wouldn't have got the help' (secondary teacher) (Rogers, 1999, op. cit.).

'The function of the team group doesn't come across that well as **supportive**. There are very different parameters that affect groups. Here there's not a lot of meshing of groups – we're working on it though – trying to get people to talk' (secondary teacher) (ibid.).

'Often, if you have a meeting, only a few (staff) turn up. It's affecting what we do with the kids as well I think. We hope this will change next year … maybe as Head of Department I should confront them. It's the weakest aspect of working here' (secondary teacher) (ibid.).

'Time's the problem, you've just about got time to do what you **have to**, let alone meet in groups. We're never "off". My faculty team, we're never off at the same time so that makes meeting with them difficult and we've got more face-to-face teaching, even my one extra class (it doesn't seem much) but it's two, three periods a week' (secondary teacher, colleague's emphasis) (ibid.).

One colleague notes that 'while obliged to attend formal meetings teams, at times we're engaged in mental absenteeism but not really working as a team.' Another colleague added, 'Well, we've all done *that* in meetings – nothing new there; except it's hard for the colleague conducting the meeting!'

'Teaming', as a loose-coupling form of colleague support, is highly valued but this concept of 'teaming' is often occurring *across* 'formal' structures. It may be expressed dyadically or in small 'informal' groupings. Such teaming goes beyond obligatory support. It was not so much that 'formal teams' (for example, faculty meetings) were a waste of time, but that they were less of a 'teaming' and more a 'meeting' process.

Close role-proximity is highly valued in colleague support; physical role-prox-imity are those colleagues one works with on a day-to-day basis. The key sub-theme of transitional and ad-hoc support was frequently cited as operating across faculty groups and teams. Colleagues often noted they would go outside their 'formal' team to get support for 'behaviour issues' as well as coping support. When issues had to be 'formalised with paperwork', say an incident report sheet for a student behaviour issue, then the lines of 'formal structural support' did occur within the year level or department teaming, while the viable and valued emotional support and needs-sharing often occurred outside such a 'team' organisation.

Purposeful teaming

The issue is not whether a school has teams, but what kind of teams they have. For what purpose? Do colleagues need to meet in 'formal' teams? If so, how do they utilise their team time? – their 'discretionary time'?

Loose teaming, as an expression of colleague support, will occur in all schools; purposeful teams and teaming as a 'formal', structural expression of colleague support is a different matter.

Teachers in several primary schools reflected on how their grade teams operate:

'We meet once a week to discuss student needs, behaviour concerns and matters relating to the curriculum. We plan together and divide all the key learning areas up into several sections (for example, Time/Space), and then discuss what we'd covered last year and extend from these. We then each take away from this process and teach within our own class group. Dividing up the curriculum in this way we try to make it as user-friendly as possible.'

One teacher, new to this school, said:

'I find the team support here outstanding. I walked into a **team** – a team that took time to explain how this place works. They don't criticise here. We cover all the key learning areas even through the one day where we specialise it gives us a chance to see other groups of, and teach other groups of, students' (colleague's emphasis).

One colleague notes the difference to 'collegiality' that *grade meetings* has made:

'You look forward to these meetings. In the past I didn't normally look forward to meetings but I look forward to these. We've always had meetings here but since we developed the **grade meetings** our time together has *taken on a more **collegial** tone*. If ever I've needed help it's come primarily from my colleagues within the team. If I want to try something new I'm not criticised – they're never critical. They see – they know you've done your best' (colleague's emphasis) (Rogers, 1999, op. cit.).

Both in the survey data and in the interviews I conducted across schools such teams were nominated and commented on as a key feature of, and a key factor in, colleague support. Staff consistently noted that professional concerns, needs and issues were met by participation in their grade teams:

'It's largely from the team I get support; the sharing and planning we do together. I mean, we preach to the kids: It's okay to fail; we, too, need to be big enough to admit that we, too, fail and it's okay. This is from the principal down' (ibid.).

'We all plan our units of work together. Everyone is listened to and encouraged to put in. I feel we're very supportive of one another. It's significant to me – working in the team. We communicate well together and talk through lots of issues, not just curriculum. Sometimes even more personally related issues.'

'I find the grade teams valuable because you're not always sure you're right, or doing the right thing. I never feel silly for asking questions. This is confirming, it gives assurance, we also give each other the "pat on the back", we whinge a bit, too, but we always have the opportunity to talk things through.'

In many of the interview sessions staff noted the way that grade teams operated was based on common values of 'trust, 'openness', 'mutual respect', as well as 'acknowledgment of fallibility' and 'failure'. One principal notes that she communicates regularly with the grade leaders (team leaders) but points out:

> 'That planning is left, by and large, to the grade team. I receive minutes of grade area meetings, so I'm informed, but I don't have to sit down and talk for ages with them about their grade teams. **Trust is important, trust to the team**' (colleague's emphasis) (Rogers, 1999, op. cit.).

One of the grade team leaders adds:

> 'The attitude is give it a try, okay? With support from the team and the principal, and **you're allowed to get on with it**. It's very important, here, if we're having problems when we go to a colleague it's not seen as a failure. You won't get "backstrapped" [here my colleague meant "put down"]. We talk it through and sometimes it mightn't work out, that's okay. The grade team is a support group – we're quite prepared to discuss a range of issues. We're quite open, and I know that what I say in confidence will be kept in confidence. We've **learned** to trust one another' (colleague's emphasis) (ibid.).

One deputy primary principal noted that:

> 'Building teamwork means building up trust, over time, through mutual-professional relationships. It means being available and approachable; seeing staff as individuals, as well as "groups"; making sure people know and are familiar with their roles; and having open respectful relationships that see people with varying strengths and interests across the range and respecting those strengths as they contribute to the well-being of the school.' (Rogers, 1999, ibid.).

The team-setting also provides for ongoing learning and professional development. 'If someone's got a great idea, it's shared, and our resources, too. We also make sure we rotate the key learning areas of focus to enable variety.' Each grade leader meets regularly with other grade team leaders and the principal.

> 'This gives a cross-school picture. There are, of course, times when we meet on a needs basis. While there's always room for improvement the school has come a long way, definitely, since we developed this kind of team approach' (Rogers, 1999, op. cit.).

The ethos of a purposeful team is also based on inclusion. In one of the schools the school secretary made this point:

> 'This is the third school I've worked for and **here** I'm included on a consultative basis. At first I thought do they really want me, like when we develop policy-making? But I was assured that it **really was** worth getting a viewpoint from other than teaching staff. People here are considerate of me. *I feel like I'm part of the school staff.* I'm also included in any in-services and I'm always invited on staff retreats. I'm not left out of anything' (colleague's emphasis) (ibid.).

The processes that enable such communication, though, are subject to the ongoing needs of staff. As one principal shared, 'If it's not working [the team] we need to examine the process; we follow [the] people here and not just the process.'

When selecting people to work in teams one principal notes:

> 'When helping staff to work "together" in teams, both in structured teams and the more ad hoc teams, you have to be subtle. ... Those I know who work better together in terms of personality and similar philosophy of teaching. Those who "determine" the curriculum and those who "meet the children's needs". I therefore give a lot of thought as to how we can structure the grades and grade teams. Prevention is better than cure!' (ibid.).

This note of *realpolitik* is important in that the differences are acknowledged, even affirmed, but staff work with those differences in establishing and engaging colleague teaming (see also pp. 96f, 124).

Peer-support teaming/transitional teaming

One form of transitional teaming that has been found to be particularly supportive in schools is the 'peer-support group; a transitional grouping for teachers with varying needs and concerns.[14] Those I have had most experience with have been first-year peer-support groups. Their purpose is to directly support colleagues through the mutual sharing of common needs and concerns, and to work on solutions together. These 'solutions' range from fundamental defusing of natural stress through 'whingeing' and 'off-loading' time, advice within the group and ideas generation. Such groups often develop more focused options that include ongoing mentoring, with the group as a reference body, so that colleagues take on a mentoring or peer-coaching role, they bring back shared insights to the larger peer-support group (see pp. 37–9). In such groups:

- participation is elective and voluntary
- trust is modelled and encouraged. The key values espoused in such groups are mutual regard (as co-professionals) and respect, equality, tolerance of differences, and trust and commitment to one another for colleague support
- teamwork is fostered when setting goals and developing plans
- structures for support are offered, particularly for struggling teachers, though the emphasis of such groups should not simply be on 'teachers who are having problems'; teachers of wide ability and experience also benefit from such peer-support groups. The emphasis is professional development in a climate of moral support
- the support group develops evaluation processes to gauge professional development needs in terms of such needs being addressed/met
- confidentiality is emphasised, especially when negative matters are disclosed
- there is also an emphasis on skill-development and professional 'risk' such as elective mentoring, peer-coaching and mutual classroom observation; even modelling and role-play (within peer-group times) as colleagues feel comfortable.

Such groups need careful and skilled facilitation, as well as thoughtful planning and monitoring. The key feature of such groups, however, is the enablement of its members to be peer-supporting rather than relying on a leader as such.

A note about the support given by office staff

Some of the office staff in this research study actually filled in surveys and expressed their wish to be interviewed. In collegially supportive schools office staff explained they felt genuinely part of the school staff; they felt valued as the teaching staff consciously affirmed their role in the overall school team.

In the interviews I conducted, teachers often shared how supportive they found the office staff, giving 'high praise' to their 'office colleagues'. At some schools the office team were described as 'the heart that pumps this place'. 'They keep this place running.' 'They are great; they'll take time out with a whole lot of "little burdens": money, form-collecting and all that. *They look out for us ...*' Colleagues often noted the theme of 'colleague watchfulness' demonstrated by their office team. I have noticed, too, the many, transitional expressions of support these women give in a single, busy day. Their role in school-wide support should not and was not minimised by many of the interviewees in this study. In my role as ongoing observer and researcher I was afforded generous, caring and patient 'colleague' support on every occasion by such office staff colleagues and other support staff in the schools in which I worked.[15]

Encouragement and feedback

As people and professionals all of us value encouragement, even a basic 'mention in dispatches' as one respondent described it. All staff valued being acknowledged and encouraged; the deceptively simple truth that 'I am valued. Others (who matter to me) acknowledge what I do, and who I am here. They see, they know, they let *me* know.' It is as if colleagues are saying, 'this encouragement shows you affirm and trust me. In this you also support me and my professional role here.'

Encouragement can occur through a few words – *en passant* – to notes, cards, flowers; as colleagues in every school noted. Such 'incidental' encouragement is always valued by all staff in all schools.

It is disconcerting – in less supportive schools – when teachers are not encouraged for their contribution, their energy, time and skill. As one colleague said, 'You can go for weeks here, months even, before a senior colleague acknowledges your effort, your energy, with a difficult class group or student … and I get no significant, supportive feedback about what I'm doing'[16] (secondary colleague).

At the most fundamental level encouragement is an expression of colleague watchfulness. (Rogers, 1999):-

'Someone who knows someone is having a rough time of it …'

'For me it's just to know you're there, you're thought of. You're not forgotten. In my other school, I didn't know what the senior staff thought.'

'Even a simple thank-you is important and given here. The parents often do that here … the other day a parent said thanks to me **via** the principal about a program I'm running.'

One colleague notes that one has to:

'Take time to remember and affirm others. Sometimes through a thank-you note, mostly it's verbally; for example, it was midnight before we wound up the musical, it is important to remember to thank the parents, too, who helped out. Sometimes it needs to be public – I know I like it myself.'

Again, while this quality of encouraging feedback can be described as professional it also has a powerful human dimension in the affirmation of the person. Another common form of encouragement occurred through 'shared talk'; dialogue that was often referred to as a way of coping with the day-to-day stresses. Such 'shared talk' often involved 'shared laughter'.

Shared talk, dyadically, or in larger groups, can also give a form of 'feedback', though such feedback is incidental (even 'accidental'), often unfocused, often not consciously linked to ongoing professional learning and development.

Feedback and encouragement have to be 'genuine' and 'meaningful': 'If it's false it's meaningless. You know when a colleague is genuine, when they've acknowledged *you* and *what you've done*' (colleague's emphasis).

My colleagues and I talked about the difference between encouragement 'just for the sake of it' and encouragement where one 'feels acknowledged'. Acknowledgment is connected with 'knowledge about' that which one is being encouraged within. That 'knowledge' affirms the recipients in that they feel that those who encourage have taken time to 'know' what it is their colleague has done, or is doing, or going through. Colleagues noted how they also appreciated children's and parents' responses as a form of, or expression of, feedback and encouragement.

Feedback

Those schools within the typology that I have termed 'consciously supportive' had made an attempt to consciously address the issue of staff feedback by recognising the supportive effect of feedback; even when feedback is considered to be 'incidental' (it is nonetheless valued for that):

- 'Mainly through talking, but it's positive feedback.'
- 'Some is very incidental, the patrol down the corridor, the unobtrusive coming to a class (not normally during instructional time, though).'
- 'The fact that people recognise my role is important to me … a recognition of my contribution … I'm valued …'
- 'Feedback helps, you can read and think you're doing okay, but you don't *really* know; you can get it wrong …'
- 'I got a Christmas card and it said, "You don't realise how much you've helped …"'
- I've been in teachers' homes where they proudly display a card, a note, or a personal letter of thanks or encouragement from their principal.
- 'There is an informal sort of appraisal I suppose … we talk about curriculum; what worked or didn't. We don't talk *specifically* about the way we teach, more *what* we teach.'
- 'I try to give as much feedback as possible, especially in their sticky situations [sic] with students. What you're trying to do is help; actively help. It's hard though if colleagues, say, have asked you to do something on their behalf, or

follow something up. It's hard to get back to them to let them know you've got things in hand, *but it's worth taking a few minutes to let them know*; or even giving a note in their pigeon hole. I have to plan this; I've got notes on my desk to remind me!' (senior teacher, colleague's emphasis) (All cited in Rogers, 1999).

Professional feedback

All staff acknowledged, however, that *professional* feedback requires more than a 'thank-you', an appreciative comment, or a note (as above).

I asked one of my secondary colleagues (a leading teacher) how she appraised her ongoing teaching and classroom management. 'Well, it's the things said in the staff room between us; we often talk about what we did say in 8D. You see them [colleagues] with folders of things. You *see* how well they're organised with their work – you see the *way* they communicate with kids at the staff room door. You *sense* it. You see what extra-curricula tasks they do without making a big deal about it' (colleague's emphasis). This form of feedback 'appraises' others through observation, and over time a 'picture', an 'understanding' of another's role and abilities and skills is built up.

Beyond such incidental observation and 'appraisal', 'consciously supportive' schools had enhanced professional feedback:

- By increasing the expectation that professional feedback is part of the teaming role.
- By consciously working on the positive benefits of feedback (even mentoring feedback). In a study on collegial mentoring, Little (1995) suggests that: 'Reticence to give advice may stem from a prevailing attitude among teachers where the giving of advice is not highly prized and that one should not assert one's self on matters of curriculum and instruction' (p. 36). I suspect this also has a great deal to do with the isolationist culture that still exists in some schools, or at least in the mind of some teachers.

One interesting understanding about feedback, often mentioned by colleagues, was the acknowledgment that in valued feedback, one is 'heard' even if the feedback is brief or transitional. In this sense feedback is often a dynamic and reciprocal concept. Such feedback and encouragement is linked with trust – trust that one will support 'the other' by acknowledging and assuring (see Figure 5.1 below).

Professional feedback is more likely to be effective when it is:

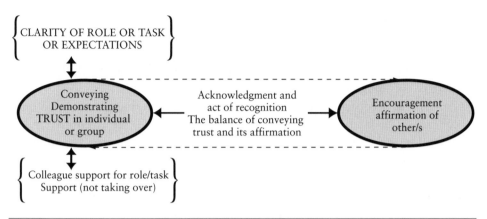

Figure 5.1 *Reciprocal nature of trust and encouragement*

- Shared within an awareness of what is actually going on. When colleagues know that 'you know they know' what they're going through, what they have done with their students in teaching/learning, then they are more likely to value any feedback. This is especially important when senior teachers give feedback to their colleagues. It comes, says a senior teacher, 'from an awareness of what's going on with the team, as well as individual colleagues within the team'.
- Distinguished from criticism (or the suggestions that one is a failing teacher). One of the problems raised by *any* feedback is the degree to which it is 'invited' or 'uninvited' by the colleague who is the feedback recipient. This is also more difficult when feedback is unasked for, but necessary in order to clarify role expectations and task expectations (see pp. 42f, 144).
- Given within a school-wide understanding of the concept of professional feedback as a purposeful means of professional reflection, ongoing teacher development and professional growth. Purposeful feedback enables teachers to move beyond hopeful approximation or guesswork about their role and practice.
- Descriptive, but consciously respectful of the person. This is critical, for example, in mentoring support that involves teachers who may be acutely aware of their struggle in teaching and discipline. In these cases feedback should focus on teacher behaviour not personality. Such feedback also needs to be focused in the present and made specific rather than abstract, being sure to give no more than people can appreciate, understand or immediately cope with. I have always found it helpful to have a shared understanding, at the outset, with a colleague – in any mentoring role – that feedback will always be given invitationally and reciprocally. Focused questions can be used to increase self-awareness, to develop self-reflection and a 'common' language. (p. 42f)

- Professional feedback is most useful, valued and effective when it is linked to common aims, and objectives, among all staff. When there is agreement on common aims and objectives *and practices*, feedback is seen as more purposeful. Any feedback will also need to address specific issues, problems, skills in a climate of non-judgmental respect.
- Professional feedback necessitates initiating and maintaining trust with one's colleagues. Such trust is dependent on mutual regard). It is effectively the mutual regard that carries to one's colleague that is remembered and valued.[17] Trust is also clearly related to encouragement (see Figure 5.1).

The collegial climate of the school has a significant effect on how these aspects of feedback are perceived, understood and utilised.[18]

Feedback and appraisal

There is some natural tension between colleagues' perception of feedback, generally with feedback as it refers to appraisal. Most of the colleagues I spoke to valued feedback from colleagues where they trusted those who gave the feedback and where such feedback was, primarily, initiated in an invitational, supportive manner. In this way colleague feedback has the potential to meet professional needs. Colleagues resonated with what Royce-Sadler (1989) terms, 'the randomness and inefficiency of trial and error learning' (p. 120). While colleagues often used transitional 'shared talk' to objectify experience – and perhaps confirm experience – it did not always mean they reflected, assessed and learned from such experience.

I believe colleagues also saw that feedback could be improved in their schools in terms of professional focus, direction and skill development. If, however, such 'professional feedback' is invested in appraisal processes, colleagues made clear that 'appraisal feedback' requires some collegial control when such 'appraisal' has 'performance' and 'competence' as elements of the appraisal process.[19]

Feedback, professional-sharing and 'appraisal' occur across a continuum from one's self-reflection to the occasional and incidental shared-talk with a collegial partner (or in a team), professional feedback expressed within teams and in mentoring, through to formal appraisal processes.

What I have noticed, broadly and widely, in the teaching profession is that teachers, generally, entail a high level of accountability to themselves and to each other and are often 'harder' on themselves than any 'outside body'.[20] Colleagues frequently noted that schools can adequately develop 'their own appraisal' – within a framework of external guidelines or parameters. It is within the school that colleagues need to develop and sustain:

- ongoing supportive feedback, both 'incidental' and more focused professional feedback
- formative as well as summative appraisal
- a teacher-learning culture expressed in elective expressions of peer-coaching and mentoring to increase the quality and focus of feedback in relation to professional development.

If teaching is so complex, and it is; if it is often demanding, and it can be; then staff ought to be looking for supportive, professional feedback to enable professional reflection, professional learning and professional development. In a more individualistic colleague culture this is less likely. The complex and demanding role of teaching and management is faced alone, with feedback dependent on self-reflection or whingeing outside of the school context; outside of the very context where others who 'know' can help.

Mentoring and peer-coaching in 'consciously supportive' schools

Mentoring and peer coaching can be positive and effective ways of supporting colleague self-reflection and professional development (see Chapter 2, p. 43f). As a concept-in-use, 'mentoring' can range from the ad-hoc, or regular, advice one seeks from a trusted colleague; the ongoing support of a 'teaching-buddy' (a term used in several schools I worked with); shared mentoring within teams where certain colleagues meet as professional guides, through to longer-term mentoring as coaching.

The concept of 'mentoring as coaching' is less commonplace in schools. In many secondary schools I have worked with, staff still perceive such mentoring as a 'form' of appraisal, rather than an opportunity for ongoing, supported, professional reflection and development. I have seen examples of mentoring by mandate in schools where the principal has 'directed' staff to work with mentors. As one colleague noted, 'it was *as if* [he] was saying "all failing teachers report to room 27 ... to find out how to begin their mentoring obligations"' (secondary teacher, colleague's emphasis).

One of my colleagues, a secondary deputy principal, concerned about such unhelpful perceptions in his staff noted that, 'Our early attempts at *any* sort of *"mentoring"* have been very relaxed, casual and not broadcast "publicly", at least not intentionally. I've offered to help with *any* classes at all this year. Not to take over – nothing like that – but I'll wander in and help with simple organisational things, as well as discipline procedures being followed fairly' (colleague's emphasis). I know a senior teacher (in secondary); he's the sort of colleague who would assist at any time. I have noticed that he is the 'quiet modeller' when working alongside teachers. For example, I have seen him diplomatically move alongside a colleague in conflict with a student and quietly distract and divert the residual tension between them. I have seen him tactfully refocus discordant voices among colleagues at one of the faculty meetings I was invited to participate in. He probably works too long, too hard and cares too much (in Rogers, 1999).

One of the teachers in this school indicated how such mentoring has assisted him and helped change his perspective on professional feedback:

'When the principal suggested a mentor approach to professional development [this is in line with the staff survey] I was all for it. It hasn't gone fully ahead yet, but we've been doing some team-teaching; it's changed the way I teach, it's helped me to be less "involved", less absorbed in it all, especially less involved in student behaviour hassles … It's also given me some helpful feedback – not always positive but that's okay. The problem, generally, with feedback is that people feel threatened. They feel they're being judged. I guess I might have done the same 10 years or so ago' (Rogers, op. cit.).

Some of the 'mentoring' (here in this school) has been based in a team-teaching model, some within a faculty framework, some by the principal networking with a 'mentor' and 'mentee' relationship.[21] The emphasis has always been on keeping the mentoring professional; giving constructive and purposeful feedback – and always keeping the emphasis supportive.[22] As one senior secondary colleague notes:

'They have to feel comfortable with me coming into the room. In my faculty [technology] safety is crucial. I know in some areas of the school colleagues would feel uncomfortable. That might change … In my area it's okay. Not enough teachers give this kind of support; I understand that **and** time is precious; but I've explained I do want (as HoD) to explore these ideas **with you in your classes** (where time permits). In this way they feel valued because *it's all about **the way it's done**!* We **make time** to discuss issues outside of class, like behaviour of students, and find ways of helping out, action plans and providing an avenue of support that can reduce stress, but also give some way of clarifying things' (Head of Department, colleague's emphasis) (ibid.).

The crucial role of the mentor/coach has to be considered when working alongside colleagues, in the long term, in their classes; their tone, manner and approach is crucial to any 'success':

'I was approached by the principal to ask if I'd mentor a colleague; the colleague was willing to have [this kind of] support and I was asked if my name could be proposed. My colleague was willing to, so I took it on. First, I let them talk. I really didn't know how to start, so we decided to work on his units of work – "getting them up to scratch" – then on to his practical lessons, themselves. We even worked on "keys words" to use with the kids, especially in classroom management situations. He said it had really helped [I've been in the classroom with him too, a number of times, and I've noticed a difference]. It's much better now. He's more confident. It's important to get the camaraderie going when coaching – that helps a lot. We still talk to one another well after the coaching. We've got a pretty good network going now' (Head of Department, senior teacher) (in Rogers, 1999).

The key point here is that my colleague decided 'with' his fellow colleague, how the mentoring could operate.

Whenever and wherever mentoring was utilised in any of the schools I worked with the following features of mentoring were present:

- The process was invitational and elective. It ought to be obvious that any 'forced', or 'required' mentoring or coaching will gain at best acquiescent compliance rather than professional reflection and change in a teacher's attitude and practice.
- Mutual goal-setting focused on particular and specific skills and approaches.
- The mentor needed to be aware of the ethical probity pertaining to a relationship that would see one's professional and personal self-esteem 'exposed'. The ability to develop and sustain a positive, professional communication with one's colleagues is crucial to effective and supportive mentoring. In this the mentor has to invite, demonstrate and sustain trustworthiness.
- Skills and techniques were developed through observation and modelling in classroom settings[23] (see also Figure 5.2).
- Mutually appraising links between an educational focus and curriculum focus (even individual lesson approaches).
- Behaviour management and discipline needs also were seriously considered as a key focus for mentoring.
- Ongoing reflection, monitoring and shared evaluation characterised the professional development in the mentoring journey.

Risk and trust

While there is naturally some 'risk' with such a level of trust, that risk can be minimised by enabling one's colleague to feel 'professionally safe' through the way mutual regard is communicated by the mentor to the 'mentee'.

Because the coaching aspect of mentoring requires some classroom observations early in the mentoring relationship, the mentor will need to consider how feedback will be shared relative to such observations. Feedback is a crucial aspect of mentor-coaching. 'Mentees' need to know in advance that feedback is a necessary feature of the mentoring journey.

Feedback is *descriptive*, never judgmental (at least not intentionally so). Its aim is to assist mentee professional reflection, and enable ongoing professional development in key skills (see Figure 5.2).

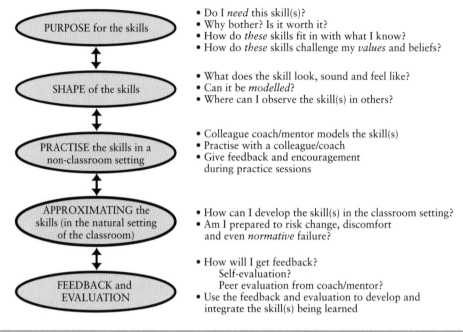

Figure 5.2   *A coaching model (skills)*

Adapted from Rogers (2000).

'Observation' (within mentoring)

The purpose of early classroom observations is to gain some understanding of classroom dynamics; typical teacher/student interactions; characteristic teacher behaviour in the area of discipline and classroom management; organisational features of the classroom such as seating plans, movement patterns of students' time-on-task; teacher engagement of student attention; motivation; and 'on-task' learning.

Even 'basic' considerations such as how the students will perceive the mentor/coach when they 'visit' the host teacher's classroom need to be planned in advance of the first 'visit'. Older students – upper primary onwards – are naturally 'suspicious' of the 'visiting teacher': 'What are you doing here? You're not our normal teacher.' My standard line to such an observation is, 'There aren't any normal teachers'. It is important to plan how the mentor/coach will be introduced by the 'mentee'; how much 'team-teaching' should be part of classroom visits (keep the context as natural as possible); when (and if) the mentor should exercise any discipline/management *while* the 'mentee' is teaching and managing a class. For example, if there is significant disruptive behaviour that the 'mentee'-teacher is not addressing, or cannot manage, there needs to be a prearranged understanding and a dignified *symbiotic cue* that can signal when the mentor will elect to 'step into the breach', as it were, and when to 'hand back' to the host teacher.

Debriefing after each class visit is crucial and will include some natural off-loading about how challenging 'some of these students can be'. If the 'mentee's' teaching and management behaviour has been significantly ineffectual or counter-productive to 'preferred practice' (see Appendix 2). The mentor needs to be careful and cautious about how much feedback to give initially; giving too much feedback may easily dissuade or discourage. Feedback is linked on the one hand to problem-description, raising concerns, but also provides a basis for goal-setting regarding necessary change (pp. 131–5).

Disengagement of the mentoring relationship will need to be mutually agreed either by setting an initial time frame for the mentoring journey, or through evaluating the ongoing development and pacing of change. Even when there is a 'formal' end to a regular mentoring journey the mentor will have an ongoing, incidental supportive role with their colleague, as a member of the grade or faculty team.

Skills – a mentoring case example (middle school)

Some of the skills may appear very 'basic' in the professional eyes of the mentor/coach. For example, a teacher with a restless class may face calling out, butting in and students talking during instructional time. Some teachers seek to discipline and engage such behaviour through questions such as, 'Were you two talking?' 'Are you calling out?' 'Why are you calling across the classroom?' 'Don't butt in when I'm talking' 'You know you're not supposed to call out, don't you?'

The teacher in question may well be unaware they are typically using interrogative questions in a management/discipline context ('Are you?' 'Were you?' 'Why were you?') when other language forms are more appropriate and effective, such as incidental directions. For example, naming the student(s) and 'incidentally' noting the behaviour: 'You're calling out and I'm trying to explain something to our class', 'A number of students are talking.' (Having 'described the reality' the teacher tactically pauses – briefly – and resumes the flow of the lesson.) This is a deceptively basic language skill, but it involves a confident and open posture, effective group-scanning, 'take-up-time', and re-engagement of the class group after giving the 'incidental' direction.

A few students are leaning (distractedly) back in their chairs:

'Jason and Bilal, you're leaning back in your seats' (incidental direction).

A simple, behavioural direction – 'Four on the floor, thanks' (like this) – is more positive, and invitationally co-operative, than the negative direction *'Don't* lean back in your chair!'

Incidental language or brief behavioural directions, combined with thoughtful eye scanning of the group, encouraging and engaging students in the dialogue or instructional time can significantly affect attentional behaviour of students. These examples are only one of several *core* language skills that can be effectively taught as key aspects of personal discipline planning and practice (Rogers, 1998, 2000). Of course, the *way* in which one communicates such low-level discipline to students is crucial and may also need to be addressed in the feedback, modelling and practice. Aspects of confidence, assertion and non-verbal behaviour expressed in tone, manner, proximity are all features of thoughtful, teacher behaviours that can be *learned*. It will also be important to address the relationship of teacher beliefs and mindset, as it affects behaviour management. This is addressed in some detail in Appendix 4.

One of the 'mentees' I worked with noted the difference that 'incidental language' (Rogers, 1998, 2000) had made with his grade 6 class:

'I no longer easily, or simply, tell the kids **what to do**. I briefly describe what's happening and leave some catch-up thinking with them; that is, the students who have "bits" of litter on the floor during an activity and it's nearly recess ... I say, "The bell's about to go soon ... there's some litter on the floor." I smile and thank them as I move off leaving them with "take-up-time" (I don't hang around "waiting")'.

The difference noted by my colleague may appear 'small', but there are many occasions when this 'incidental language' is a more effective form of 'discipline' than merely telling or asking a question (for example, 'Why is there litter on the floor?' or frequently using negative demands: 'Don't leave that litter ...').

With any coaching the 'mentee' colleague needs to see purpose, benefit and meaning in both the skills being addressed and the process of coaching itself. In this sense what *really matters* in the professional development process cannot merely be mandated. One cannot say 'you must teach and discipline like this in order to be effective'. (Well, you can 'mandate', but it is not likely to assist, or effect, genuine change in practice!) Inherent purpose and meaning are essential to personal commitment in professional development and change, and need to be worked through at every stage in the mentoring journey. (See Figure 5.2)

Beginning teachers

Beginning teachers will naturally be apprehensive about their first 'real' school and their first classes. Younger first-year teachers also talked about the 'natural anxiety' of facing the 'responsibilities' of teaching and managing their grade class (or classes) and the concern they had about educational outcomes of their students. Beginning teachers of any age have to engage not only the culture of schools, education and teaching, but the culture of *this* – their first – school.

One school describes its support of first-year teachers in this way:

'We make sure they have adequate resources for literacy and numeracy, where they're available. Even paper, pens, even seats(!). Sounds basic but it is important. We emphasise to them that our policy procedures and our decision-making is all shared.' 'We make sure they have an ongoing "teaching-buddy" – actually we call them "teaching neighbours". This is normal here for new staff **including** casual relief teachers.'

'With **all** teachers new to the school we literally walk them around the school, give a list names of staff and rooms etc., give a map, explain the key programs in the school, such as reading programs/literacy hour and how we use the Curriculum Standards Frameworks' (cited in Rogers, 1999).

One fundamental way of supporting several beginning teachers (in a large school) is to establish a peer-support group (see p. 37). These groups can provide an essential forum for the sharing of *common* experiences and concerns, common struggles affirmed (You too?!) and reframing of the new possibilities generated.

Such groups need encouraging leadership that can allow rapport, off-loading and sharing, as well as offering new insights into student behaviour, classroom management and teaching practice. For example, how to engage and sustain attention and motivation; how to utilise class discussion, particularly questions; how to move productively from instructional time to 'on-task' time; how to deal with task-avoidance; and noise levels etc.

Such groups, in the early meetings, often address deceptively mundane concerns about organisational aspects of the school such as how to 'mark work'; dealing with 'lateness'; how to 'run detentions'; management issues like whether, 'I should let a student go to the toilet after being in class for just a few minutes ...?'; how to manage time-out with dignity; how to follow-up with students when you have a concern about a student's behaviour or learning needs. These meetings give assurance that 'one is basically on the right track', 'that my peers share the *same* concerns as me', 'that I'm not the only one who struggles with 8D!'

In one secondary school a first-year teacher who had experienced some informal mentoring qualifies the kind of mentoring he found helpful:

'It would be more helpful if they [the admin.] could concentrate more on classes with mentor support, especially at the beginning of the year. It could help you be more independent. There should be more discussion and feedback on this ... It's important to do it [informal mentoring] without damaging your reputation in the school ... Don't just tell me what to do, *it's got to be practical*. When Charlie comes into my room it's like we're working together on those things we've discussed about behaviour and teaching' (colleague's emphasis, shared interview) (in Rogers, 1999).

Casual relief teachers

Casual relief teachers get a hard time of it in some schools. Arriving early enough (hopefully) they go to the office to ask what class they've got ... 'Oh, um, see the cleaner he normally knows what's going on around here'. They may not be given a timetable, or a 'teaching buddy' for the day (or week); they may not be introduced to the staff (at morning tea) or even introduced to their class (or grade). In some schools, casual teachers do need to 'feel', or be treated as if, they are 'genuine' teachers rather than 'de-facto' teachers or 'babysitters'.

In the 'less consciously supportive' schools I worked with, whenever I raised the issue of support given to beginning teachers and casual teachers, senior teachers I interviewed on this topic noted that, beyond a 'friendly chat' and an 'assurance that a senior teacher was available in a crisis', there was not a lot of *conscious*, or *planned*, support given to casual relief teachers.

Time constraint was the most cited reason for lack of *conscious* support in this area, particularly in secondary schools, rather than unwillingness to provide support to casual relief teachers. It was the same when discussing how colleagues supported 'new teachers'. Most of the support was incidental and ad-hoc. There was no actual 'structure' or 'process of induction'.

The important issue regarding colleague support for beginning teachers and casual teachers is not to leave their induction to 'chance', as it were, but 'factor' in procedures and opportunities for both moral support (off-loading and sharing) and professional support (needs-analysis, problem-solving, feedback, action planning etc.).

As was noted in several primary schools (in Rogers, 1999):

'We have a folder for casual teachers (map, bell times). We tee up a relationship with a "teaching neighbour" to give advice, help when you're not sure. We physically walk them through the school. We also make sure:
- there is a whole-school introduction at assembly time and in the classroom
- there is a folder (in **every** classroom). This contains a map, bell times, medical concerns for particular students etc.
- we have a card system for exit from the room for disruptive students who may need time-out
- the leader of each grade department "takes them under their wing"; and organises an introduction to a colleague next door as a "buddy". We also introduce them to the office staff (a small but important point).
Our key question is, does "it" (what we do for casual relief teachers and new teachers)

makes sense to them and help ease them into the way we do things here and give them a genuine sense of support?' (primary school principal).

These deceptively small points are very important and highly appreciated and valued by visiting, relief teachers, as well as first-year teachers. **See also Rogers, 2003.**

New teachers covering an existing class

In some schools new teachers, particularly first-year teachers, are 'welcomed' to school, and to their first serious teaching experience with a timetable allocation that has the known most-challenging groupings, or grade: 'Welcome to our school, you've got 9D, 10E for double maths on Friday in the portable classroom (five "light years" from the staff room and the nearest toilet!)'.

I've heard some experienced teachers say things like, 'Well, we were given hard class groupings when we started teaching, why shouldn't they? It was "done to us", so …'. I find such comments professionally disturbing and disconcerting. Such an attitude indicates a singular lack of welfare consideration for our colleagues.

Those who supervise and manage timetables need to be supportively aware of how class groups are allocated. Unless it is unavoidable, what is the point of giving a *known* difficult-to-manage grouping to a first-year teacher? or to teachers who may not have the experience, confidence or knowledge and ability (at least at this stage of their career) to effectively cope and manage with such a group? If, for example, a new teacher comes in to replace a teacher on sick leave (stress leave?) and their class is a particularly challenging class, it is my view that the re-establishment of the class with the new teacher should be a supported process involving some initial 'teaming'. This 'teaming' would involve planning how to:

- introduce the 'change-over teacher'
- re-establish a sense of shared purpose in learning and behaviour (a 'fresh-start' for the class group)
- link in the previous teacher's best practice with the new teacher's discipline, management and teaching
- re-organise seating options
- 'time-out' options for fractious and repeatedly disruptive students (should the need arise).

Even the way the support teacher works with the new teacher in the first few lessons is collaboratively planned out.

The support teacher in such a situation needs to know the students well, have 'credibility' with the class group, and work with the new teacher in such a way as not to diminish their own initial leadership credibility. My colleagues and I normally do this through 'introductions' to the class: 'I'd like to introduce Mr/Ms X to you. Mr/Ms X will be your teacher and will be leading your class while Ms/Mr Y is away.'

This 'introduction' gives a 'reason' for the support colleague to stay in the room for the first session with the class. 'Let me hand you over to Mr/Ms X to explain, and discuss with you some of the topics and projects you'll be covering this term and ...' While the new teacher is introducing him/herself and beginning the discussion with the group about 'how we will be working together this term', the support colleague respectfully stands to one side – not 'watching the class' but in a *symbiotic* teaming with his or her colleague at the front of the room. The last 'message' the support colleague needs to communicate is that of standing, watching and scanning the class group *while* the colleague is talking with the class (as if to say I'm the one who's got the 'real control here!').

Later, in the 'on-task' phase of the lesson, both teachers will move around the room 'getting to know' the students, reframing work tasks, encouraging, disciplining (as is necessary). The new teacher is receiving moral support from his or her colleague's presence and also receiving some incidental mentoring as he or she observes how the support colleague interacts and deals with behaviour management and discipline issues, as well as observing the support colleague's normative teaching and encouragement. The students are beginning to relate to the new teacher 'through' the teacher they know, as it were.

This relaxed, but consciously planned, teaming enables a kind of 'credibility by proxy' (Rogers, 1997). In the next few lessons the support colleague will 'incidentally' drop in to the class group (to see how things are going). Both colleagues will debrief that day.

If any student needs to be followed-up beyond the classroom setting regarding behaviour/learning issues, the support colleague will 'sit-in' to give moral support without taking over. At all times, this kind of initial support-teaming needs to keep the professional integrity of the new teacher's leadership in mind at all times.

Struggling teachers and colleague support

'There's nothing worse than talking about a colleague you know is struggling – even failing – yet not really supporting them' (senior secondary teacher) (in Rogers, 1999).

A colleague contrasts her struggle in a previous school with that of her present school:

'I really appreciate the support I received here, now. I have been in situations where I have felt the "lesser" of the group [sic]. This shattered my confidence and I've felt the many skills I had were squashed by stress and self-doubt. I know I must take responsibility for the way I respond and am affected by others. However, the positive environment in **this** school is **so** enriching and brings out the best in all associated' (primary teacher) (op. cit.).

Support for struggling teachers was one of the more sensitive aspects raised in this research study. It was a key question in both the survey and the interviews. In several of the schools where I conducted the research, I was actually involved, directly, with teachers who self-elected to have colleague support relative to the 'struggle' in their current teaching and, more particularly, their classroom discipline and behaviour management. Our aim in supporting struggling teachers was always to encourage them not to think they were 'alone' in their struggle.

Senior teachers often noted they felt somewhat inadequate and lacked skills in supporting colleagues whose classroom discipline and 'classroom control' were a cause of great concern. Staff also distinguished between those colleagues who asked for, and invited, support in this area and those who did not – or refused to acknowledge they needed support, when they would clearly have benefited from some focused colleague support. Of particular concern, also, were teachers who presented with emotional problems related to their teaching or that were interrelated between home and school.

I was, however, encouraged by the almost universal willingness of teachers to help such colleagues; to engage in some 'perspective-talking' and to offer practical support wherever they could. As one colleague (a senior teacher) noted:

> 'I'm aware that some teachers are teaching for survival. My aim is to support them, help them and link this with our overall aim – the benefit and welfare of our children. Sometimes it is helpful to invite them to work with another colleague, utilising their experience ("Who would you be comfortable working with?"), a sort of "relaxed-mentoring"' (in Rogers, 1999).

Another senior teacher adds, 'You want to acknowledge the good things that are happening with the teacher in that class; how difficult teaching can be; that the person is not alone; that severe discipline problems are *the whole school's responsibility* – don't take it personally.'

My colleague then went on to detail a suggested plan of action; she expanded on the sort of support the school would offer. 'In the school ... being relatively small, we're sort of alert to those sorts of problems and can nearly always offer help early, and ongoing in small steps [sic].'

That 'alertness', however, can operate just as efficiently in large schools through faculty teams.

In summarising the issue of support to struggling teachers, staff almost always referred to an approach that needs to include:

- senior teacher involvement: often the senior teacher can link a colleague to a peer for support in a way that is invitational, confidential, discreet and, wherever possible, elective in response
- invitational support emphasis: that the colleague(s) in question have the opportunity to share their concerns, needs and problems; to pursue the issue with professional honesty and balance. It is also important to emphasise the positive aspects of their teaching practice
- wherever possible, *any* support offered, or requested, which should be 'early-intervention' before a spiral of low self-esteem sets in
- where appropriate, senior staff will initiate an *ongoing* plan of support, developed with the colleague in question and wherever possible include some mentoring to enable that ongoing support. Included in the mentor role is often some 'stop-gap', 'structural', support such as a 'supported time-out' plan for the more disruptive students. (See also p. 113f.)

As a colleague in one of the 'tougher' schools noted:

> 'One colleague (in our department) who I know is having trouble – really struggling: 'missiles', noise-level, kids swearing, you know ... I go into the class quietly, take a few kids out (just one or two). It helps settle things down. Most teachers don't like this **so I only do it with a prior understanding and do it carefully; low key. I** don't make a song and dance about it' (colleague's emphasis; see also p. 113f.) (in Rogers, 1999).

He went on to talk about ongoing mentoring within the 'comfort zone' of the colleague in question. Ongoing mentoring is normally only effective if it is elective, includes some shared in-class observation and descriptive feedback geared to skill development, action planning and shared review (see p. 135f.).

'*Availability*', '*understanding*' and 'lack of *blame*' were consistently cited in terms of offering support to struggling teachers. Most of all, staff acknowledged that the situation ought not to occur where issue of a teacher's ongoing struggle is just 'let go' in the hope that things 'will fix themselves' – they won't. Staff, while acknowledging the difficulty of supporting 'some teachers', acknowledged that support should be 'offered' first and then be 'ongoing', rather than just 'talking *to*' or 'talking *about*' such colleagues. As secondary colleagues noted:

> 'Peer support has really helped. I have listened to my peers, their ideas and advice; they have especially helped when I've had to use time-out procedures ... I've also been able to reassess my teaching skills through this peer-support approach ... learning to take a middle path.' [Here my colleague meant not swinging from one extreme reaction, to another, when managing his classes.] (Rogers, 1999, ibid.)

At the end of the day it is a balance between providing support and encouraging professional responsibility.

> 'I acknowledge their struggle, their humanity, their questioning and their learning. I also say, time and again, if I've been expecting too much let me know. I delegate whatever I can and respect that readiness to take on responsibilities (that often stretches them) but that's where trust is.' (Rogers, op. cit.)

> 'What we're trying to do is to enable reflection on teacher practice through team meetings; with team planning; and even self-reflection (this is not always that strong), but **never** an inferior/superior focus' (senior secondary teacher, colleague's emphasis) (ibid.).

As noted earlier, colleague support can meet basic needs. Colleagues noted, however, that some teachers' expression of needs are confused with unreasonable demands. There is a small percentage of teachers whose 'struggle' exists (in teaching, organisation or management) because they want to be 'wet nursed'; who expect all assistance and no personal change where such change is necessary; who refuse to co-labour (collaborate) with others in whole-school practice; who 'white-ant' rather than professionally disagree; who dissent rather than problem-solve; and who characteristically whinge and say that such support, as was on offer, 'would not work for *me*'.[24]

As some described their fellow colleagues in this way, there was *still*, by and large, a sense of professional concern for such colleagues; rarely any vindictiveness, just natural frustration. Colleagues often admitted there are 'some staff we have to work around'.

As one colleague pointed out:

> 'Some teachers are not suited for the job personality wise. They don't get along with kids, really. Maybe it's not their fault. That's the way they are; maybe they shouldn't have chosen teaching. In teaching you need patience, flexibility and [to] be relaxed about things and not let things get to you too easily. If you let every little thing get to you, you'll very easily get stressed' (in Rogers, ibid.).

There will, in reality, be some colleagues who may need counselling support out of the profession of teaching, while others may be so resistant (yet so 'noisome') that their characteristically unprofessional behaviours may need to be supportively confronted through diminished work performance processes. To use a gardening simile from Shakespeare's *Richard III* ... 'the noisome weeds, that without profit suck the soil's fertility from wholesome flowers' Act 3, (iv).

Ideally, when any teacher is struggling, the earlier the support offered the more likely it is that such support will be accepted and utilised. The more supportive the 'ecology' or 'culture' of the school, the more likely a colleague will either seek moral and professional support, or be more willing to receive it when it is offered in good faith.

End notes

1 This is not dissimilar to Aristotle's 'conception of concord'. He argued that concord 'is realised' when 'men are in harmony with both themselves and with one another, having pretty much the same ground to stand upon.' It is the 'shared ground' as well as the realisation of self (as individual) and other in a common context. Aristotle: *Ethics* p. 271 (Trans. Thompson, 1969).

2 This was a firm recommendation of the report *Teacher Stress in Victoria* (1989):
> 'That each school be required to have a published discipline policy (developed in consultation with parents, students and staff), and to develop mechanisms to ensure that it is understood and applied consistently within the school, and that the Ministry support it in implementing this policy' (p. 44).

See, also, Rogers (1995).

3 'Many teachers complain bitterly that they are not backed-up when they find themselves with problems of this kind (confrontation with unco-operative, dysfunctional, violent, abusive, rebellious, anti-social students or their parents) ... indeed this lack of confidence that their authority will be supported appears to be one of the commonest causes of low morale with the profession' (Morgan, 1991, pp. 7–8).

4 See Rogers (1997).

5 See Rogers (2000).

6 See Rogers (2000) and Rogers (1997).

7 Accountability conferences are discussed at length in Rogers (1997) and (2000).

8 Henri Nouwen makes a universal point about teaching. 'A few years ago I met an old professor at the University of Notre Dame. Looking back on his long life of teaching he said, with a funny twinkle in his eye, "I have always complained that my work was constantly interrupted until I slowly discovered that my interruptions were my work".'

9 Little (1993) observes, 'Teachers' central reasons and opportunities for professional development begin with the teaching assignments they acquire, the allocation of discretionary time, and the other work conditions encountered day-by-day' (p. 147).

10 A school secretary at one of the primary schools relates, 'I came from a school where I didn't attend any staff meetings. I got typing handed to me. I sat at the front office. I wasn't invited to staff meetings. There was no consultations with staff re: budgeting or accounts ... Now, I attend all meetings and I'm a part of the consultative group. Until this new principal came I didn't even have a diary of day-to-day events ...'

11 This was a highly valued aspect of leadership particularly in the smaller, primary schools. A recent Boston University study of staff cynicism says '80% of US employees do not trust management'. When asked what influenced their levels of trust in the workplace, employees identified five factors: openness, autonomy, feedback, shared values and congruity. And what is the communication mechanism that generates the most trust, according to employees? Face-to-face communication (in Finger, 1993).

12 Obviously, it is a rare principal who demonstrates all these qualities. As Bernard (1990) notes, 'there seems to be a sense that for a school to have a good "organisational climate" the array of leadership characteristics should be distributed among the school's leadership team' (p. 314).

13 As noted in Buchanan and Huczynski (1985), such teams consider themselves to be part of 'an identifiable unit [sic] who relate to each other in a meaningful fashion and who share dispositions through their shared sense of identity' (in Dunford, 1992, p. 103). Wildblood (1968) argues that people work more readily in teams when values are obviously shared and when differences in values are articulated and accounted for in the relationships between people in the organisation.

14 Rogers (1996); O'Brien (1998); Bernard (1990) note that such groups also have a powerful function in reducing workplace stress.

15 When working in the United Kingdom some years ago a head teacher introduced me to some cleaners and cooks as, 'the domestic staff' (sic) – not 'staff who are part of our collegial community'. Contrast this with a school secretary at one of the primary schools who saw herself as a member of the total staff. 'It's a staff here, not just teachers'.

16 This was an issue raised in the report *Teacher Stress in Victoria* (1989), regarding the lack of evaluation and feedback on performance and lack of recognition for a job well done.

17 Skiffington and Zeus (1999) argue that 'confidentiality' is an essential feature of any 'coaching role' and that within such confidentiality a 'person's needs' are met.

18 'Teachers, like members of any working community, need to have the benefit of a quality of professional relationships that supports development ... characterised by respect, empathy and genuineness, acceptance of individuality, open communication, shared responsibility, willingness to change and permission to make mistakes ...' (Swift and Thomas, 1994, p. 59).

19 Kyriacou (1981) notes that: 'It is essential that teachers being appraised feel they have ownership of the process' (p. 132).

20 Shulman (1988) notes that what teachers are interested in is identifying the qualities in their teaching practices that show evidence of change over time, rather than merely periodic assessment. See Ingvarson and Chadbourne (1994). One experienced primary teacher shares her struggle with the 'one-off' formal appraisal:

> '... trying to find the right words for the things you do, and if you don't fill in the black bits of paper (you know those "item categories") when *you've really done it*. It's difficult to describe what you do as a teacher; I mean apart from the *actual* teaching part of it you're such an important part of the children's lives – how you talk to the kids, how you treat them, and you can't put that down in a few sentences in your appraisal that you've helped some child along the way ... it's a draining, but crucial, part of our life, but just because you haven't filled out certain professional development categories you look as if you might not be doing it'. (Rogers, 1999)

21 The term 'mentee' is one my colleagues and I have, jokingly, utilised working as consultant within these schools.

22 Hays, Gerber and Minchinello (1999) note that: 'The concept of mentorship is critical to quality education because it fosters the development of and growth of individuals,

and is essential in this "passing-on" of skills and professional standards to the next generation' (p. 84). The Elton Report (1989) notes:

'The most talented, "natural" teachers may need little training or advice because they learn so quickly from experience. At the other extreme there are a few teachers for whom training and advice will not be properly effective because their personalities do not match the needs of the job. It is clear, however, that the majority of teachers can become more effective classroom managers as a result of the right kinds of training, experience and support' (p. 69).

23 Even in non-classroom, duty-of-care settings, such as playground supervision.

24 This 'self-immolation' is often resistant to offers of colleague support. In the survey on *Teacher Stress in Victoria* (1989), it was noted that some teachers on WorkCare offered 'self-defeating' patterns of explaining their difficult situations in schools, often showing 'a tendency towards blaming external factors when things did not go well' (p. 30). 'Almost all respondents mentioned this aspect related to issues of teacher incompetence and laziness, high absenteeism, abuse of the system and lack of peer-support' (p. 29).

Shaw (1987) notes that with respect to some teachers who have settled resistance to necessary change (in self or in collaboration with others) '... there is always a group of traditionalists on the staff to whom resigned tolerance is extended until they retire' (p. 789).

CHAPTER 6

COLLEAGUE SUPPORT AND THE PROCESS OF CHANGE

'You cannot step twice into the same river, for other waters are continually flowing in.'
Heraclitus Fragments (21) (c. 500 BCE)

'Life is change. Growth is optional. Choose wisely.'
Karen Kaiser Clark b. 1938. American legislator and feminist

'Change is always a mix of broader forces and the interaction of individuals with them. People, individually or in combination, shape these broader forces and factors in order to influence the way in which a change effort turns out.'
Scott (1998)[1]

When a school embraces significant change in attitude, policy or practice it is rarely a smooth or easy 'run'. If change is an 'event' at all it is more like a cross-country run than a 100-metre dash. I have worked with some school leaders who believe that 'if we start the change process with a clear beginning, have a plan, direct resources, and time and mandate the requirements then change *will* happen.' It is as if there is a 'starting line' and a 'finish line' and we go forward to the finish line and change, subsequently and consequently, *happens*.

My experiences of change relate more easily, more realistically, with the metaphor of a cross-country run for 'less-fit runners', where a significant number of teachers do not even realise there is a 'run on' ('I didn't know anything about a run!'), are unaware of the course ('I haven't got a map!' 'I can't read a map!') and who don't always feel up to it ('I'm not well' 'I'm too unfit!' 'My knees are sore!' 'I'll catch up with you later!').

Any effective and purposeful movement in the direction of change, even man-dated change, requires more than a decision *to* change; whether at the level of classroom change or whole-school change. Any 'top-down' decisions to change also need to be able to engage, and 'carry', those for whom the changes will inevitably impact and affect.

Michael Fullan in his writings on change (1991, 1993) has noted that change is not merely 'an event' it is a 'process'; a process that needs to identify staff concerns about those aspects, and features of the change that create anxiety and uncertainty. It is also important that staff understand and accept that feelings of concern, anxiety and even frustration are normal in change processes. Staff need to be clear about the reasons for any changes, particularly those changes from without the school – 'mandated change' from the Department of Education.

Staff also need to be a significant part of the process of change through open communication about natural concerns and uncertainties. When staff genuinely believe that the change process is consultative and collaborative – and that their views, needs, concerns are taken seriously – they will more likely 'come aboard' (as one senior colleague put it).

There are 'events' relevant to change that we may well have no direct control over: a new policy, a new program, a new direction in curriculum, evaluation and even class sizes. Staff will need to understand what elements or features of required changes they can and cannot directly 'control' or manage; this is *realpolitik*, not admission of weakness.

A significant aspect of 'resourcing' for change also requires equipping staff with the necessary skills for taking on new programs, new practices, even if the skill development is only 'fine-tuning' or 'modifying' the existing practices. Most importantly, it will be the quality, utility and extent of colleague support that will enable colleagues to come to terms with the change imperatives. As one senior primary colleague notes:

> 'We emphasised from the outset collaborative processes (at staff, team and co-ordinator meetings). Ownership of the process empowers. In our discussion on change processes in the school my colleague went on to point out that, "we work the mandate at the local level ... so we own it here"' (Rogers, 1999).

Supporting colleagues who struggle with changes (notably in recent years with the onset of information technology/computers in every aspect of schooling) means allowing time, normative struggle and ongoing development of the change requirements. When a 'big change requirement comes, while we *have* to take it on board; *the actual changes* are more incremental' (senior colleague's emphasis).

All staff in all schools within this study acknowledged the pressure of outside-of-school changes from the Department of Education. As one senior secondary colleague noted, 'Teacher morale is down across the board; generally, I mean, any changes from the Department are seen as largely negative.' We had a long discussion about past and current Department of Education changes as they affect general morale and the difference the individual school can make on receipt of imposed changes. This is a regular sub-agenda in any school; I see it across the country where teachers, as public servants, cope with varying cycles of change over time from differing political persuasions and emphases. Many of those change demands are also arising from a currently, constrained economic landscape.

> 'It's difficult at times – coping with what "has to be" – or so we're told. It helps when we get a chance to talk out the changes and why and what we can do here at school. There's many changes over the whole of society – not just education. At school we need to have structures and processes in place to work **with** that change. Mind you a whinge is helpful – even though it may not [directly] solve anything as such!' (senior secondary teacher) (Rogers, 1999, op. cit.).

When a school addresses any significant change it needs to be seen as change from the 'inside out', as well as the 'outside in'. Purposeful and embedded change; 'owned' change *within* a school cannot simply occur by *fiat*; those affected by change need to 'own' the process and translate the process to their situation. This 'collegial mindset' was most notably present when the leadership in these schools had:

- acknowledged the normative stresses that come with any significant change, let alone mandated change(s)
- explained the need and reasons for the change(s), particularly imposed mandates
- acknowledged that small steps towards core change is more realistic than grand change forced quickly 'on paper but not in real-time behaviour'; allowing time for the process of change to engage attitude, mind-set and changed practice. As one primary colleague notes, 'We distinguish between a "buffer zone" and ongoing change; the team gives one a "buffer zone" and one can go back to digest and work through implications for us as individuals. This is in contrast to isolating ourselves from each and other and the change requirements' (Rogers, 1999, ibid.).
- developed more open, face-to-face and consultative communication generally, and more consciously, within a *teaming focus*. The team focus enabled staff to share the natural, common pressures and concerns associated with the changes
- enabled supportive processes as to carry the changes over time through resourcing, teaming and professional development
- linked change imperatives and processes to appropriate delegation and responsibilities to engage the 'challenge of change' (as one senior primary colleague put it).

Most importantly, the leadership had maintained an ongoing emphasis on colleague support through precept, practice and necessary collegial structures that sought to meet colleagues' support needs.

In 'owning the change', and the necessary change processes, the leaders in those consciously supportive schools particularly emphasised the moral purpose[2] and meaning within the changes. As O'Brien (1998) notes:

> 'A cohesive collective consciousness will be articulated through the school aims and the methods by which they are implemented. Most importantly, aims should be driven by an agreed concept of what is of **worth** to the school community. Clarity about collective worth can enable teachers to mediate experiences, provide a positive ethos, and promote individual and communal growth' (p. 53).

Change within a concept of shared meaning and purpose, rather than the merely utilitarian necessity of change, is a feature of supportive colleague cultures as they own the change process. One of the primary school principals went to some pains to emphasise that 'their mission was not simply subservient to the task'.

Transitional culture changes

Meaningful change in the colleague culture within a school occurs when the staff, with their leadership team, acknowledge areas in school organising policy and practice, even in normative professional behaviour, that are not adequately meeting colleague needs (see p. 74).

As a school begins to reassess colleague support needs (in its widest sense), the culture itself begins to change as its relational and professional life more consciously acknowledge how moral and personal support impact on, and enable, the daily purposes of teaching and learning. I have termed this process 'transitional school-culture'; that time in a school's journey where staff awareness and readiness coalesce in internal change as their structures, policy and processes move towards a more consciously collegially supportive culture.

A school's culture is not a fixed, permanent expression of how a particular group of teachers relate and work. A school culture is not merely an accidental happenstance; it is the visible, characteristic, explanation of how people value each other; relate to each other and work together; how they communicate and collaborate as a team; how they engage in supportive and helpful feedback; how they embrace shared understandings and behaviours that contribute to colleague welfare and their shared purposes as professionals.

The schools I was involved with who had sought to consciously determine how they wanted their 'colleague culture' to be were aware of where they had come from (and how) and they were aware of how they had sought to address colleague needs. Even then these schools realised they needed to re-address their colleague culture from time to time to see if and how they were meeting espoused needs of staff.[3]

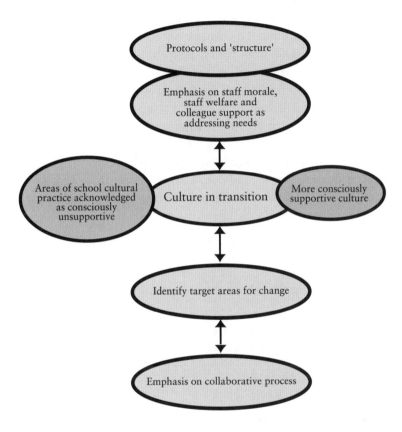

Figure 6.1 *Culture in transition*

Readiness for change

One primary principle notes: 'I was lucky; the school was ready for change'. I asked her how she identified this 'luck' and 'harnessed' it:

- 'I met with staff individually and as a group to *understand* their concerns and needs.'
- 'I shared my concerns but also what I wanted *our* vision to be with respect to our core values and concerns as a school.'

- 'I encouraged them to see that I've had to face mandated change from the department, but *we*, as a staff, could *own* it and transform it at the school level so that *we* manage the mandate. *It* doesn't manage us!'
- 'We developed a more conscious teaming approach, across the grades, to enhance the change process and give the necessary moral and practical support needed to carry and translate the changes.'
- 'Most of all we emphasised, from the onset, collaborative processes at whole staff meetings, at grade meetings and at co-ordinator meetings, and, where appropriate, with parents and students. They too are affected by change(s) and need a chance to understand where we're going as a school and why. It was this understanding of the process that empowered the staff.'

Change is not simply a 'process', 'event', or 'structure'; it involves people having a sense of shared aims and purpose, and behaving and working in light of these aims and purposes. This, of course, is the difference between 'surface' (and paper change) and 'embedded' change.

> 'Changes occur quickly, sometimes you can't always communicate all aspects of the changes to everyone's satisfaction. You have to trust admin., when and where you can't always collaborate. Sometimes we've got to sort information out into what's important, what's really important; and avoid "overwhelmingness"' [sic] (senior secondary teacher) (in Rogers, 1999).

> 'After a school-wide review, which, as you know, has included some outside consultancy, we had a strong sense of **we could change this culture**, especially with respect to staff welfare. I believe welfare and morale go together; from the way staff conduct meetings to how we support each other in discipline situations. We've come a long way in the last few years' (senior primary teacher) (ibid.).

> *'It is important not to over-control events* or colleague contributions. It's a sign of trust; risk too sometimes. I encourage my co-ordinators **within a range of options**. We were, last year, making policy on the run **while we were doing it**. This year we have made some changes. It's no good saying I'll skirt around you, or around the problems, when we *need* the information, then take **time** going into key areas to validate **what's** going on. The time we've put into this **one** proposal for basic structural change whole-school; even these "structural proposals" take time' (senior secondary teacher, colleague's emphasis) (ibid.).

One of the 'buzz-phrases' in the past 10 years in education has been the use of the term 'whole-school approach'. While this is an important feature of both whole-school policy and practice, as well as colleague support, it is important to address what is meant by the terminology 'whole-school'. A senior secondary colleague shares some of his natural frustrations in this area of change:

'When they talk about whole-school approach some of the teachers here are basically saying **my** whole-school approach. They'll say, for example, "it's terrible in the playground on duty", and yet not even take their duty seriously you know?' (Rogers, 1999, op. cit.).

'We've got this process, we've set it up, for behaviour management but some teachers by-pass it when it doesn't suit them. **The process does, it can, give support** but staff need to work with it and support it **by their involvement**' (colleague's emphasis) (ibid.).

The senior staff and the 'middle management' in this school; in fact, many of the teachers had accepted the reality that the concept of 'whole team', and 'whole-school' when applied to any policy or practice means about 80% of staff at most, for most of the time (bad days notwithstanding).

Colleague support is a crucial factor and determinant in any school's transitional culture. Most staff acknowledge that while they affirm the value of current colleague support in their personal and professional coping, a more conscious, even 'structural' aspect, to colleague support could improve morale, welfare and professional development. 'Structures', or processes are often the 'easier' aspects of the change process, and if staff believe such 'structures' are needs-meeting they are more likely to address essential areas of personal and group attitude, behaviour and practice necessary to the change process.

Colleague support gives a kind of 'buffer', softening the perceived impact of change, acting as a 'clearing house' for identifying 'what really needs to happen with the changes' and the practical demands of 'how we do it' at the 'local level'.

'We all get threatened by change at times and six heads are better than one. From that flows the way we put things together; the encouragement we give each other that **change is not life threatening**. It's stressful, though, but the load is more manageable and distress is diminished when we look at the changes together – that includes a whinge. Toss it around together and get a plan of action going then modify what we **have to do** (like the Curriculum Standards Framework, especially at the moment) and the record-keeping and assessment part of it all. While a lot of things change [teaching] by looking at it together **and** sharing the load, it helps' (senior secondary teacher, team leader) (Rogers, 1999, ibid.).

The process of change

In the ongoing observation and dialogue with these schools it was clear that when the normative situation and organisation began to change there were stresses expressed in frustration and doubt. This doubt for some, took the form of 'operational doubt': 'Will these changes and this new system and organisation work?' 'Is it *really* necessary?' 'How will *we* work in the new system?' 'What will be *my* role in this new structure?' For others there was an 'ethical and ideological doubt': 'Is this *fair*, is it *right?*' 'Is it appropriate?'

These doubts and anxieties are normative in the cycle of change as circumstances, context and demand affect a formerly more 'comfortable' social and professional dynamic now embracing the natural concerns and anxieties that change can bring.

It may be that such doubts arise out of a 'settled complacency' of a former culture under perceived threat as schools have to face mandated, organisational and educational change. What these schools (see p. 153f.) have done is to revisit their vision and purpose as a school and from there develop programs, 'structures' and professional development opportunities, to enable a more consciously supportive environment for staff and students in the now changed context.

The degree to which there will be an ongoing supportive culture in these schools depends on the degree to which the schools' policies, structures and programs have a genuine sense of collegial cohesion; a workable sense of cohesion developed *and sustained* out of collaborative, shared goals and a common mindset and shared practice.

Senior colleagues in the primary schools I researched made the point that unless the vision and practices of the school, in terms of colleague support, is revisited, reviewed and reaffirmed, they, as a school staff, could easily become complacent. Such complacency, where it is redolent of 'know-it-all attitudes' and 'we have achieved all we need to', can contribute to 'operational doubt', even a decline, or regression, of positive features and practices in a colleague culture.

I have sought to outline the main features of this process of transitional change as it works in a more positive, or a more negative, direction in Figure 6.2. In reference to this model those schools that I have termed 'consciously unsupportive' have certainly had their 'uphill struggle', as it were, they have not 'descended', however, into a state of significant doubt. Those schools 'in transition' between 'consciously unsupportive' and 'consciously supportive' (see Chapter 3) had acknowledged their normative doubts, and those doubts have been aired, discussed and are being worked through, to the extent that these schools can be typified as standing transitionally between 'consciously unsupportive' in some elements and features of their school culture, and 'consciously supportive' in other elements (see Figure 6.1).

A paradigm shift with cultures in transition

Schools' cultures have to address many changes, on many fronts. It is often natural for the 'immediacy of tasks' to overly engage the day-to-day focus. There is external pressure, and normative daily pressure, in many a school organisation that can 'eat up a school day'. 'Task paradigm' is evident when the pressure and need for change is expected – even demanded – creating a tension between imposed change and the need to collaborate, own and 'pace' the change at the local setting. Such tension is exacerbated when individuals in a school overly focus on a 'task paradigm', to the exclusion of a conscious 'people paradigm' and 'purpose paradigm'.

As asserted earlier, the function of colleague support as it affects, and is affected by, change is to meet colleague needs. Any 'form', 'process', 'procedure', 'organisation' or 'policy' that a school factors into its normative culture ought to thoughtfully and consciously consider how such structures attempt to meet colleague needs; their moral and professional needs.

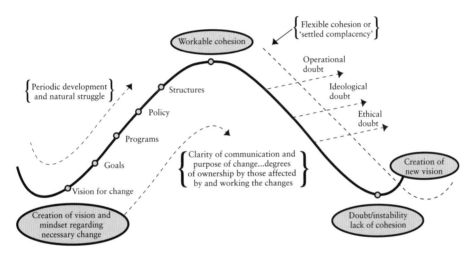

Figure 6.2 *Transitional change dynamics in an organisation or group*[4]

End notes

1   Scott (1998) in Ashdown (1999, p. 12).
2   Fullan (1993) speaks of an: '... authentic shared vision (as it relates to change agentry such), vision [is built] through moral purpose, inquiry, mastery and collaboration' (p. 31). Quoting Louis and Miles he adds, '... strategy is viewed as a flexible tool, rather that a semi-permanent expansion of the mission' (p. 31).
3   Nias et. al (1989) note that teacher interdependence in professional learning has its main impetus deriving from the shared belief that existed in all the schools [they studied], that practice could always be improved and hence that professional development was a never-ending process, a way of life.
4   I am indebted to my colleague Neville Webster for this model as represented in Fig. 6:2. As such, 'cultures', and 'systems within cultures', need to be seen as 'interdependent'.

Kelly (1996) asserts that 'members of a social system should be viewed as interdependent ... adaptive (some traditions, rules, and relationship histories constrain some behaviours and facilitate others). Cultures are also "successive" – environments are constantly changing, because systems lie within systems and have a natural progression through maturation ...' (in Hobfoll, 1998).

CHAPTER 7

TOWARDS ADAPTIVE UTILITY:
a framework for colleague support in schools

'A cord of three strands is not quickly broken.'   Ecclesiastes 4: 12

'It's about tackling something together: binding staff together, pulling staff together, celebrating success, observing – sensing when things are not right and tactfully offering, inviting the right support …'   (Primary teacher) (in Rogers, 1999)

'It's experience, over time, of knowing how trust will be given … of knowing how it will be received. It doesn't come easy, or cheap.'   (Senior primary teacher) (in Rogers, 1999)

Every school has some degree or expression of colleague support. The degree to which such support is consciously addressing colleagues' needs varies widely among schools. The degree of variance, I believe, is related to:

- the degree of 'consciousness' within a school culture about colleague support (see Chapters 3 and 4)
- characteristic expressions, 'forms' and structures of support across the school organisation and practice (see Chapter 5)
- the espoused values and 'protocols' that undergird colleague support (see Chapter 4)
- how school leadership values model, engage and encourage ownership of the more 'formal' expressions of support (see Chapter 6). Who owns the processes of colleague support? This, in terms of 'form and structure', is an important question in assessing how realistically colleague support operates in a school.[1]

Adaptive facility: implications for schools

Working daily with schools, as I do for a living, I was keen to see how a school's colleague support could be enhanced or improved as a result of this study's findings (Rogers, 1999). I believe that colleague support is an underrated aspect of a school's existence and mission. I further believe that colleague support can give (and does give) an integrative function to teacher morale and professional practice not always acknowledged or affirmed in some schools.

At the heart of any adaptive facility (arising from the research in this area) is the 'consciousness of support' demonstrated in school leadership making a concerted effort to reappraise how it address the many aspects of colleague support and collegiality in its school community. Further, such leadership can encourage colleague ownership of the change process necessary to increase the function and utility of colleague support. In the process of adapting the school culture towards increased supportive collegiality, the leadership will be aware of the need 'to risk', 'to trust one another', to engage and work with value differences and bring out into the open those issues, concerns and problems that are often selectively not addressed in less supportive cultures.

Consciousness of colleague support

Consciousness of support finds its valued expression, by staff, when it actually meets espoused needs; in this sense 'form' follows 'function' (see p. 74f.); such 'consciousness' has a school-wide application beyond any transitional expressions of support. As noted earlier, the transitional expressions of support are highly valued by teachers.[2]

In addressing colleague support at a more conscious school-wide level, a school leadership needs to extend its 'ad-hoc' and 'transitional' expressions of support into useful 'structures' and 'forms' that can address colleague needs. It is the positive inter-relationship between supportive relationships and supportive structures that characterise a supportive culture.

Consciousness of support also seeks to address the professional needs of staff, including ongoing professional feedback; such feedback can be 'incidental' or ongoing within professional appraisal. In order to be professionally supportive, however, feedback needs to be more than 'chance' or *merely* incidental.

Colleague support consciously addresses collaborative collegiality in shared decision-making and reciprocal communication at every 'level' across the school. Purposeful teaming can provide significant opportunity for ongoing professional communication in a school. This often includes a reassessment of how 'teams' actually function in terms of shared values, goals, parallel planning, team problem-solving and direct team support beyond the 'group formation' itself. Kilman (1985) notes the signal differences between 'a group' and 'a team' in terms of adaptive cultures:

'One has merely to experience the energy that flows from shared commitments among group members to know it – the power that emanates from mutual influence and *esprit de corps*. Why does one organisation have a very adaptive culture while another has a culture mired in the past? Is one a case of good fortune and the other a result of bad luck? On the contrary, it seems that any organisation can find itself with an outdated culture if the culture itself is not managed explicitly. I have found that unattended, a company's culture almost always becomes dysfunctional. Normal human fear, insecurity, over-sensitivity, dependency and paranoia seem to take over unless there is a concerted effort to establish an adaptive culture' (p. 65).

When colleague cultures are consciously supportive, certain features of school management and colleague behaviour are present:

- A consciously supportive leadership will address both the values as well as the utility of support. They will espouse and hopefully model those values, particularly those redolent in valuing others: 'mutual regard' and 'mutual respect'.
- A consciously supportive school will develop 'structures' of support that directly serve colleague needs and that proceed from a collegial needs analysis. Because the benefits of colleague support as it relates to stress-buffering are so well established senior staff can utilise a 'stress and (morale) auditing' process that addresses staff feedback and concerns (see p. 168). Such a process, in turn, becomes preventative as well as responsive and supportive. The ownership of support in this case is based on staff collaboration rather than an administrative mandate.
- A consciously supportive school has 'structures' and 'processes' to encourage and enable support. Colleague support does not depend on the reciprocal goodwill of individuals alone for the existence of support and welfare.
- A consciously supportive school will also be sensitive to those teachers struggling in their teaching and classroom management. A consciously supportive community will support struggling teachers through early intervention and ongoing support. It will emphasise support that encourages responsibility through shared needs-analysis and through professional development (mentoring/coaching is often offered as part of such professional development).
- A consciously supportive school will directly acknowledge the special needs of first-year teachers. In particular, senior staff will not give first-year teachers the 'worst' classes in the 'worst timetable slot'.
- A consciously supportive school will also address the special needs of casual relief (supply) teachers.

Most of all, a consciously supportive school will not rate the request or expression of support as an indication of professional weakness.[3] It is the climate of acceptance of shared struggle and common need that encourages confidence to share with others. Acknowledgement of a shared humanity and common needs, present in our stressful profession, will go a long way to endorsing confident colleague sharing.

A framework addressing 'consciousness of support', across a school community, is offered below (see p. 170f.). This framework has, in part, an awareness-raising function and is, in part, a diagnostic 'mechanism'.

The tension of colleague support

Any change occasioned in a school culture such that it becomes more consciously supportive means encouraging its individuals to reassess the purpose, meaning and utility of support. Every survey I took, every school I have worked in long term and every colleague I interviewed – even the most cynical – saw some value and utility in colleague support. Many also saw the value of extending individual expressions of support to encompass more whole-school expressions.

There will always be limits to how colleague support can operate in a school; notwithstanding the vagaries of human fallibility, temperament and personality. Closing the gap between espoused needs and how individuals, teams, structures and processes can assist in meeting them is no mean feat. The 'consciousness' regarding a school's efforts and practices relative to support is the difference between how what is espoused, or hoped for, becomes more 'real' in practice.

The framework for reviewing and developing a more consciously purposeful colleague culture (offered later) is based on the research primarily conducted in suburban schools in Melbourne, and a long-term observation and reflection about colleague support and school cultures across Australia. This long-term view (based in national and international consulting) has afforded an understanding of how schools vary in their colleague cultures. This framework is one I have been using for over a decade with schools to review, assess and assist in the shaping of policy, practice and encouragement of collaborative, colleague support. It is offered as a suggested framework for reviewing and assessing the 'consciousness of colleague support', and how school staff perceive the function and form of colleague support in their school with a view to better assessing and addressing their colleague needs.

Plato's *Republic* records a dialogue about the 'ideal' and the 'real' that acknowledges the creative tension in any human expression of theory and reality:[4]

> '... haven't we been painting a word picture of the ideal state? True. Is our picture any the worse drawn, then, because we can't show how it can be realised in fact? ... Does practice ever square with theory? Is it not in the nature of things that, whatever people think, practice should come less close to truth than theory? Do you agree or not? I agree' (Plato, *Republic,* Book 5, p. 472).

Not all colleagues want support; even in supportive schools. Not all colleagues want to give support either. Some colleagues will give support because the culture in the schools makes giving of support easier, or even because one perceives it as a personal or professional duty arising from 'mutual regard'. Within a school culture there are complex relationships between personalities, structures and the demands of one's role. Those who do give, and give unstintingly, the time and energy to support others speak about the stress of the given support, as well as the benefit of support enjoyed by recipients.[5] It will be important for schools to acknowledge such tensions in not just the receiving but the giving of support.

One effective way of addressing such natural tension seems to be in how purposeful teaming occurs within formal teams, and how whole-school processes and policies increase *shared professional dependency and coping*, rather than relying on transitional coping alone. This is a characteristic feature of support I have noticed particularly in schools with challenging student populations. The school-wide opportunities for 'structural', dependable, support offered in such schools is *crucial* to the coping ability of individuals and groups, even of the school as a community in its local setting (Breheny et al., 1996). The kind, nature and extent of such support can significantly affect well-being, a sense of professional purpose and cohesion, and even the basic energy to engage the 'day-after-day-after-day-ness of it all'.

Fullan and Hargreaves (1991) describe two types of exhaustion that exist in schools. This observation resonates well with my experience and that of my collegial peers:

'One arises from lonely battles, unappreciated efforts, losing ground, and a growing and gnawing feeling of hopelessness that you cannot make a difference. The other type of exhaustion is the kind of thorough tiredness that accompanies hard work as part of a team, a growing recognition that you are engaged in a struggle that is worth the effort, and a recognition that what you are doing makes a critical difference for a recalcitrant child or a discouraged colleague. The former type of exhaustion ineluctably takes its toll on the motivation of the most enthusiastic teacher; the latter has its own inner reserve that allows us to bounce back after a good night's sleep. Indeed, the first type of exhaustion causes anxiety and sleeplessness, while the second induces rest and a regeneration of energy. School cultures make a difference in what kind of tiredness we experience' (p. 107).

A grounded theory of colleague support

In terms of the grounded theory developed in this study (Rogers, 1999) colleague support can be expressed as developing a more consciously supportive colleague culture, observed in the following:

- meeting needs: these needs may be generic or specific. They can be met transitionally and individually, or in a more developed, sustained whole-school way as through teams
- enabling the management of normative day-to-day stress by having colleagues you can rely on, and formal, as well as informal, opportunities and 'structures' within which such 'reliance' can be expressed. In this sense, colleague support can enable a 'buffering effect' relative to such stress, as well as providing a coping 'mechanism' for managing such stress[6]
- when colleague support is consciously addressed within a school culture, in terms of meeting needs, such support decreases the isolation that often leads to stress (see p. 14f.). As O'Brien (1998) notes:

    '... a teacher should not have to be in a position where they feel that they cannot face going to work because of the invisibility or lack of interest of a school support system that has not picked up the early warning signals. The situation is made worse if the teacher has requested support but not received it. In this context, the "sickie" day is often not an indication of a medical ailment but a description of feelings brought on by stress. "I'm sick" can be interpreted as "I'm sick of the difficulties I experience in isolation and the lack of support that I am receiving". The actual existence of a system that claims to support staff is not enough because being supported is a multi-sensory experience that extends beyond systems provision. Teachers should feel supported; they should see evidence of support, and hear that those who are offering support are doing so in a non-judgmental fashion' (pp. 110–11).

- an increase in professionalism in conscious and purposeful ways. A notable difference in school-wide consciousness in this area can be demonstrated in how a school utilises teaming and teams (see p. 123f.). Teams can provide an ongoing collegial forum for discussion of common professional concerns about teaching, management and curriculum planning
- the formal expression of colleague support in productive policies, practices and 'structures' on a whole-school basis. This 'formal' expression of support needs a dependability for it to be needs-meeting.

Beyond any 'formal' support there are times when teachers feel the need to 'offload', to share concerns, to seek reassurance, clarification; obviously, as an individual, one needs to speak up, invite and request support where it is felt it is needed. Colleagues may not always know, or sense, a fellow colleague needs support.[7] Yet the protocol of 'watchfulness' (noted earlier on p. 97f.) and the value of 'mutual regard' increases the likelihood of reciprocity in the requesting of, or offering of, support.

Sometimes this is as basic as the 'informal' 'How's it going?' or the more extended informal 'How's it going with 8D?' or 'That student (so and so)?' It may even be a little more specific, such as the quiet aside, 'Look I noticed … do you want to have a chat about …?'

Where the 'ethos' of support affirms the protocols of support noted earlier (see Chapter 4) the 'climate', or 'ecology', enables such transitional exchanges, as those noted above, to be well meant. At the 'end of the day' one has to be essentially able to trust one's colleagues, as well as the processes developed by our colleagues to engender such trust. Climate and ethos, of course, are present in both the 'ad-hoc', transitional exchanges of support and the more 'structural' forms of support, such as shared-policy and purposeful teaming. When both are present, then staff feel valued and that their needs are being addressed, even met. Conscious colleague support, in this sense, is not something 'forced' or 'done' to colleagues.[8] As colleagues often noted:

> 'You can't really mandate, nor can you make people want support, especially re: difficult classes, behaviour management, lesson-delivery, teaching style. You can have structures to assist such likelihood but forcing it won't work' (secondary teacher) (in Rogers, 1999).

> 'What makes colleague support a sort of chicken and egg situation is [that] you need the people to make the culture that is supportive to the people. *They make the environment; it's the people, the quality of the people; it's the people who make their school*' (senior secondary teacher, colleague's emphasis) (ibid.).

In a consciously supportive culture, colleagues seem able to rely on both the structures and each other in an interdependent relationship.

Leadership and management of stress

Consistent with the research on stress and colleague support (noted in Chapter 2), leaders in collegially supportive schools evidence characteristics of supportive leadership such as:

- Leaders/managers communicate their expectations to staff in ways that are meaningful, as distinct from those managers/leaders who over-rely on printed communication rather than face-to-face contact.[9] This includes role clarity that expresses realistic responsibilities and objectives, it also includes appropriate consultation and review on role clarity. One would need to add that such expectations derive from common values and realistic understandings about one's professional obligations and practice.
- Leaders/managers are prepared to genuinely listen to their staff and provide feedback about staff concerns, suggestions and misunderstandings. Feedback is critical for staff in order to know how their practice corresponds to shared expectations. Such feedback needs to also address aspects of organisational health and

welfare, particularly in areas that impact on stress.
- Leaders/managers are readily available to 'their employees' (their colleagues); keeping channels of communication open. One of the major factors in staff understanding of colleague support and change in this study was closely allied to 'positive', 'open', 'non-judgmental' and 'opportune' communication processes.

One of my colleagues shared with me how colleague support, especially from a senior colleague, had enabled him both to cope and re-evaluate his role in the school. He was struggling, he said, as an 'older post-50 teacher', with some of the newer demands of the Curriculum Standards Framework (CSF), and evaluation and some aspects of behaviour management. He had thought it might give 'it away' and had rated himself quite harshly as not doing a thorough or effective job. He was surprised and heartened by several phone calls at home, indicating both their support for him – he had shared his concerns and whinges, incidentally, many times at school – and asking particularly if there were aspects of his role they could modify, or, help with or even change. 'We don't want to lose you! We really value you here.'

It was this demonstration of understanding, trust and practical willingness to assist in fine-tuning his role, when going through this 'rough patch', that encouraged him to stay on in a profession he loved. What he said he valued most was the fact that his colleagues – even the principal – took time to talk *with* him and let him tell his story.

- Leaders/managers understand the climate of their organisation and their colleague culture; this particularly includes monitoring for stress factors in the workplace. A 'stress audit' can indicate where physical and situational stress factors exist across a school. Even 'minor' concerns such as stuck doors and windows; lack of shelf space; inadequate toilets; flickering lights; jamming doors, windows and cupboards; space; poor photocopying possibilities; as well as organisational and procedural factors such as timetable loads and allocation of class groups, teaching area allocations, policy processes and collaborative and decision-making factors can be addressed in such an 'audit'.[10]

Stress auditing

The 'stress audit' (conducted yearly, or in times of perceived need) gives assurance that staff are being listened to and that, wherever possible, *reasonable* and *possible action* is taken. In this, staff feel valued, believe that their needs are addressed and hence cope more effectively. The process entails:

- Identifying the workplace stressors in terms of frequency, intensity and generality of stressful effect or impact through a survey, or small-group discussion via staff meetings.

- Allowing staff input and negotiation on how to improve the working environment so that it best serves the school community's needs; that is, staff and students' needs.
- Deciding what needs to be modified, 'fine-tuned' or changed in order to reduce occupational, environmental and organisational stress. This will also include, for example, arranging staff levels and ratios in terms of matching teachers and classes so that first-year teachers do not routinely get the harder-to-manage classes.
- Determining what is realistically achievable in both the short and the longer term (and learning to live with that!).
- Developing an action plan and time-schedule, with key personnel, to achieve those aims of reducing and more effectively managing acknowledged stress.
- Reviewing and evaluating the plan.

By reducing the impact of natural and normative workplace stress, schools act preventatively as well as supportively. When unaudited and unaddressed stressors are coupled with poor communication and unclear rationale for change there is an increase in staff anxiety and uncertainty. 'Stress auditing', coupled with conscious colleague support, can increase the psychological and situational safety margins relative to stress.

Levels of consciousness and the process of change

Schools, clearly, are at different levels of 'consciousness' about how and whether colleague support is meeting the needs of staff: their transitional coping needs, needs for shared planning, professional feedback and for assured back-up in situations and circumstances where colleagues are 'struggling' with teaching and discipline in their classes.

Because schools are at different levels of school-wide consciousness regarding colleague support, the degree of needs analysis and review will vary considerably.[11] An axiomatic finding in this research is that colleague support is, fundamentally, about being *consciously* aware of colleague needs, and inviting, encouraging and developing opportunities, forums and 'structures' and 'forms' to meet those needs wherever possible.

Those schools that are less consciously supportive will need a more extensive needs-analysis as their 'structure' and 'forms' of support may be limited, unhelpful or not focused on or meeting colleague needs. In such schools, awareness-raising about the benefits of focused colleague support, as well as addressing appropriate 'forms' and 'structures', will also be helpful.

Such schools, when aware of the need to address colleague support more widely than its transitional or ad-hoc expressions, can often benefit from outside-of-school consultancy support. Often the 'outsider' can bring fresh insights and perspectives. Any outside consultancy will need to be ongoing, be able to 'enter into' and have some genuine 'shared awareness' about the school's particular situation, social context and cultural norms.

Those schools that have developed a more conscious awareness of what they are doing – or not doing – regarding colleague support will also need to pursue needs identification or, at least, evaluate their current provision. The 'less consciously' supportive schools often require substantial needs analysis to address the needs-provision gap (see Figure 7.1).

Those 'more consciously supportive' schools will often be evaluating their current expressions and provision of colleague support. Some schools may only need to fine-tune or adapt current structures or policies – even revise them. Other schools will need to engage in substantial change.

Colleague support and school-wide review

In pursuing some adaptive facility, from the 'typology of consciousness of support', schools will benefit from some school-wide review:

- Where is the school now in terms of its 'consciousness' of colleague support?
- How *acknowledged* are the individual and collective needs of colleagues?
- What changes need to be made to address, and seek to meet, staff colleague-support needs?
- What changes to current 'forms', 'structures' or processes, or plans will we need to make? (See Appendix 3.)

While the review process will vary in degree, the fundamental process is noted in Figure 7.1 and developed in Figure 7.2.

Preparing for changes in school-wide colleague support (see Figure 7.2)

1 Acknowledge the need for colleague support

Preparing for any change towards a more 'consciously supportive culture' means acknowledging and affirming the basic and common need for colleague support in the school community. Some needs will be based in structural dependency (for

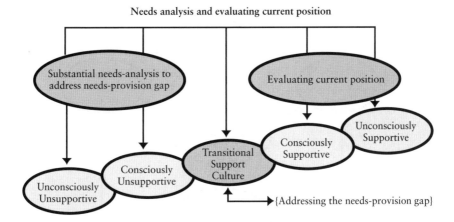

Figure 7.1   *Needs-analysis 'continuum' and consciousness of support*

example, discipline plans and playground management plans) and some will be based in fundamental professional interdependency as in purposeful teaming. Indeed *any* 'structural forms' of support find their accepted utility, at best, when the shared values and practices of 'mutual respect' and 'mutual regard' enables such interdependency.[12]

As noted earlier, no pursuing of change in school culture or practice is 'value free'. At some stage in the change process it will be important to address the fundamental values that underpin the very concept of colleague support. The 'protocols of colleague support' (noted in Chapter 4) can be a useful reference point for exploring how shared values practically underpin a school community.[13]

It is my experience that schools which are 'consciously unsupportive' may benefit, early in the change process, from more visibly 'structural' aspects of support. As staff believe their immediate needs are met they are more likely to entertain and pursue a more holistic whole-school approach to the issue of colleague support and welfare.

Effectively, staff have to see a common purpose for any proposed changes when they address, support and see what the underlying values and aims are for those changes. In identifying areas for change, schools will obviously be selective in terms of priorities for change. Often schools will employ a deliberate awareness-raising process to engage such 'prioritising'. Such awareness-raising often runs concurrently with, say, a specific needs-analysis and review. In practice this involves consciously building into the organisational and relational culture of a school opportunity the means for staff to rethink their common purpose, their operational methods and evaluating how they work to support their primary mission.

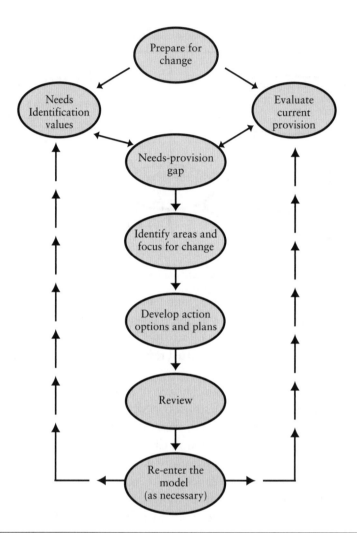

Figure 7.2   *Needs-analysis process*

Change often sees natural anxiety in those affected by change, as well as those who are changed by the implementation at the local level. Such anxiety is more acute when the change is 'imposed' from without and where such 'imposition' (or perceived imposition) does not comfortably fit with teachers' perception of purposeful, pedagogical or organisational change.

The degree of 'consciousness of colleague support' is also related to how aware the members of a school community are about its culture. Fullan (1993) suggests that an understanding of one's school culture needs to extend to an understanding of what it values. There is a moral purpose in change that extends beyond the utility of change or even the imperative of change. In fact, if the imperative of change is not consistent with the moral purpose of change, the change as such is not likely to be effectively 'embedded',[14] or genuinely affect what a school does. With reference to espoused values of collaboration and generic collegiality, the change process will need to both express and extend what the school values about colleague support. In this way, the 'gap' between espoused and 'ideal' and 'real' can be addressed.

While there can be no formulaic or guaranteed model of support, I note time and again that when schools *consciously* address what they value and affirm about colleague support, and then seek to consciously address support needs, then staff consciously act more supportively of one another.

2 Identifying needs/evaluating needs-provision

In light of a grounded theory of 'consciousness of support' (see p. 165f.), as it is matched to the common needs of staff, review questions will need to address:

- How *consciously* supportive is the school in terms of colleague support 'provision' beyond 'transitional' and 'dyadic' support?
- How open, and effective, and responsive is our communication and decision-making?
- How effectively do we work in teams (as distinct from transitional teaming)?[15]
- How are struggling teachers assisted? (Does the school promote 'collective and shared regard' or covertly value 'competitive self-interest'?) I have noticed in those 'consciously unsupportive' schools in which I've worked that the covert message of some of its senior staff is, 'If you've got problems in your classes it must be your fault, and don't pass *your* problems on to the admin.'
- How strong is the consciousness of 'mutual regard' and in what ways it is expressed?[16]

The more consciously supportive schools will – in their journey of change – address needs-provision in some way, but all schools can benefit from an evaluation of needs-provision. In identifying or evaluating needs, senior staff can use a range of approaches and 'entry-points' from surveys and one-to-one interviewing, and small-group dialogue and feedback to prioritising issues of common concern.

3 Appraise the needs-provision gap

In this staff are to define the 'gaps', as it were, between identified needs and existing provision. The nature, extent and scope of the 'gap' between the range of needs and meeting them is rarely easy. Old memories, even 'old scores' (and 'promises not kept') can hinder how genuinely staff believe any commitment to change will be; again an outside consultancy can sometimes help to 'keep the process honest'.[17]

4 Deciding the focus for change

This is where the school takes on the features of transitional culture from a 'less' to 'more' conscious school-wide belief in, and practice of, colleague support (see p. 154f.).

Senior staff will need to have:

- explained the purpose for any changes to organisation, structure and policy; the fundamental assumption being that people *and* environments can change where there is a conscious and school-wide emphasis on 'mutual responsiveness' and mutual regard for our 'common lot'. The clarity for, the workability derived from, and the utility of any new 'structures' (or revised structures or 'forms' of support) will increase motivation for change
- secured staff commitment; a task made easier when staff believe the commitment of senior staff to the identification of needs and willingness to seek to address such needs is genuine
- acknowledged that some needs will be more generic and some more specific. Generic needs can be expressed as: 'belonging', 'self-esteem', 'affirmation', 'acceptance', non-judgmental' feedback and 'mutual respect' (see pp. 74–6)
- a clear understanding that in schools which are 'more consciously supportive', an honest appraisal of the school's current position regarding colleague support is an important step in any necessary change. From this, staff can set realistic 'targets' and 'processes' for 'structures' that can further enable realistic colleague support.[18]

5 Develop action options and plans

By stating options and developing specific plans and 'structures' a school gains direction and motivates task-engagement and workable change. It is important to recognise that there will be aspects of (one's) role, task or situation over which individuals and groups have clear and direct control, some negotiated control and at times no direct control. A good deal of government policy, with respect to Education, is mandated; schools (as civil-servant bodies) have to carry the government mandates. In this sense the school, and its staff, have no direct control over the *initial* mandate for curriculum standards frameworks, testing procedures or professional accountability.

In collegially supportive schools, however, senior staff (with their colleagues) work with the external demands, or requirements, for change to see how and where they can control, rework and manage the external mandate to reduce unnecessary negativism and stress, and enhance school-based empowerment of its mission – consistent with the imperatives and responsibilities in the mandates.

6 Undertake an ongoing review

Any plan or policy needs *ongoing* review, addressing:

- the extent to which staff believe their needs are being met[19]
- how effectively the 'needs-provision gap' has been narrowed
- the viability and utility of current 'structures' and 'forms' of support. Are they adequate and realistic? If not, how and what do we need to adapt or fine-tune such 'structures'?

In a school's ongoing journey, as it reappraises how colleague support is addressing staff needs, the model, noted in Figure 7.2[20] can be re-entered at any stage in a school's review journey. The primary focus will always be: 'how is our current provision, in stated belief and practice, meeting espoused colleague needs, and enabling our core mission and professional responsibilities?'

Endnotes

1 A point acknowledged in the *Elton Report* on school discipline (1989):
'The way in which a school is run can be changed. We know this is not easy. Changing the nature of an institution can be a long, complicated and uncomfortable process. We recognise that the difficulties involved in breaking into the vicious circle of ineffective performance and low morale can be very great, and that some schools may need a great deal of help in achieving this breakthrough. We are convinced however from what we have seen in schools, from research evidence, and from experiences described to us in other countries that successful change can be achieved. The first or important requirement is a positive commitment to change by the head teacher and other senior staff. The second is for them to carry as many of the rest of the staff as possible with them and to be open to their suggestions' (p. 90).

2 All the teachers I discussed this issue with valued highly the 'ad-hoc' and 'transitional' expressions of colleague support. They saw such support as meeting needs related to 'dependability', 'assurance' (of being there), 'back-up' and 'social affiliation'.

3 So many colleagues gave a qualifying caveat to their interview responses, such as 'without blame', 'not feeling a dill or stupid', 'I don't feel like it's my fault when I share concerns ...', 'I'm not the only one' (see Chapter 4, p. 95f.).

4 This fundamental acknowledgement resonates with the protocols noted earlier: 'the certainty of uncertainty' and the 'acceptance of fallibility'.

5 Mortimer (1989) notes that the world is roughly divided between 'nurses' and 'patients'. It can be tiring for those who always seem to be playing the role of 'nurse'.

6 This has been acknowledged widely in the literature (see Chapter 2, p. 25f).

7 Although if one walks past a class 'out-of-control', for example, it should not take too much 'nous' to sense the need for some immediate support, as one, transitionally, sees the 'pain' in a colleague's eyes through the thin glass separating you and them!

8 Fullan and Hargreaves (1991) point out that 'many staff initiatives take the form of something that is done to teachers [sic], rather than with them, still less by them' (p. 17).

9 It is worth pointing out that the term 'manager' is increasingly (and annoyingly) being used in secondary schools.

10 Schools can now develop similar 'stress-auditing' by utilising the 'Occupational Health and Safety Systems in Schools' available from the state Department of Education. However, if such 'auditing' reveals significant physical–structural stressors in the school workplace, then funding and resourcing also needs to be a significant part of an ongoing addressing of morale and support (especially in summer, in a portable classroom without air-conditioning and 30 or more students facing West!). The importance of an attractive and stimulating environment within the 'teaching and learning workplace' is noted by a number of commentators to be an important factor in stress-minimisation and staff morale. See Breheney et al. (1996) and Rogers (1996).

11 See notably Axworthy et al. (1989). A healthy organisation responds neither passively nor rebelliously to demands from outside. Because it equates growth with a collaborative style, it is likely to measure goals from a flexible stance, but with a keen eye for that which is good from the past; not mere change for change's sake as a new form of pedantry. Collaboration is a means of adaptation; in this it has *in place* problem-solving mechanisms enabling it to critically face new pressures and demands.

12 'Structures' or 'forms' of support need to be reviewed by asking, 'What do they do?' 'What and whom do they serve?' 'In what context?' The 'how' of structures will also indicate whether staff feel that a given 'structure' is meeting needs in any meaningful way at all.

13 In exploring shared values, colleagues will need to address the core values that give a sense of community and professional identity, as well as those values that are more 'peripheral' to their vision. Further, they will need to ask how such values (if at all) are authentically reflected in the school's current policies and practices.

14 See Fullan (1993, p. 72) and Fullan and Hargreaves (1991). Dobson and Swift (1994) note: 'for better or worse culture is a powerful force ... trying to shape it, change it, or fight it can have serious repercussions ...'. They go on to suggest that principals (when addressing changes in culture) 'begin by asking, "What is the culture of the school; its values, traditions, assumptions, beliefs and ways?"' (p. 12).

15 One of the key findings of the research I undertook in this area was that the more 'consciously supportive' the school, the more purposeful was the concept and practice of teams and teaming.

16 A more comprehensive set of questions, as well as a question framework, is set out in Appendix 3 for schools to adapt in a school-wide needs-analysis or review.

17 As one colleague put it to me recently, 'For some here [in this school] the memories are deep and long' [with respect to the amalgamation of the formerly technical schools into the post-primary secondary organisation and culture].

18 Always remembering that colleague support, as such, cannot actually be mandated or simply instituted by *fiat*. The very notion of support depends on prior concepts of 'mutual regard' and 'interdependence'.

19 This includes student needs. I noted many times in discussion with teachers how they often linked their provision of colleague support with meeting of student needs as well as staff needs.

20 I am indebted to my colleague John Swift for the practical simplicity of the developmental model (Figure 7.2) that I have adapted here.

CHAPTER **8**

CONCLUSION

'Colleague support? It's life. It's being able to share the good and the bad alike ...'
(Primary teacher) (in Rogers, 1999)

A parable from nature: As each bird flaps its wings – by flying in a V-formation – the whole flock adds over 70% flying range than if each bird flew alone. Lesson? People who share a common direction and sense of community can get where they are going quicker and easier because they are travelling on the thrust of one another.
A lesson from 'The Geese' – in Issue 27 of Boos, M. W. Agricultural Notes (ECLA)
Omaha Province Newsletter.

Colleague support can be described and attenuated in many ways. In seeking to hear the voice of my colleagues and convey their understandings, and meanings more widely, I am aware of the complex nature of collegiality and colleague support. I am further aware of the temptation to simplification. As the maxim goes: 'For every complex problem there is a simple solution – and that solution is wrong'.

It does seem clear from all the participants I surveyed, interviewed and had long discussions with, and from the ongoing observation in many schools, that colleague support is, perhaps, underrated in the literature as an integrating feature in a school culture. The individual, and the school community, significantly benefit from conscious colleague support. My colleagues affirm that the kind of support they receive can meet their moral and professional needs and their transitional and long-term coping.

In terms of the emerging typology of colleague support (see Chapter 3), colleagues confirm, and affirm, that colleague support – when consciously valued in precept and practice across the school – makes a difference to their planning, coping and teaching;

the management of student behaviour and 'their overall stress level'. This is consistent with the literature on the buffering effects of social support in relationship to stress, the literature on change processes in schools and the literature on management and discipline in schools (Rogers, 1996, 1997, 1999, 2000).

Where schools consciously utilise 'structures' and 'processes' to enhance support they are also conscious of certain 'protocols' that typify the expression of that support – so that what emerges is 'an ecology', or culture, built around shared ways of believing, valuing, affirming and 'doing' colleague support.

In observing the schools in this study, particularly in their management of change, their capacity to both come to terms with and manage the demands and stresses brought about by change is clearly related to the nature, viability and utility of support existing in a given school.

Such support cannot be 'forced', or merely mandated, though it substantially benefits from thoughtful 'structure' and 'form'. That 'form' can occur widely from ad-hoc teaming to shared planning and purposeful teams, through to supportive mentoring and appraisal; from consideration of physical environment through to whole-school policy. No single focus stands alone. The 'protocols of support' affirm that whether the support is moral, professional or 'structural' in expression, at its heart it is the acknowledgement of our shared humanity that is significant. It is within that frame of understanding that essential meaning is conveyed and fundamental needs can be met.

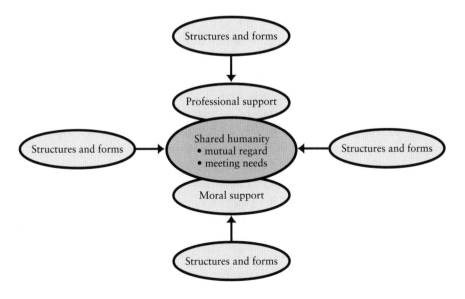

Figure 8. 1 *Colleague support: Between the dimensions*

Two metaphors,[1] one message

At the end of the day the overriding dimension of colleague support that stays with me is that of 'moral support' – the 'human element' so frequently cited by my colleagues.

When colleagues expressed value in the differing dimensions of support they almost always spoke about 'how' such support was given as well as why. The essential message coming through was that such support affirms and meets needs – a continuum of needs from emotional support and transitional assurance to professional feedback.

'Black dot – white square'

Earlier, in Chapter 4 (p. 78), I noted that one of my senior colleagues reminded me in an interview that we had discussed the metaphor of 'black dot'–'white square' at a recent staff workshop. With his colleagues this metaphor seemed to represent a central message about colleague support. The 'black dot' represented the normal and daily stresses and strains of teaching; the 'white square' represented the safety-margin of colleague support.

The 'black dot' (the day-to-day grind) can appear to be more significantly stressful than the large-surrounding 'white space', so that the dot is all we see, all we focus on (or over-focus on). We hypothesised that this metaphor could well represent the 'unconsciously unsupportive school', where staff mostly see only the 'black dot' to the exclusion of the 'white space'.

When an individual or a group is facing difficulties or stressors it sometimes appears – expressed as a metaphor – as a 'black dot' on a 'white square'. The individual or group perception, and psychological energy, over-focuses on the 'black dot' to the exclusion of the 'white page' as it were. The 'black dot' represents the difficult, stressful, painful features, circumstances or relationships we often face as teachers. The 'white page' represents the positive, good, enjoyable, worthwhile aspects of our school here, and the positive, worthwhile things we do.

I have shared this metaphor widely and have heard colleagues say, 'Yes, but sometimes the "black dot" is too big!' I have had other colleagues thoughtfully add, 'Well, how can we make the "white square" bigger?' This is not mere badinage; the 'white square' is not fixed. Colleague support is a critical factor in the viability, the extent and the utility of the 'white square' happenings, whether it be the listening ear; the few minutes of advice or counsel,[2] the shared laughter, the problem-solving, the back-up of a team, the assurance a colleague gives 'that you are on the right track' or, as one colleague added, '… the few drinks and off-loading in our faculty area on Fridays!'

Teachers in this study also made a number of references to the effect that school and teaching was an important 'part' of their life – but not 'their whole life'. Supportive administration in schools consciously emphasises the importance of 'balance' so that staff are less stressed '*from* work', '*about* work' or '*because* of work'. A positive *life* outside of teaching gives a healthy 'white square' within which to creatively manage the 'thousand natural shocks that flesh is heir to …' (*Hamlet*, Act 3 Scene 1: 52).

The 'white square' in this metaphor is the needed balance between the negative and unpleasant aspects of teaching experience and those that are positive, rewarding and affirming. The 'white square' can give the needed perspective. I have noticed that 'stuck schools' (Stoll, 1998) and schools who perceive themselves as 'under threat' often have a 'black dot consciousness'. The 'dot' is over-emphasised, over-focused on, and the school culture moves into those self-defeating explanations for their condition and 'status': 'It will always be like this, things will never change'. Blame, then, becomes an easy, perhaps, natural coping strategy: 'It's the fault of these kids', 'the government',' the Department of Education', 'the parents', 'the curriculum', 'the area we teach in …'

This is particularly important in times of imposed change where leaders can enable and support a sense of collegial *sangfroid* – in the sense of colleague 'composure', 'calmness and resilience' when living with inevitable 'uncertainty'. It is interesting to note the difference in a school's 'cultural composure' and 'coping ability' where the school-wide response to change is often reactive, stressful, disparate, and with no commitment to that interdependency that can engage and enable the change process.[3]

A 'consciously supportive' school, with colleagues who endorse and affirm the 'protocols of support' within a school culture, and provide 'forms' and 'structures' to enable colleagues to give one another support, are both giving and strengthening the 'white space' that meets the fundamental needs of colleagues in their workplace; particularly on those 'bad days'.

Same table – share the spoons

Tim Costello, in a social comment on the nature of mutual regard, civic respect and social justice, resurrects an old fable that, for me, is metaphorical with regard to colleague support:

'There is a fable that when God was asked to tell what Hell was like the answer came back that it is a huge table with a large and delicious-smelling bowl of soup in the middle, but the spoons that are set on the table have such very long handles that no guest can spoon any of the soup into their mouth. Asked what heaven was like, the answer was that it is the same room with the same soup and long spoons, but it is where the people have learned to use the spoons to feed each other' (*The Age*, 18 October, 1998, p. 25).[4]

Supportive teachers in supportive schools share the same table, the same food and 'the same spoons'.

At the end of every program and protocol, at the end of every 'structure' and policy within a school, is a group of colleagues working with the vagaries of time, pressure, stress and their workload. They do this by supporting and sharing the common load, the common task and their common mission.

If this study can assist teachers' welfare by increasing productive colleague support to address stress, coping and professionalism, it will be time well spent. It is to that end that this book is offered.

End notes

1   Metaphors are fundamentally about transference – a carrying across – from one arena to another. Aristotle in the *Poetics* affirms that, 'the greatest thing by far (in communication) is to have a command of metaphor … to employ metaphors happily and effectively it [is] necessary to have an eye for resemblances'. As Partridge (1980) notes, 'we all live and speak only through our eye for resemblances. Without it we should perish early … As individuals we gain our command of metaphor just as we learn whatever else makes us distinctly human' (p. 184).

2   'Your needful counsel which craves the instant use …' Shakespeare, *King Lear*.

3   This seems to resonate with what Jarvis (1975) says:

'Evidence from many sciences shows that penalties are suffered by people who habitually allow themselves to be dominated by destructive emotions such as anger, hatred, depression, helplessness, jealousy, cynicism, despair and fear. By contrast creative feelings like love, faith, joy, peace, compassion and delight, bring countless benefits. I think we can best summarise these principles by considering the kinds of debits which are likely to increase when disruptive emotions become typical of us. By contrast an opposite credit comes to those who cultivate creative emotional habits' (p. 90).

4   Costello uses this 'fable' to remind his readers of the consequences of 'unfettered rugged individualism' and the more traditionally Australian cultural 'creed' of 'a fair go and mateship'. Quoting Adam Smith (the eighteenth-century Scottish moral philosopher and political economist) he suggests that moral empathy to one another implies 'a sense of connectedness to one another'.

APPENDIX 1

The purpose of educational research

The purpose of educational research – in the qualitative methodology used in this study – was to carefully describe and attempt to share a substantial longitudinal teacher narrative about colleague support so that interested readers could:

- share in other teachers' accounts of their own thinking and experience of colleague support. This sharing of itself can, at the very least, serve to clarify another's thinking or understanding
- elaborate existing concepts of colleague support as developed in the educational literature and in the research (Rogers, 1999)
- challenge existing concepts of colleague support as highlighted by teachers concerning the nature, strengths, limitations and practice about colleague support within their schools. This challenge can also extend particular views and understandings beyond their current, published, usage
- explore new meanings and engender new concepts about colleague support
- generalise beyond the setting and research gathered in this study to a 'grounded understanding' about colleague support. The search for generalisations is not the delivering of outcomes with absolute certainty; it is a valid description of the reality researched (rather an exhaustive description). As Warwick (1973) notes:

  '... every method of data collection is only an approximation to knowledge. Each provides a different, and usually valid glimpse of reality and all are limited when used alone' (p. 190).

- encourage change behaviour of individuals and groups indirectly through the description of reality in a given area. Highlighting needs, issues or concerns that are problematic and to explore possibilities for change – in action research terms.

From these research emphases one can make reasonable generalisations about complex reality: the resonance of a repetitive voice across a number of school settings in this study; the comparing of those 'teacher voices' within and across those settings; and the utilising of shared methodologies – qualitative and quantitative – to give a productive basis for grounded theory.

It is important, too, to remember that the 'consumer', to use Harter's term (1989), has the responsibility to generalise beyond the research offered. Assuming the researcher has researched within the professional constructs of any research paradigm, and with ethical probity and rigour, it is the consumer of the research, not only the author, who does the generalising. It is up to the 'consumer' of the research to decide what aspects of the case apply in a new context (Peshkin, 1993 p. 26).

What I have sought to do in Chapter 7 is make some firm generalisations (from my own thinking and experience about colleague support) and suggestions for adaptive facility more widely beyond this research study. It is also my hope that there will continue to be developmental outcome possibilities that schools will find beneficial from a review of colleague support in their school.

APPENDIX 2

Behaviour management: A whole-school framework[1]

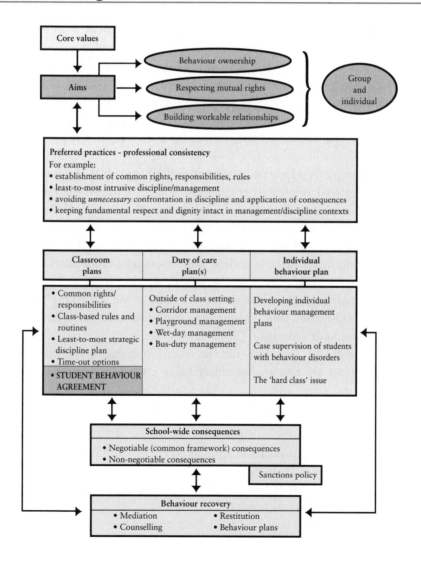

The concept of preferred practices within a whole-school approach to behaviour-management

The concept of 'preferred practices' relates to a school-wide consciousness about the way we, as teachers, characteristically manage student behaviour on a day-to-day basis.

The term *preferred* is deliberate; there are some behaviour management practices we prefer (when it comes to management and discipline) because of certain core values we hold. These *core* values, such as mutual regard, mutual respect and dignity of the individual, give a focus and direction to our management and discipline practice.

In relating our preferred practices back to our core values we also give *meaning* and purpose to why we discipline in the way we do (our *characteristic* practices). Discipline practice becomes purpose-driven, not merely task-driven.

The following preferred practices are outlined for staff discussion. It is also worth noting that each practice implies a conception and utility of teachers' skills. For example, the preferred practice (3) (p. 187) *The Language of Discipline....* and *least to most intrusive* management implies a teacher's wide repertoire of positive corrective language.

A basic example is where two students are talking while the teacher is talking during instructional time. Rather than say, 'Lucas, Mark, *stop* talking.' Or 'Lucas, are you talking?' (Interrogative questions, such as 'Why are you?' 'Are you?' are the least helpful questions to ask in a discipline context.) The teacher could better say, 'Lucas, Mark, you're talking ...' (this *briefly* describes what they are doing that is disruptive). This 'description of reality' is often enough. Sometimes we might need to add a brief *behavioural* direction: 'Facing this way and listening now. Thank you.' This is one small example of many that could be given. Of course the *mere* words are hardly enough; one's tone, manner and expectation all carry conviction, confidence, expectation or indecision (Rogers, 2000).

Preferred practice (2), (p. 187) implies a skill in managing *potential* conflict in a way that does not see the teacher engaging in emotional brow-beating, sarcasm, 'cheap-shots' and other unnecessary, 'un-adult' behaviour. Even when we need to communicate appropriate anger we can do so by:

- assertion rather than verbal aggression
- communicating our frustration, even anger, briefly (on issues that really matter, not trifling issues)
- focusing on the behaviour or issue rather than attacking the student
- de-escalating the natural tension
- allowing appropriate cool-off time (even 'time-out')

- engaging in repairing and rebuilding at a later stage.

The *skills* of positive correction can be learned and the skills of thoughtful follow-up with applied consequences can be learned. *Preferred* practice can imply commitment to skilled discipline and management practice.

Central aim

Within a whole-school plan for behaviour management: teachers will agree on common behaviour management and discipline practices at the classroom level and 'duty-of-care' level, and take *active* but supported responsibility for management and discipline.

Preferred practices

1   Each teacher will establish and clarify classroom rules and consequences, based on a year-level framework and known 3R s (rights, responsibilities and rules). These will be developed with the students in the 'establishment phase' of the year.

   The school-wide 3Rs will be the *basis* for corrective, consequential and supportive management/discipline, and those 3Rs will be expressed in the *student code of behaviour*, or in a *student behaviour agreement.* The aims of all discipline and management are to enable the student(s) to own their behaviour, to respect mutual rights and to do so within the context of workable relationships. The teacher will consciously discipline within these aims in order that the core business of the classroom (teaching and learning) can take place.

2   Minimise unnecessary confrontation in management and discipline; (ie, undue and unfair criticism, sarcasm, ridicule, embarrassment and public shaming).

3   When developing and utilising corrective discipline:
   a   plan the 'Language of Discipline' (think about words and meaning with respect to typical discipline language)
   b   balance 'Language of Discipline' with 'Language of Encouragement'
   c   use a 'least-to-most intrusive' intervention approach when managing and disciplining individuals and groups.

4   In addressing disruptive behaviour, keep the focus on the 'primary behaviour' or 'primary issue' and avoid arguing, debating with or over-servicing 'secondary behaviours' or side issues wherever possible.

   Where possible take the student aside from his or her peers in a heated conflict situation and allow 'cool-off' time. Some consequences will need to be deferred until after 'cool-off' time.

5   When developing and applying *behaviour consequences*, avoid using unrelated consequences. Establish a year-level approach to the use of consequences for common
rule-breaking behaviours; emphasise reparation, restitution and reconciliation as
the norm. Also, emphasise student behaviour as a 'choice'. Distinguish between
'negotiable' and 'non-negotiable' consequences. When applying consequences
emphasise the *certainty* of the consequences, rather than the mere severity of the
consequences; remember to keep the fundamental respect intact when *applying* the
consequence.

When establishing behaviour consequences, try to gain a relatedness
between the disruptive behaviour and the outcome; where appropriate, ask such
students what they think they should do to fix up 'x', 'y' ... At the school-wide
level employ *degrees of seriousness* with respect to consequences; especially deten-
tion practices.

6   Separate the behaviour from the student, emphasise respect as an 'action
towards others'.

7   Actively *promote* positive behaviours through verbal, relational and symbolic
encouragement. Consider the range of possible 'incentives' and public recognition programs.

8   'Exit' and 'time-out' procedures: establish year-level and school-wide due
processes for exit, time-out (cool-off time) and follow-up of a student whose disruptive behaviour has necessitated 'exit' from the classroom (ie, for safety,
persistent refusal to work within the fair rules and within reasonable teacher
direction or verbal abuse). Plan fundamentals such as: How? To whom? How
long should they stay in time-out? What happens when students refuse to leave
the classroom for time-out? Where do they go for time-out? What happens
during time-out? On what basis do they renegotiate entry back to the classroom?

Class/subject teachers are responsible for follow-up of time-out procedures *with*
support of senior peers. Emphasise the importance of re-establishing working relationships and reconciliation – avoid holding grudges, tempting as that may be!
Where the relational issues are serious, utilise supporting mediation from other
colleagues for resolution processes.

Clarify *roles* in the discipline/pastoral sense (that is, of class/subject teacher
through to head teacher). Establish clear communication processes for follow-
through of discipline incidents. It is important that the grade or subject teacher be
directly involved in the follow-up and follow-through of disruptive behaviour.

Where possible involve parents (case-by-case), through diaries, phone calls,
parent/teacher conference – let them know positive outcomes, too!

Emphasise collegial, responsibility of duty-of-care management: 'relaxed vigilance' in out-of-class contexts (eg, corridors, 'wet-day', playground or bus-supervision).

Most of all, build and utilise a supportive colleague culture for problem-solving and structural support. Colleague support is essential in the management of difficult students and students with emotional and behavioural disorders. The 'hard-class syndrome' and playground supervision are also crucial areas that benefit from focused and ongoing colleague support.

These preferred practices, and shared expectations, need to be expressed in a common policy within a common classroom discipline framework at the classroom level and at a common 'duty-of-care' level. Due processes for consequences, counselling and 'contracting' for long-term behaviour change with students who have ongoing disruptive patterns of behaviour need to be established as normative and whole-school in practice.

End note

1   Adapted from *Behaviour Management: A Whole-School Approach*. Scholastic © Dr William A. Rogers (1995, second edition 2006).

APPENDIX 3

A survey framework for colleague support

The overriding purpose of a periodic needs-analysis is to ascertain what colleagues currently understand and value about colleague support, including 'formal' and 'structural' expressions of support. The most fundamental questions could concentrate on the well-known 'three w's':

- What is working well with regard to colleague support in a our school? *And why?*
- What is not working so well *and why?*
- What can we do to improve (enable and encourage) colleague support (fine-tune, adapt, modify or change)? *And how?*

Some suggested questions that could frame a survey or questionnaire used in a need-awareness/needs-analysis process:

1 *What do our staff mean by colleague support generally, and what is its relevance at our school?* What factors do they rate as defining a collegially supportive school? What do colleagues note as the major benefit of colleague support, generally? In past teaching experience? In their current school?

2 *How does colleague support normally (characteristically) operate in our school?* Do our current expressions, even our practices, of support help to build a more humane and collegially supportive school culture? Do they help colleagues cope with the daily demands of teaching, discipline, management etc.?

3 *What 'structures', or more 'formal processes', do we specifically target as being linked to colleague support?* Another way of framing this question is to list those 'structures', or programs or policies, that staff believe are collegially supportive and ask staff to rate them.

    In what ways do colleagues provide their peers with a sense of professional 'safety' and 'security', particularly in discipline situations? What are our policies and 'structures' *serving* with regard to colleague support? For example, if we have a structure/policy like 'time-out', do colleagues feel they are 'ineffective', 'weak' or 'failing' if they call on a colleague to 'escort' a disruptive student from the classroom for a period of 'cool-off time'?

4 *How does collegiality and* teamwork *operate in this school?* Do our staff plan and problem-solve purposefully in teams? What role do 'teams' provide in ongoing professional support (such as professional discussion and professional feedback and planning)?

5 *What are the* expressed needs *colleagues note that specifically relate to colleague support (that is, professional sharing, discipline concerns, supportive feedback), and in what way do our current practices and 'structures' seek to meet those needs?* What areas require reassessment? How are the needs of struggling teachers met?

6 *What is the current relationship between colleague support and professional development?* In what ways are skills, abilities, contributions and worth generally acknowledged in the school? How is *professional feedback* normally given (if at all)?

7 *How are casual relief teachers supported in our school?* How could such support be improved?

8 *How do we specifically support teachers new to the school? And first-year teachers?* Through planned and ongoing induction? A peer-support group?

9 *It can help to ask staff what kinds of realistic support they ought to – normally – expect from*:
  • Teaching colleagues, particularly in grade, faculty, teams
  • Year-level or team leader, head of department, grade leader
  • Deputy and principal
  • Structural expressions and forms of support? Professional support.

10 *Ask staff for open suggestions on how we could develop or improve the 'culture of support' in 'our school'.*

APPENDIX 4

TEACHER BELIEFS, COGNITION AND BEHAVIOUR MANAGEMENT

Individuals, and even groups, can sometimes fall foul of self-defeating mindsets in the face of difficult to manage situations. This is understandable; when one is faced daily with challenging students and students with emotional–behavioural disorders it is no wonder that we sometimes latch on to negative, even self-defeating, perceptions of reality.

I have sat with many, many, teachers (and groups of teachers) to discuss challenging student behaviours and very-difficult-to-manage group behaviours. In *some* schools I often hear teachers saying things like:–

- *'I'll* never *be able to manage that class ...'*
- *'They* never *listen ...' 'They're* always *lazy or ...'*
- 'No one *pays* any *attention to what I say ...'*
- 'No one *cares about me ...'*
- *'They're* all *animals in 8D!!'*
- *'Children* should *do what I say ...'* (*'without answering back ...' 'without sighing, pouting'* or *'eyes to the ceiling'* or *'whining, moaning, complaining and tut-tutting!')*
- *'I should be able to ... "manage them"; "control them"; "get through to them ..."'*
- *'It's* all *my fault ...'*
- *'I shouldn't get upset or angry about ...'*

While it is important to 'let off steam', and defuse natural and residual tensions in our profession, these perceptions and ways of explaining stressful reality can become self-defeating. If a teacher (or a group of teachers) easily, and *characteristically*, describe(s) their reality in 'demanding' and 'absolutist' terms it makes that reality more stressful; makes coping with that reality more difficult and often results in patterns of self-defeating behaviour. Such self-talk will also negatively affect the nature of the relationship between the teacher and individual students and the teacher and the group.

When engaged in regular peer-group discussions on student behaviour (p. 128f), or engaged in longer-term mentoring (p. 135f) the issue of teacher 'beliefs', 'perceptions' and self-talk will often need to be addressed alongside any changes in one's practice. If a teacher is *characteristically* engaged in 'demanding' belief statements about student behaviour: *'They* must *not answer back'* [– when they do ... at times], *'They* should *respect me!!'* [when their behaviour indicates that immediate respect is not always easily forthcoming ...] then such beliefs can be as stressful as the reality itself.

It is not enough to mentor a colleague for improved (or new) teaching and management skills – important as that is. Underlying self-talk, and perceptions, may need to be addressed to enable colleagues to be aware of how they *typically*, *characteristically*, explain stressful teaching experiences to themselves and to each other. In this regard my colleagues, and I, have found the R.E.T. (rational emotive therapy) model very helpful in challenging maladaptive thinking and reducing the distress that can arise from dysfunctional beliefs about our professional dynamic.

R.E.T. is based on the philosophical underpinning that we are not simply disturbed by events, circumstance, situations *alone – by themselves* as it were. The kind of, and the *degree* of, emotional arousal, disturbance and stress is also significantly affected by the beliefs and self-talk we bring to those events. When people believe that *activating events* (a student's behaviour, a difficult event, task, circumstance, a poor relationship ...) of *themselves* directly create their disturbing emotions they are often unaware that their beliefs (*characteristic* self-talk, underlying beliefs and attitudes) also significantly contribute to one's emotional state. (Bernard, 1990; Walen, Di Guiseppe and Wessler, 1980; Seligman, 1991). To more effectively manage one's stressful life [the R.E.T. model asserts] we need to be aware of, and challenge, our 'irrational beliefs' and learn to address, and dispute sabotaging self-talk to re-effect more 'rational', 'realistic', beliefs about one's role and relationships as a teacher-leader in classrooms.

Typical case examples – Teachers (A) and (B)

Some attentional student behaviours can be *tactically* ignored when it does not affect the overall learning or safety of students.

For example: A student (year 7) throws an eraser at another student (during the on-task phase of the lesson), the student on the receiving end 'drops the catch'. The 'bowler' calls out – loudly – *'You silly bitch!!'*

Teacher A says – *'Get over here Chantelle, get over here now!!'* Chantelle starts whining and whingeing ... *What did I do – nothing!!'* Her face is sulky; skewed eye contact, folded arms ... The teacher is getting very annoyed, *'Don't argue!! You know what you did just get over here – now!'*

Chantelle saunters over, eyes to the ceiling, sighing – full *dramatis personae*. She stands next to the teacher, rolls her eyes again, arms folded, legs akimbo … All these behaviours ('secondary' to the issue of the thrown eraser and the loud 'silly bitch' comment) are 'over-focused on' by the teacher who is (now) more annoyed by how the student stands, looks, and her tone, manner and body language …

(Teacher)	*'Don't you roll your eyes at me!! Look at me when Im talking to you …'*
(Student)	*'What'd I do? What's the big deal – hassling me!'*
(Teacher)	*'You know what you did! And don't you talk to me like that!'*
(Student)	*'Like what? Gees, get real!'*
(Teacher)	*'Don't you ever swear in my class.'*
(Student)	*'Swear!! What are you talking about? I didn't swear!'*
(Teacher)	*'You know what you said, when you shouted at Susanna …!'*
(Student)	*'She don't care if I say that, that's not swearing!'*
(Teacher)	*'It is in my class!'*
(Student)	*'Whatever!'* (here Chantelle rolls her eyes again, clicks her tongue). Her insouciant tone starts off another round of counter arguing by the teacher. Meanwhile the *primary* issue (the thrown eraser and the inappropriate language) are bypassed.

Of course this student's behaviour is frustrating; at times *very* frustrating. While the issue could have been dealt with more skilfully the teacher's 'frustration tolerance' and their resultant behaviour is also affected by their *typical beliefs* about student behaviour.

- *'Children must do what I say the first time …'* (Chantelle had 'argued' about coming across to the teacher when called …). A more preferential, realistic and reasonable belief would say 'While I don't like it when children don't immediately, or even quickly, do what I ask it doesn't mean I'm a poor (or bad) teacher. While it is unpleasant – annoying even – it's not awful and terrible!'
To insist on immediate obedience at all times is not sound psychology or pedagogy; nor is it likely to be effected. (Bernard and Joyce, 1985). One will *never* have total control of anyone (even themselves!).
- *'Children should not be rude to their teachers …'* They *are* sometimes; in some schools quite often – at least in the early relationship-building/establishment phase. *Over-focusing* on all aspects of a child's behaviour such as the rolling of eyes, clicking of the tongue, cavalier tone of voice, only increases stressful arousal and bypasses the core issue of discipline *at that point* (Rogers, 1998). Some aspects of the child's behaviour can be *tactically ignored* (particularly when an audience of

peers is watching). If necessary a *brief* 'I statement' about the rudeness is enough and then a *refocus* (by the teacher) to the 'primary' issue. Of course some rudeness is unacceptable and (at times) unpleasant but as *adults* we can more skilfully address this in our public discipline and our follow-up (one-to-one) with the student. (Rogers, 2000). Demanding that children '*should just not*(!)' be rude is, in itself, an unrealistic belief.

- '*Children should not answer back.*' Children *do* answer back; the skilful teacher learns to refocus to the main discipline issue at that point; sometimes by *tactical* ignoring, sometimes by 'blocking' the argumentative words and redirecting the student to the core rule, right or expectation at that point (Rogers, 1998).

- '*I can't stand it …*' ['when children are rude', 'annoying', 'disruptive', 'smart alecs', 'answer back' and 'show disrespect'…] Our feelings are *significantly affected by our thoughts* – particularly our characteristic, frequent, self-talk in times of stressful arousal. The problem behaviour *by itself* cannot merely make one so upset that they 'can't stand it'. This is not mere badinage; what we say to ourselves is part of our overall coping behaviour.

  I am not saying, here, that we merely shrug such stressful experiences off as if 'it doesn't matter' – it does. The frustration and (at times) even the pain of stress arising from our demanding professional life is real; it is significant. We have 'bad-days', and 'worse days'! However the *degree*, and *extent*, of our stress, and the resultant effect on our coping ability and relational life is also significantly affected by the personal cognitive domain.

- '*I must be able to control my class, and individuals at all times …*' Many factors of a child's behaviour are out of our direct control: home background, diet, TV, peer group socialisation, parenting styles, parent support, family dysfunction … (Howell, 1993; Rogers, 2000). Sometimes we will need to use cool-off time and time-out options for some students so they can regain some self-control. In some situations we will even need to call in a colleague to support such time-out options as when a very disturbing, (and disturbed child or children) are holding a class – effectively – 'to ransom' (Rogers 1997, 1998). When engaged in daily behaviour management it is not so much a matter of *controlling others* but using our adult leadership and relational power to help the students control themselves. This is where the real skills of behaviour management are evidenced (Rogers, 2000).

Teacher B

Going back to the example of the student (Chantelle) throwing the eraser (p. 193). Teacher B (in a similar situation) calls Chantelle over (away from her immediate 'Greek chorus' audience – no offence to classical Greeks you understand …).

'*Chantelle* (…) *Chantelle* (…)' [she tactically pauses to allow some 'registration of attention' across the room]. '*See you over here for a moment thanks.*' She drops her eye contact (across the room) and resumes her support for a few students she is working with (it is on-task learning time). This dropping of the eyes from the disruptive student signals 'expectation of compliance' and avoids a kind of psychological 'stand-off' that is easily effected when a teacher calls a student and *keeps staring* and toe-tapping *until* they come. Having given some 'take-up-time' (Rogers, 1998) the student still doesn't come. The teacher is not fazed, she *repeats* (redirecting a second time) the call to come across the room to where she is; she *tactically* ignores Chantelle's huffing, puffing, sighing and 'What'd I do? …' comments.

Chantelle saunters across to her (the teacher can see her in her peripheral vision but is still talking to the students she is working with at that point). As Chantelle stands near her teacher, sighing, rolling her eyes – adding an insouciant '*Yes?*' – the teacher excuses herself from her teaching group, beckons Chantelle aside, and quietly says '*I called you away from your group Chantelle because I saw you throw an eraser at Susanna and because you called her a silly bitch.*' In this she is briefly *describing* the incident, not immediately judging, or arguing with her, or asking her (fruitlessly) '*Why* …' she threw her eraser and … The teacher's tone is clear, quietly firm, even positive – she does not *sound*, or *look*, threatened by Chantelle's 'secondary behaviours' but she is still exercising effective discipline.

Chantelle says (with a throw-away line) '*She don't care if I say that – it's no big deal. Gees!*'

'*Maybe Susanna doesn't care, I don't know, I care* (…) *What's our class agreement about* considerate language?' The teacher does not get drawn into this avoidance 'secondary' behaviour; she keeps the focus calmly on the *primary* issue (the thrown eraser and the loud comment) by *partially* agreeing and refocusing with a *direct question* to the classroom agreement (re: the rights, rules and responsibilities for learning and behaviour).

Chantelle fully understands the teacher's question and sarcastically adds '*Sorreeee!*', with an *ex parte* eye roll and pout. Again the teacher *tactically* ignores most of Chantelle's behaviour adding, '*Chantelle I don't speak to you nastily I don't expect you to speak to me nastily.*' This brief, firm 'I statement' is enough [she will have a more extended 'chat' with Chantelle after class, later – away from her 'audience']. Chantelle sighs, mutters '*Whatever*' adding '*Can I go back to my seat now* … ?'

NB If Chantelle had refused to come across (in the first instance) the teacher would have used a *deferred* consequence (following-up later) eg '*If you choose not to come across now – Chantelle – I'll have to speak to you at recess*' (said in a non-threatening tone, leaving the consequences with the student …).

This discipline incident did not take long to address (far less than Teacher A). It takes longer to 'unpack' it in print. It is not 'merely' that Teacher B had more 'nous', more inter-personal skill, perhaps more active 'emotional intelligence' or more behaviour management skill.

Teacher A was making demands on annoying reality that reality does not easily, or always, (or even often!) acquiesce to. It is also more than 'bad-day-syndrome' – all teachers have bad days as it were. Teacher B interprets such incidents as annoying, even frustrating but not *'terrible!', 'awful!'* and *'can't stand it'*. She does not sabotage her self-talk with beliefs about herself, or students, couched in demands (*'I must!', 'they* must*!', 'they* shouldn't*!'* … *'I'm a* failure *if I can't … or don't …'*) When she catches herself 'mentally kicking herself', (Edwards, 1977), she reframes such self-talk and feels less stressed and generally more forgiving of herself and more able, and focused, on doing something constructive about 'failure' and normative, stressful, discipline issues.

I know, I've worked with both teachers.

A more unpleasant discipline example is that of swearing. In some schools it is not uncommon to hear students drop a range of expletives – most commonly in frustration, sometimes in abuse to teachers.

A teacher directs a student back to his seat during on-task learning time (he has been 'wandering', engaged in task avoidance and hassling others …). On receipt of the teacher's direction to 'resume his seat …' the student drops the f__ word (well above *sotto voce*). He walks off in a habituated sulk and flops down into his seat sulking, arms folded. Of course this student's behaviour is unacceptable, it is probably 'learned', even 'habituated' behaviour. Of course it is important to discipline the student now and, later, away from his peer audience.

How effectively such a situation is addressed depends in part on the teacher's skill in management and discipline and how supportive the school discipline policy is in relation to such incidents. The effectiveness of the teachers' discipline and their coping strategies (at this point) is also affected by their beliefs about swearing. I have had teachers (after such incidents) say things like *'Well they* shouldn't *swear!'* *'It's* terrible *when children swear!'*

Maybe they 'shouldn't' swear in an ideal world, in an environment where each student has a supportive family modelling; has high frustration tolerance; is secure in their self-esteem and doesn't need to 'pose' to seek social power in confronting ways …

When discussing swearing with some colleagues they are quite trenchant in their beliefs …

'But they shouldn't *swear …!'* After a supportive, shared whinge I often add, '… *but they* do *swear.' 'They* did *swear.' 'But they* shouldn't*!'* (is still the insistent reply).

'But they do ...' '*I don't like it* (reality) *but they do, sometimes, swear'*; this is reality.

A universal, trenchant, demand that they *'should not* swear' does not change reality, what it in fact does is to increase the stressful arousal (as the demand – *'shouldn't swear'* – is not met). Further, the demanding belief and self-talk affect the management dynamic in a self-defeating way: – *'How* dare *you swear!! Who the hell do you think you are! I* am a teacher; *I have been teaching for 197 years! Is that how you speak to your parents ...?'* (It may well be.)

It is not a simple cause and effect, eg: – swearing = high-stress outcome. Behaviour management skill coupled with a less insistent, absolutist, belief *about* swearing enables a more effective management of swearing incidents.

It does not mean we approve of swearing, or ignore it, it means we are *realistic* about its reality: *'I don't like it when young people swear. How can I address it in both short-term immediacy, longer-term student discussion, and even educational discussion about the nature – even probity – of language?'*

When developing skills with teachers – in any 'coaching' environment – it is not enough to merely describe, model, rehearse and seek to develop a *new skill repertoire.* It is also important to be aware of, and sensitive to, a colleague's beliefs and 'explanatory style' as they cope with the challenge (even the imperative) of change in behaviour.

Take a deceptively simple behaviour management skill like *tactical* ignoring: – if a teacher seeks to employ this skill say for some types of calling-out behaviours, or some aspects of 'secondary behaviours' (such as a student's sulky, 'pouty', body language) a teacher needs also to be aware of their own frustration tolerance when engaged in such 'ignoring'. *Tactical* ignoring needs to be balanced by selective attendance ie: when the student does put his hand up without calling out the teacher will attend to him. If a teacher seeks to *tactically* ignore *some* disruptive behaviours while at the same time saying things to themselves such as *'He* shouldn't *be calling out!'* '*Good teachers* shouldn't *get angry ...'* 'I should *be in control at all times,'* then the effectiveness of the *tactical* teacher behaviour will be often mis-cued by the students and, further, leave the teacher frustrated by a useful (but context-dependent) management skill.

If we could tune-in to a teacher's *characteristic* self-talk the variance between the more demanding, and absolutist self-talk, in contrast to preferential and reality–contingent self-talk we would also often see a correlation with patterns of stress (particularly frustration, upset and anger). That stress (even heightened negative arousal) then hampers effective professional behaviour (Bernard and Joyce, 1985; Rogers 1996, 2000).

DEVELOPING NEW SKILLS IN BEHAVIOUR MANAGEMENT AND DISCIPLINE

Learning my new skill, even fine-tuning old skills, takes time and some natural 'discomfort'. Some colleagues will interpret this discomfort as 'failure'.

Learning any new ways of communicating with students, developing any specific forms of discipline language (particularly assertive behaviours) doesn't always come easily for some teachers. It is important to support colleagues in their perceived 'failure' so they do not easily label their failure in self-defeating ways. *'It's* just *me'*, *'*I never *get it right'*, *'It* (my failure, my struggle) *will affect* everything I *do ...'* Natural feelings of failure are normal. It is important to *re-label* unpleasant feelings as annoying, even painful at times rather than to label them in 'stable', 'global' and 'universal' terms. Sometimes it is a lapse in judgement, sometimes plain 'bad-day syndrome' sometimes a mistake; an acknowledgment of our fallibility (and that of others) (p. 95). Relabelling one's failure assists in learning meaningfully from our failure (Rogers, 2000) *'Okay I did get it wrong; I should have done "x", "y", or "z" – I didn't ... what can I do next time in a similar situation?' 'What support do I need to move on from here?'* Redirecting one's cognitive and emotional energy is an important step in coping meaningfully with personal failure. Tuning in to one's negative self-talk is not easy, it is a *learned* behaviour. Negative self-talk is also learned behaviour even if the genesis, and context of such learning is 'lost to us'.

Failure in our professional (or personal) life is something that can cause us all to feel hurt, or 'momentary helplessness ... like a punch in the stomach ...' (Seligman, 1991, p. 45) – for some people that hurt can affect them significantly and for a long time.

Seligman (ibid.) describes 'learned helplessness' as deriving from an explanatory style that explains difficult and bad events within dimensions such as permanence, pervasiveness and personally focused: – *'It's* just *me;* all *my fault ...'*, *'*I never *get it right ...'*, *'I'll* never *be able to ...'*, *'It* (the failure, its context, its effects) *will* last for-ever ...', 'It ... *will affect* everything I *do ...'*

When working with colleagues who quickly, and easily, explain difficult and stressful events in this way, we need to supportively address the annoyance and even the pain of some failure but challenge them to move beyond frequently ascribing abiding traits to incidences, and circumstances, of failure.

Learning to 'qualify' and 're-label' is an important part of overall learning: *'Yes ... I did get it wrong ... and yes it is unpleasant to fail ... I haven't been up to scratch with my lesson plans ... so ... what do I need to do to ...?'* This realistic, and rational, kind of self-talk is a precursor to moving beyond the pain of failure; redefining failure as that – failure (*'I have failed in ...'* not *'I am a failure ...'*).

It is the habits of self-talk and 'self-explaining' that can have a self-guiding and regulatory function that can work for, or against, personal and professional coping. If the *residual* and explanatory style that one falls back on is overly pessimistic, global, and stable (*'all', 'always', 'never', 'no one'* ...) that, *in itself*, can significantly affect one's feeling, moods and coping behaviours.

Supportively disputing, and helping colleagues to 'dispute', maladaptive thinking patterns is often an important part of the mentoring journey. In this the work of R.E.T. (rational emotive therapy) provides a useful, theoretical and practical framework for mentors and peergroup leaders.

Learned optimism is not positive thinking; it is realistic –non-negative thinking. It doesn't deny how stressful the stressful event is but acts to avoid putting the worst construction on that event. It changes the *focus* and the direction of thinking as well (as the explanations) by disputing those elements of the explanations that *overfocus*, that are inaccurate, that are global (rather than specific) that imply it will always be this way. As Roberts (1989) notes, 'optimism training ... gives people three cognitive tools to use when things go badly at work'.

- Avoid blaming yourself for your failures;
- Realise that mistakes usually have a temporary effect; and
- *Don't let mishaps or down days infringe on other areas of life* (in Rogers, 1996, p. 43). 'That was a stupid thing to do but ...' The *but* prefaces the reframing of how we perceive events.

This process is not some self-immolation. Uncountered negative thinking can become a habit – a bad habit. As the Roman poet Ovid has said, 'Habits change into characters.'

Nor is it merely a matter of being naively optimistic. As George Eliot replied when asked the question 'Are you an optimist or a pessimist?' 'Neither,' came the reply, 'I am a meliorist.' (In Potter, 1950, p. 81). I wasn't sure what a *meliorist* was, I had to look that one up. A meliorist (n) is someone who believes things can 'grow better' that 'things can improve with persistent and practical effort'.

I am not arguing for some quiescent, passive, acceptance of stress as a *fait accompli*; quite the reverse. Stress is *natural* to work, to living, to life, as C.S. Lewis has observed (1970): 'No organisation or way of life whatever has a natural tendency to go right.' (p. 284). There *are*, 'the thousand natural shocks that flesh is heir to' (*Hamlet*). And if I cannot always change (directly) the stressful condition or situation, at least I can change *how I think about* stressful conditions, whatever they may be. I cannot choose my emotions, but I can learn to choose my perceptions.

There are many ways in which we can manage stress, from exercise and meditation, through to social support (avoid Valium sandwiches!). But the role of cognition, belief and self-talk, is a crucial factor in how we characteristically perceive, interpret and respond to stressful situations. If we are vigorous in countering negative and dysfunctional thinking, and refocusing the 'musts' and 'shoulds', the 'alwayses' and 'nevers' that lurk behind those stressful emotions, then odds on we'll not get as upset, as often, as long.

REFERENCES

AITKEN, J. (1996) From Values and Beliefs About Learning to Principles and Practice. *Seminar Series: Paper No. 54* IARTV, May, pp. 3–24.

ANDERSON, L.W. and BURNS, R.B. (1989) *Research in Classrooms: The Study of Teachers, Teaching and Instruction.* Oxford: Pergamon Press.

ANTONOVSKY, A. (1979) *Health, Stress and Coping.* California: Jossey-Bass.

ARGYRIS, C. and SCHON, D. (1978) *Organisational Learning.* Reading, Massachusetts: Addison-Wesley.

ARISTOTLE, *The Ethics of Aristotle: The Nichomachean Ethics.* Trans. Thompson, J.A.K. (1969) London: Penguin Classics.

ASHDOWN, C. (1997) Call for Talks to Tackle the Future of Teaching. *Education Review*, Vol, 1. No. 1, March, pp. 1, 2.

ASHDOWN, C. (1997) Your Brilliant Careers. *Education Review.* Vol. 1, No. 8, October.

ASHDOWN, C. (1999) Change and Leadership. *Education Review*, February, Vol. 3, No. 1, pp. 11–14.

AXWORTHY, D., OLNEY, H. and HAMILTON, P. (1989) Managing Student Behaviour: A Whole School Approach, in *Addressing Behaviour Problems in Australian Schools.* Camberwell, Vic: ACER Press.

BARNES, R.H. (1999) *Positive Teaching, Positive Learning.* London: Routledge.

BERNARD, M. (1990) *Taking the Stress Out of Teaching.* Melbourne: Collins Dove.

BERNARD, M. and JOYCE, M. (1984) *Rational Emotive Therapy with Children and Adolescents: Theory, Treatment Strategies, Preventative Methods.* New York: J. Wiley.

BLUMER, H. (1969) The Methodological Position of Symbolic Interactionism, in Blumer, H. [ed.] *Symbolic Interactionism: Perspective and Method.* Englewood Cliffs, NJ: Prentice-Hall.

BOGDAN, R. and TAYLOR, S.J. (1975) *Introduction to Qualitative Research Methods: A Phenomenological Approach to Social Sciences.* New York: J. Wiley.

BOOS, M.W. A *Lesson From the Geese.* Agricultural Notes (ECLA) Omaha Province Newsletter. Issue No. 27.

BOUCHON, M. (1999) Change is Here to Stay. *Management Today* January/February, pp. 21–4.

BRADSHAW, P. (1981) *The Management of Self Esteem*. New York: Prentice-Hall.

BRAMSON, R.M. (1981) *Coping With Difficult People*. Melbourne: The Business Library Press.

BRAUD, W. and ANDERSON, R. (1998) *Transpersonal Research Methods For the Social Sciences: Honouring Human Experience*. London: Sage Publications.

BREHENEY, C., MACKRILL, V. and GRADY, N. (1996) *Making Peace at Mayfield: A Whole-School Approach to Behaviour Management*. Armadale, Victoria: Eleanor Curtin.

BROWN, S., FINLAY-JONES, R. and McHALE, (1984) Measuring Teacher Stress in Western Australia. (Official Publication of the WA Institute of Educational Administrators), 14, pp. 28–40.

BUBER, M. (1958) *I and Thou* (trans. R.G. Smith) New York: Charles Scribner Sons.

BURFORD, C. (Winter 1987) Humour of Principals and its Impact on Teachers and the School. *Journal of Educational Administration*, Vol. 25, No. 1, pp. 29–54.

BURNS, R.C. (1994) *Introduction to Research Methods*. Melbourne: Longman.

CALDWELL, B.J. and CARTER, E.M.A. (1993) *The Return of the Mentor: Strategies for Workplace Learning*. London: Falmer Press.

CAMBOURNE, B. (1995) Buddy Can You Paradigm, *IRA Institute* No. 19, May, Anaheim, Cal.

CARR, W. (ed.) (1989) *Quality in Teaching*. Sussex, England: Falmer Press.

CLARK, M. (1991) *The Quest For Grace*. Ringwood, Victoria: Penguin.

COOLEY, C.H. (1926) The Roots of Social Knowledge, *American Journal of Sociology*, pp. 32, 59–79.

COOPERSMITH, S. (1967) *The Antecedents of Self Esteem*. San Francisco: Freeman.

CORNETT, C.E. (1986) *Learning through Laughter: Humor in the Classroom*. Indiana: Phi Delta Kappa Educational Foundation.

COSTELLO, T. (1998) *The Age*. 18 October, p. 25.

CURTIS, S. (1988) *Identifying and Solving the Research Problems Encountered in the Naturalistic Paradigm*. Wollongong: Wollongong University.

DIAMOND, C. (1986) Avoiding Burnout and Rustout: A Dependency Grid Study of Teacher Stress, in *Theory, Structure and Action in Education Papers of the Annual Conference of the Australian Association For Research in Education*, Ormond Coll. The University of Melbourne, Nov., Melbourne: Australian Association For Research in Education.

DOBSON, B. and SWIFT, J. (1994) *Skills For Life: Core manual–A handbook for Managers and Co-ordinators*. London: HMSO.

DOUGLAS, T. (2001) Poll Reveals High Levels of Support for State's Teachers.

Australian Education Union News (Victorian Branch), 8 March, Vol. 17, No. 3, pp. 1–2.

DREIKURS, R. (1968) *Psychology in the Classroom* (2nd edn). New York: Harper and Row.

DREIKURS, R., GRUNWALD, B. and PEPPER, F. (1982) *Maintaining Sanity in the Classroom* (2nd edn). New York: Harper and Row.

DUNFORD, R.W. (1992) *Organisational Behaviour: An Organisational Analysis Perspective.* Sydney: Addison-Wesley.

DUNHAM, J. (Feb. 1987) Caring for the Pastoral Carers. *Pastoral Care in Education*, pp. 15–21.

DUNNETTE, M.D. (ed.) (1986) *Handbook of Industrial and Organisational Psychology.* Chicago: Rand McNally.

EDWARDS, C. R.E.T. in the high school, *Rational Living*, 1977, *12*, pp. 10–12.

EISNER, E.W. (1979) *The Educational Imagination.* New York: Macmillan.

EISNER, E.W. and PESHKIN, A. (eds) (1990) *Qualitative Enquiry in Education.* New York: Teachers College Press.

EKMAN, P. (1989) A Smile's a Smile. Underneath we're all the same. (June 1989) *Psychology Today.*

ELTON REPORT (1989) *Discipline in Schools, Report of the Committee of Inquiry* London: Her Majesty's Stationery Office.

ELY, M. and ANZUL, A. (1991) *Doing Qualitative Research: Circles Without Circles.* London: Falmer Press.

ERIKSON, E.H. (1963) *Childhood and Society* (2nd edn). New York: Norton Press.

ERIKSON, E.H. (1968) *Identity: Youth and Crisis.* New York: Norton Press.

ETZION, D. (1984) Moderating Effect of Social Support on the Stress-Burnout Relationship. *Journal of Applied Psychology,* 69: 4, pp. 615–22.

FARRELL, H. (1991) Success Oriented Classrooms and Student Responsibility. *Compak Professional.* July, pp. 17–22.

FILEY, A. (1975) *Interpersonal Conflict Resolution.* Glenview, Illinois: Scott Foresman.

FINGER, J. (1993) *Managing Your School Vol. 1.* Brisbane, Qld: Fernfawn Publications.

FINGER, J. (1993) *Managing Your School Vol. 2.* Brisbane, Qld: Fernfawn Publications.

FIRESTONE, W. (1987) Meaning in Method: The Rhetoric of Quantitative and Qualitative Research. *Educational Researcher.* 16, pp. 16–21.

FORRISTAL, B. and ROGERS, B. (1988) *Developing Peer Support Among First Year Teachers.* Fawkner School Support Centre Ministry of Education, Victoria.

FRANCIS, D. and YOUNG, D. (1979) *Improving Work Groups: A Practical Manual for Team Building*. London: University Associates.

FRANKYL, V. (1963) *Man's Search for Meaning: An Introduction to Logotherapy*. New York: Simon and Schuster.

FREEMAN, A. (1987) The Coping Teacher. *Research in Education*, No. 38, pp. 1–16.

FULLAN, M. (1991) *The New Meaning of Educational Change* (2nd edn). New York: Teachers College Press; London: Falmer Press.

FULLAN, M. (1993) *Change Forces: Probing the Depths of Educational Reform*. London: Falmer Press.

FULLAN, M. and HARGREAVES, A. (1991) *What's Worth Fighting For?: Working Together For Your School*. Toronto: Ontario Public School Teachers' Federation.

GETZELS, J.W., LIPHAM, J.M. and CAMPBELL, R.F (1968) *Educational Administration as Social Process*. New York: Harper and Row.

GLASER, B.G. and STRAUSS, A.L. (1967) *The Discovery of Grounded Theory: Strategies for Qualitative Research*. New York: Adeline Press.

GLASSER, W. (1992) *The Quality School*. New York: HarperCollins.

GLICKMAN, C. (1991) Pretending Not to Know What We Know. *Educational Leadership*. May, pp. 4–9.

GOLEMAN, D. (1996) *Emotional Intelligence*. London: Bloomsbury.

GOSSEN, D. and ANDERSON, J. (1995) *Creating the Conditions For Quality Schools*. New Conneticut: New View Publications.

GREEN, D. (April, 1983) Framework for Considering the Burnout Syndrome. *The Journal of Counselling, Guidance and Clinical Services*, pp. 10–13.

GREIGER, R.M. and BOYD, J.D. (1980) *Rational Emotive Therapy: A Skills-Based Approach*. New York: Van Nostrand Reinhold.

GRIMMET, P. and CREHAN, E.P. (1991) The Nature of Collegiality in Teacher Development, in M. FULLAN and A. HARGREAVES (eds) *Professional Development in the Reform Era*. New York: Falmer Press (in Unicorn).

GUBA, E. and LINCOLN, Y. (1981) *Effective Evaluation: Improving the Usefulness of Evaluation Results through Responsive and Naturalistic Approaches*. San Francisco: Jossey Bass.

GUBA, E. and LINCOLN, Y. (1989) *Fourth Generation Evaluation*. California: Sage.

GUINESS, O. (1973) *The Dust of Death*. Leicester (UK): IVF Press.

GUSKEY, T.R. (1986) Staff Development and the Process of Teacher Change. *Educational Review*. Vol. 15 (5) May, pp. 5–12.

HANNAN, E. (1997) Stressing the Obvious: Workplace Pressure Has Forced One in Four Australian Employees to Take Time Off to Recover. *The Age*, 18 October, pp. 1–2 (Section 8).

HARGREAVES, A. (1991) Continued Collegiality: A Micropolitical Analysis, in BLASE, J. (ed.) *The Policies of Life in Schools*. New York: Sage.

HARGREAVES, A. (1994) Restructuring Restructuring: Post-Modernity and the Prospects for Individual Change. *Journal of Education Policy*, Vol. 9, No. 1, pp. 47–65.

HARGREAVES, A. (1997) in ASHDOWN, C. Where to From Here? in *Education Review*, May.

HARGREAVES, D. (1993) *The New Professionalism in Reflections on Practice*. The Centre For Advanced Teaching Studies, May.

HARPER, T. (1988) A System of Support for Teachers – Description and Evaluation, in SLEE, R. (ed.) *Discipline in Schools: A Curriculum Perspective*. South Melbourne: Macmillan.

HART, P.M. (1992) Stress, Morale and Teachers. *Education Quarterly* No. 8, October.

HART, P.M. (1994) Teacher Quality of Life: Integrating Work Experiences, Psychological Distress and Morale. *Journal of Occupational and Organisational Psychology*, 67, pp.109–39.

HART, P.M., WEARING, A.J. and CONN, M. (1993) Evaluation of a Whole-School Approach to Discipline – Conventional Wisdom is a Poor Predictor of the Relationship Between Discipline Policy, Student Misbehaviour and Teacher Stress. Paper presented at the Annual Conference of the Australian Association of Research in Education, Fremantle, 22–25 November.

HART, P.M., WEARING, A.J. and CONN, M. (1995) Wisdom is a Poor Predictor of the Relationship between Discipline Policy, Student Misbehaviour and Teacher Stress. *British Journal of Educational Psychology*. 1195, 65, pp. 27–48.

HARTER, P.D, (1989) Curriculum Innovation and Implementation: A Grounded Study of the Change Agent's Role. Paper presented at the Annual Meeting of the American Research Association, San Francisco.

HAYS, T. GERBER, R. and MINCHINELLO, V. (1999) Mentoring: A Revision of the Concept. *Unicorn*, Vol. 25, No. 2, September, pp. 84–95.

HEARN, J.J. (1974) Alienation: Another Administration Agency. *Contemporary Education* 45, pp. 132–36.

HILL, F. and PARSONS, L. (2000) *Teamwork in the Management of Emotional and Behavioural Difficulties: Developing Peer Support Systems for Teachers in Mainstream and Special Schools*. London: David Fulton.

HOBFOLL, S.E. (1998) *Stress, Culture and Community: The Psychology and Philosophy of Stress*. New York: Plenum Press.

HOPKINS, D. (1991) School Improvement in an Era of Change, in RIBBINS, P. and WHALE, E. (eds) (1992) *The Issue is Quality*. London: Cassell.

HOWARD, B.C. and ARNEZ, N.L. (1982) *School-Based Administrator Networking and Professional Development Program for More Effective Schools*. Washington, D.C.: Harvard University Press.

HOWE, K. (1996) Against the Qualitative–Quantitative Incompatibility Thesis–or Dogmas Die Hard. *Educational Researcher* pp. 10–16.

HOWELL, K. (1993) Eligibility and Need: Is There a Difference between Being Disturbed and Being Disturbing, in *Student Behaviour Problems: Positive Initiatives and New Frontiers*, EVANS, D., MYHILL, M. and IZARD, J. (eds) Camberwell, Victoria: ACER Press.

HOY, W.K. and MISKEL, C.G. (1978) *Educational Administration. Theory, Research and Practice*. New York: Random House.

HUBERMAN, A.M. and MILES, M.B. (1984) *Innovation Up Close*. New York: Plenum Press.

HUGHES, J. (1980) *The Philosophy of Social Research*. London: Longman.

INGVARSON, L. and CHADBOURNE, R. (eds) (1994) *Valuing Teachers' Work: New Directions in Teacher Appraisals*. Camberwell, Vic.: ACER.

JARVIS, W. (1975) *Discover Yourself and Live*. Ontario: Thomas Nelson.

JOHNSON, D.W. (1972) Reaching Out: Interpersonal Effectiveness and Self-Actualisation (5th edn). Boston: Allyn and Bacon.

JOHNSON, D.W. and JOHNSON, B.T. (1989) *Leading the Co-operative School*. Minnesota: Interaction Book Co.

JOHNSON, N. (1996) School Leadership and the Management of Change. *A Paper in Seminar Series No. 55*. Melbourne: IARTV. July, pp. 1–14.

JOSSELSON, R. (ed.) (1996) *Ethics and Process in the Narrative Study of Lives*. London: Sage Publications.

JOYCE, B.R. (1986) *Improving America's Schools*. New York: Longman.

JOYCE, B.R., BUSH, R. and MCKIBBIN, M. (1981) *The California Staff Development Study: The Compact Report*. Sacramento: California State Department of Education.

KILMANN, R. (1985) Organisations and Change. *Psychology Today*, April, pp. 62-7.

KOHN, A. (1986) How To Succeed Without Even Vying. *Psychology Today*, September, pp. 23–8.

KRYGIER, M. (1997) A Civil Society is Much More Than Just a Polite One. *The Age*, 21 November, p. 19.

KUBLER-ROSS, E. (1971) *On Death and Dying*. London: Collins-Macmillan.

KYRIACOU, C. (1980) Coping Actions and Occupational Stress Among School

Teachers. *Research in Education*, 24, 57–61, November.

KYRIACOU, C. (1981) Social Support and Occupational Stress Among School Teachers. *Educational Studies,* Vol. 7, pp. 55–60.

KYRIACOU, C. (1986) *Effective Teaching in Schools*. Oxford: Basil Blackwell.

KYRIACOU, C. (1987) Teacher Appraisal in the Classroom: Can It Be Done? *School Organisation*, Vol. 7, No.2, pp. 139–44.

KYRIACOU, C. (1987) Teacher Stress and Burnout: An International Review. *Educational Research*, Vol. 29, No. 2, pp. 145–52.

LANE, W.R., CORWIN, R.G. and MONAHAN, W.G. (1967) *Foundations of Educational Administration: A Behavioural Analysis*. New York: Macmillan.

LAZARUS, R.S. (1981) Little Hassles Can Be Hazardous to Health. *Psychology Today,* July, pp. 58–62.

LAZARUS, S. and FOLKMAN, S. (1984) *Stress, Appraisal and Coping*. New York: Springer.

LEANA, C.R. (1987) Power Relinquishment Versus Power Sharing: Theoretical Clarification and Empirical Comparison of Delegation and Participation. *Journal of Applied Psychology*, 72, No. 2, pp. 228–53.

Learning to Succeed: A Radical Look at Education Today and a Strategy for the Future. (1983) National Commission of Education, London: Heinemann.

LEE MARKS, M. (1986) The Question of Quality Circles. *Psychology Today*, March, pp. 36–46.

LEIBERMAN, A. (ed.) (1990) *School as Collaborative Cultures: Creating the Future Now*. Basingstoke: Falmer Press.

LEIBERMAN, M.A. (1982) The Effects of Social Support on Responses to Stress, in GOLDBERGER, L. and BREZNITZ, (eds) *Handbook of Stress: Theoretical and Clinical*. New York: Free Press.

LEWIS, C.S. (1970) *God in the Dock: Essays on Theology and Ethics*. Michigan: William Eerdmans Publishing Co.

LIEF, B. (1989) Underneath We're All the Same. *Psychology Today*, June.

LINCOLN, Y. and GUBA, E. (1985) *Naturalistic Inquiry*. Beverly Hills, CA.: Sage Publications.

LITTLE, J. W. (1982) Norms of Collegiality and Experimentation: Workplace Conditions of School Success. *American Education Research Journal*, 19, 3, pp. 325–40.

LITTLE, J.W. (1985) Teachers as Teacher Advisors: The Delicacy of Collegial Leadership. *Educational Leadership*, November, pp. 34–42.

LITTLE, J.W. (1990) Teachers as Colleagues, in LEIBERMAN, A. (ed.) *Schools as Collaborative Cultures*, Basingstoke: Falmer Press.

LITTLE, J.W. (1990) The Persistence of Privacy: Autonomy and Initiative in

Teachers' Professional Relations, in *Teachers College Record*, 91 (4) pp. 508–36.

LITTLE, J.W. (1993) Teachers' Professional Development in a Climate of Educational Reform, in *Educational Evaluation and Policy Analysis*, 15 (2) pp. 129–51.

LORTIE, D.C. (1975) *School Teacher: A Sociological Study*. Chicago: University of Chicago Press.

LOUGHRAN, J. (1996) *Developing Reflective Practice: Learning about Teaching and Learning through Modelling*. London: Falmer Press.

LOWE, J. and ISTANCE, D. (1989) *Schools and Quality: An International Report*. Paris: OECD.

MACKEN, J. (1998) The Corporate Seers. *The Australian Financial Review Magazine*, 4 October, pp.15–22.

MacLEOD, R. (1987) *Strategies for Tackling Teacher Stress*. Richmond, Vic.: Teachers' Federation of Victoria.

MARKHAM, U. (1993) *How to Deal With Difficult People*. London: Thorson Press.

MASLACH, C. (1976) Burned Out, in *Human Behaviour*, September, pp. 6–10.

MASLACH, C. and JACKSON, S.E. (1986) *Maslach Burnout Inventory*. Palo Alto, California: Consulting Psychologists' Press.

MASLOW, A. (1968) *Towards a Psychology of Being* (2nd edn). Princeton, NY: Harper and Row.

MASLOW, A. (1985) *Motivation and Personality*. New York: Harper.

McGOUGH, R. (1993) *Defying Gravity*. London: Penguin Poetry.

McINERNEY, D.M. and McINERNEY, V. (1994) *Educational Psychology – Constructing Learning*. Sydney: Prentice-Hall.

McLAUGHLIN, (1990) The Rand Change Agent Revisited. *Educational Researcher,* 5, pp. 11–16.

MELTZER, M., PETRAS, J.W. and REYNOLDS, L.T. (1975) *Symbolic Interactionism: Genesis, Varieties and Criticism*. London: Routledge and Kegan Paul.

MIDDLEBROOK, P. (1974) *Social Psychology and Modern Life*. New York: A.A. Knopf.

MILES, M.B. and HUBERMAN, A.M. (1987) *Qualitative Data Analysis: A Source Book of New Methods*. Beverly Hills, CA.: Sage Publications.

MILLER, A. (1996) *Pupil Behaviour and Teacher Culture*. London: Cassell.

MOODIE, R. (1998) Managing Stress in the workplace. *The Age*, 22 August, p. 2 (Section F).

MORGAN, S.R. (1991) *At Risk Youth in Crisis: A Team Approach in Schools*. Austin, TX: Pro-Ed Inc.

MORROW, L. (1981) The Burnout of Almost Everyone. *Time*, 21 September.

MORTIMER, J. (1989) *Clinging to the Wreckage*. London: Penguin Books.

MYKLEHUN, R.J. (1984) Teacher Stress: Perceived and Objective Sources and Quality of Life. *Scandinavian Journal of Educational Research*, Vol. 28(1), March, pp. 17–45.

MYSS, C. (1988) *Why People Don't Heal and How They Can*. London: Bantam Books.

NASH, P. (1968) *Models of Man Explorations in the Western Educational Tradition*. New York: John Wiley & Sons.

NELSON, J. (1981) *Positive Discipline*. New York: Ballantyne Books.

NIAS, J. (1989) *Primary Teachers Talking*. London and New York: Routledge.

NIAS, J., SOUTHWORTH, G. and YEOMANS, R. (1989) *Staff Relationships in the Primary School*. London and New York: Cassell.

NOBLE, G. and WATKINS, M. (1988) Teachers' Work: Morale in Public Education. *Education Australia*, Issue 2, pp. 11–13.

O'BRIEN, T. (1998) *Promoting Positive Behaviour*. London: David Fulton Publishers.

OTTO, R. (1985) *Teachers Under Stress*. Melbourne: Hill of Content.

Oxford English Dictionary Vol. 2 (1978) Oxford: Clarendon Press.

PARKES, J. and ROGERS, B. (1987) *Peer Support: A School-Based Program for New Teachers*. Ardeer High School Publication, Ardeer H.S., Ardeer, Vic.

PARKES, K.P. (1988) Locus of Control in Three Behavioural Domains: Factor Structure and Correlation of the 'Spheres of Control' Scale. *Personal and Individual Differences Journal*, Vol. 9, No. 3, pp. 631–43.

PARKES, K.R. (1986) Coping With Stressful Episodes: The Role of Individual Differences, Environmental Factors and Situation Characteristics. *Journal of Personality and Social Psychology*, Vol. 51, No. 6, pp. 1277–292.

PARTRIDGE, E. (1980) *Usage and Abusage: A Guide to Good English*. London: Hamish Hamilton Ltd.

PAULSEN, M.B. and FELDMAN, K.A. (1995) *Taking Teaching Seriously: Meeting the Challenge of Institutional Improvement*. Washington, D.C.: George Washington University Press.

PESHKIN, A. (1993) The Goodness of Qualitative Research. *Educational Researcher*, March, 22(2) pp. 23–9.

PETERSON, M.L. (1989) *Philosophy of Education: Issues and Options*. Illinois: I.V.P. Press.

PLATO. *The Republic*. Trans. Lee, D. (1980) London: Penguin Classics.

POTTER, S. (1950) *Our Language*. London: Pelican.

POWELL, J. (1976) *Fully Human, Fully Alive*. Chicago, Illinois: Argus Communications.

Professional Recognition Programme (For Teachers): Guidelines (1996) State of Victoria: Education Victoria, DoE.

PURKEY, W.W. and NOVAK, J.M. (1984) *Inviting School Success: A Self Concept Approach to Teaching and Learning*. California: Wadsworth Publishing Co.

REBER, A.S. (1985) *The Penguin Dictionary of Psychology*. New York: Penguin.

ROBERTSON, H.J. (1992) Teacher Development and Gender Enquiry, in HARGREAVES, A. and FULLAN, M.G. (eds) *Understanding Teacher Development*. London: Cassell.

ROBERTSON, J. (1996) *Effective Classroom Control: Understanding Teacher–Pupil Relationships*. London: Hodder & Stoughton.

ROGERS, B. (1993) 'Black Dot, White Square': Managing Stress. A paper delivered to the 1993 conference *Student Behaviour Problems: Positive Initiatives and New Frontiers*. Evans, D., Myhill, M. and Izard, J. Camberwell, Victoria: ACER Press.

ROGERS, B. (1994) *Behaviour Recovery: A Whole-School Program for Mainstream Schools*. Camberwell: ACER Press. Published in the UK by Paul Chapman Publishing: London. 2nd ed., 2004.

ROGERS, B. (1995) *Behaviour Management: A Whole School Approach*. Sydney: Scholastic. (In the UK published by Paul Chapman Publishing: London, 1999.) Second Edition, 2006.

ROGERS, B. (1996) *Managing Teachers Stress*. London: Paul Chapman Publishing. (Published in Australia as *Supporting Teachers in the Workplace* 1992).

ROGERS, B. (1997) *Cracking the Hard Class: Strategies For Managing the Harder Than Average Class*. Sydney: Scholastic. (In the UK published by Paul Chapman Publishing: London, 1999.) Second Edition, 2006.

ROGERS, B. (1998) *You Know the Fair Rule and More*. Melbourne: ACER Press. (In the UK published by Pittman: London.)

ROGERS, B. (1999) Unpublished doctoral dissertation: Towards a Model for Colleague Support: Matching Support to Needs and Contexts (Melbourne University).

ROGERS, B. (2000) *Classroom Behaviour: A Practical Guide to Effective Teaching, Behaviour Management and Colleague Support*. London: Books Education.

ROGERS, B. (2003) *Effective Supply Teaching*. London: Paul Chapman Publishing.

ROSENHOLZ, S.J. (1989) *Teachers' Workplace: The Social Organisation of Schools*. New York: Longman.

ROYCE-SADLER, D. (1989) Formative Assessment and the Design of Instructional Systems. *Science Education*, 21, pp. 119–44.

RUDDUCK, J. (1991) *Innovation and Change*. Buckingham: Open University Press.

RUSSELL, D.W., ALTIMAIER, E. and VAN VELZEN D. (1987) Job-Related Stress, Social Support and Burnout Among Classroom Teachers. *Journal of Applied Psychology*, Vol. 72, No. 2, pp. 269–74.

RUTTER, M. (1981) Stress, Coping and Development: Some Issues and Questions. *Journal of Child Psychology and Psychiatry*, 22, 4, pp. 323–56.

RUTTER, M., MAUGHAN, B., MORTIMER, P. and OUSTEN, J. (1979) *Fifteen Thousand Hours: Secondary schools and Their Effects on Children*. London: Open Books.

SACKS, O. (1990) *Awakenings*. London: Harper-Collins.

SAUL, R. (1990) *The Unconscious Civilization*. Ringwood, Victoria: Penguin.

SCHÖN, D.A. (1983) *The Reflective Practitioner: How Professionals Think in Action*. New York: Basic Books.

SCHÖN, D.A. (1987) *Educating the Reflective Practitioner: Toward a New Design For Teaching and Learning in the Profession*. San Francisco: Jossey-Bass.

SCHOPENHAUER, A. (1976) *Essays and Aphorisms*. Trans. Hollingdale, R.J. London: Penguin.

SCOTT, K. (1992) Ruining or Developing Team-work – Take Your Choice. *The Practising Manager*, Vol. 13, No. 1, October.

SCOTT-PECK, M. (1978) *The Road Less Travelled*. London: Arrow Books.

SCOTT-PECK, M. (1993) *A World Waiting To Be Born: Civility Rediscovered*. New York: Bantam Books.

SELIGMAN, M. (1991) *Learned Optimism*. Sydney: Random House.

SHAW, K.E. (1987) Skills, Control and the Mass Professions. *The Sociological Review*, Vol. 25, No. 4, pp. 775–94.

SHRATZ, M. (ed.) (1993) *Qualitative Voices in Educational Research*. London: Falmer Press.

SHULMAN, L.S. (1986) Those Who Understand: Knowledge Growth in Teaching. *Educational Researcher*, 15, 2, pp. 4–14.

SHULMAN, L.S. (1988) A Union of Insufficiencies: Strategies for Teacher Assessment in a Period of Reform. *Education Leadership*, 46 (3), pp. 36–41.

SIMONS, F. (1998) Heroes, Leaders, Managers. *The Australian Financial Review*, 4 October, pp. 26–31.

SIMPSON, M.E. (1980) Societal Support and Education, in KUTASH, IRWIN L., SCHLESINGER, LOUIS B. and ASSOCIATES (eds) *Handbook on Stress and Anxiety*. San Francisco, CA.: Jossey-Bass.

SKIFFINGTON, S. and ZEUS, P. (1999) User-Friendly Interactive Interfaces. *Management Today*, March, p. 40.

SMYTH, J. (1983) Supervision – cleaning up a dirty word. *Education News*, Vol. 18, No. 3, pp. 27–30.

STOLL, L. (1997) Successful Schools: Linking School Effectiveness and School Improvement. Paper presented at Successful Schools: Building on School of the Future Conference June, *Education Victoria*, pp. 1–27.

STOLL, L. (1998) Supporting School Improvement. OECD paper presented at

Christchurch Conference, 'Combating Failure at School' Christchurch, NZ, 1–5 Feb. 199, pp. 1–19.

STOLL, L. and FINK, D. (1996) *Changing Our Schools: Linking School Effectiveness and School Improvement*. Buckingham: Open University Press.

SWIFT, J. and DOBSON, B. (1994) *Skills for Life* (core manual) Dept of Education, Oldham, UK.

SYMON, G. and CASSELL, C. (eds) (1998) *Qualitative Methods and Analysis in Organisational Research*. London: Sage Publications.

TAUBER, R. (1995) *Classroom Management: Theory and Practice*. Philadelphia: Harcourt Brace.

Teacher Stress in Victoria: A Survey of Teachers' Views: Summary and Recommendations. (1989) A Report Victoria: Ministry of Education.

THEOBOLD, R. (1997) The Future of Work Vol. 1 and 2. *ABC Audio Tapes*.

THODY, A. GRAY, B. and BOWDEN, D. (2000) *The Teacher's Survival Guide: How Do I Deal with Difficult Behaviour? How Do I Cope with the Stress of Work? How Do I Manage My Workload and other School Commitments and Still Have a Life?* London: Continuum Press.

THOMAS, K.W. and KILMAN, R.H. (1989) *The Thomas–Kilman Conflict Mode Instrument*. Sterling Forest, New York: Xicom, Inc.

Those Having Torches. Teacher Appraisal: A Study (1996) Suffolk Education Department (DFES) Suffolk.

TOURNIER (1970) *The Meaning of Persons: Perceptions on a Psychiatrist's Casebook*. London: S.C.M. Press.

WALEN, S., DI GUISEPPE, R. and WESSLER, R.L. (1980) *A Practitioner's Guide to Rational Emotive Therapy*. New York: Oxford University Press.

WALSH, D. (1972) Sociology in the Social World in FILMER, P., SILVERMAN, D., (eds) *New Directions in Sociological Theory.* New York: Collier-MacMillan.

WARWICK, D.P. (1973) Survey Research and Participant Observation: A Benefit-Cost Analysis, in WARWICK, D.P. and OSHERSHON (eds) *Comparative Research Methods*. Englewood Cliffs, NJ: Prentice-Hall.

WATKINS, C. and WAGNER, P. (1987) *School Discipline: A Whole-School Approach* Oxford: Blackwell.

WEISS, R. (1974) in RUBIN, Z. (ed.) *Doing Unto Others*. Englewood Cliffs, NJ: Prentice-Hall.

WILDBLOOD, P. (1968) *Leading From Within*. St Leonards, NSW: Allen & Unwin.

WILSON, B.L. and CORCORAN, T.B. (1988) *Successful Secondary Schools: Visions of Excellence in American Public Education*. London: Falmer Press.

INDEX

DATE DUE